Samuel Woodworth Cozzens

Crossing the Quicksands

Or, the veritable adventures of Hal and Ned upon the Pacific slope

Samuel Woodworth Cozzens

Crossing the Quicksands
Or, the veritable adventures of Hal and Ned upon the Pacific slope

ISBN/EAN: 9783337075316

Printed in Europe, USA, Canada, Australia, Japan

Cover: Foto ©Andreas Hilbeck / pixelio.de

More available books at **www.hansebooks.com**

The Trail Hunters Series.

Crossing the Quicksands

Boston
LEE & SHEPARD

THE YOUNG TRAIL HUNTERS' SERIES.

CROSSING THE QUICKSANDS;

OR, THE

VERITABLE ADVENTURES OF HAL AND NED UPON THE PACIFIC SLOPE.

BY

SAMUEL WOODWORTH COZZENS,

AUTHOR OF "THE MARVELLOUS COUNTRY," "THE YOUNG TRAIL HUNTERS," ETC.

ILLUSTRATED.

BOSTON:
LEE AND SHEPARD, PUBLISHERS.
NEW YORK: CHARLES T. DILLINGHAM.
1877.

COPYRIGHT.
BY LEE AND SHEPARD.
1877.

Electrotyped and Printed by
Rand, Avery, and Company,
117 Franklin Street,
Boston.

TO YOUNG AMERICA.

THE very flattering reception that has been accorded "The Young Trail Hunters" inclines my publishers to the belief that a series, of which the present constitutes the second volume, will meet with a like generous welcome at your hands.

I have therefore prepared for your kind approbation, "CROSSING THE QUICKSANDS;" which will in due time be followed by other volumes, narrating some of the hazardous adventures, curious experiences, and deadly perils, encountered by Hal and Ned, while travelling through that first-civilized, but now wildest, portion of our continent,— the SILVER LAND OF NORTH AMERICA.

These volumes will give a truthful account of actual experiences upon the road, through a country, the greater portion of the way inhabited only by hostile savages, and infested by wild beasts, yet containing old cities, teeming with a vast population, whose strange habits, customs, and peculiarities have for centuries furnished a fruitful theme for the Spanish historian, poet and novelist.

With the belief that the series will prove instructive, as well as amusing and interesting, I offer the present volume for your friendly consideration.

THE AUTHOR.

CONTENTS.

CHAPTER I.
PAGE

The Ranch. — Bears. — The Trap. — How we made it. — A Bee-Tree. — "Burnt Honey and Bars." — Old Jerry explains. — The Dead Log 11

CHAPTER II.

Hal discourses on Bears. — Jerry's Story about Grizzlies. — The Trap is sprung: who can tell what's in it? 18

CHAPTER III.

Ephraim caught. — Patsey's Tip-Out. — A *Rodeo* in Contemplation. — The *Vaquero* and his Dress. — Splendid Riders. — The Gathering. — Branding Cattle. — A Fandango. — The Result. 24

CHAPTER IV.

A New Acquaintance. — Sile Carter and Jerry. — A Visit to the Trap. — The Wild Bulls. — Hal and Ned turn *Vaqueros*. — The Chase and a Fall. — A Pony gored. — A Suggestion, and what came of it 31

CHAPTER V.

A Trip suggested. — A Hunt. — The Result. — How we jerked our Meat. — Organizing a Pack-Train. — A Stampede. — On the Road. — Hal and Ned in a Fix. — Crossing the Quicksands 39

CONTENTS.

CHAPTER VI.

The Old Mission of San Diego. — Olive-Trees. — How we made Waterproof Matches. — How Sile "got ketched," and how the Grizzly warmed him. — Indians coming 47

CHAPTER VII.

Indian Visitors. — Digger Manners. — A Grasshopper Hunt. — A Lame Mule. — A Visit to a Pai Ute Camp. — Caged Rattlesnakes. — Poisoned Arrows. — Cooking in a Basket. — A Diet of Wasps. — Fishing 56

CHAPTER VIII.

The Story of the Wolves. — The Ute Medicine-Man. — The Incantation. — The Dance-House. — The Black Wolf digs, and what he found. — A Surprise. — Indian Jugglery. — A Wonderful Feat. — Spiritual Mediums 65

CHAPTER IX.

The Mystic Rite. — The Wolf-Dance. — A Picture. — Our Return to Camp. — Hal and Ned. — Sile explains Medicine-Men. — Who and What they are. — Indian Skill in Shooting. — Hal's Offer. — Why he didn't set up his Hat 73

CHAPTER X.

Dangerous Shooting. — Revolvers *vs.* Arrows. — Hal's Trial of Skill. — Comanche shooting. — What the Great Spirit did. — Our Visitors' Departure. — Vamose. — Getting ready for a Start. 82

CHAPTER XI.

An Old California Ranch. — The Proprietor and his People. — His House. — His Possessions. — A most wonderful Exhibition of Skill with the Lasso. — Superior Horsemanship. — The Don says it is Nothing. — Once More on the Road. — Our Trail forks. — No-account People. — Addios . . . 89

CONTENTS.

CHAPTER XII.

Hal discusses the Situation. — The Mission Indians. — Their probable Number. — Hal discourses on Grizzlies. — Sile's Advice. — Hal boasts. — Sile's Hunt. — His Skill in Shooting. — Three Bullets in One Hole. — The Split Shot. — Our Doubts. — Sile's Success. — His Promise 98

CHAPTER XIII.

Sile goes Deer-Hunting. — Fresh Meat for Supper. — The Promise. — Sile's Story. — Down in Maine. — On the Mississippi. — Trapping in the Rocky Mountains. — Peter A. Sarpy. — "Early to Bed, and Early to Rise." — The Panther's Cry. — To Bed 109

CHAPTER XIV.

A Suggestion. — Hal wants a Grizzly-Hunt. — A Surprise. — Ned shoots a Cub. — Hal's Explanations. — We are attacked by a Grizzly. — The Boys Return. — Why they left. — Sile's Query. — Two Cubs 118

CHAPTER XV.

Our Conclusions. — Ned's Statement. — A Grizzly's a Grizzly, Big or Little. — How to Dress Skins. — The Process. — Whose Brains. — Which shall it be ? — Sile's Opinion. — He thinks Hal ignorant of the Subject of Tanning . . . 128

CHAPTER XVI.

Trappers and Trapping. — Ike McKenzie and the Silver Fox. — How to set a Fox-Trap. — Smoke and Lye. — The Value of Skins. — How to Manage a Pack-Train. — "'Tend to yer own Bizness if Yer want it 'tended to." — Hal doubts Fox and Geese 137

CHAPTER XVII.

Sile shoots a Deer. — Trapping. — How Indian Braves become Warriors. — Description of the Initiation, by an Eye-Witness. — A Terrible Scene. — The Buffalo Bull Dance. — The Medicine-Man. — "It does a Fellow Good tew holler when he feels like it" 145

CONTENTS.

CHAPTER XVIII.

Brained and Packed. — Sile's Stew. — An Unexpected Sight. — The White Horse and its Rider. — We shoot a Lion. — A Search and Discovery. — "Whar's me Hoorse?" — Dennis Burke and his Shillalah. — A "Pumel" and what came of it. — A Search for the Horse, and then a Search for Dennis. — Camp 155

CHAPTER XIX.

Hunting for the Lost. — He is found. — Prefers to "walk afoot." — His History. — "Ould Maverick's Ranch." — Ould Sam. — "Ma'am and the Gals." — We move Camp. — "A California Buck." — A Boy with the "Genii." — Hal and Ned. — The Dispute. — "You hear me now" 166

CHAPTER XX.

The Maverick Family. — Dipping. — Music. — The Shots. — "It's a Grizzly." — A Rush for Camp. — The Cinnamon Bear, and who shot it? — "And you aimin' at the Eye of the Baste." — Old Sam's Word. — We make a Trade. — Who was scared? 175

CHAPTER XXI.

A Camp in a Big Tree. — Sile's Cinnamon Bear Story. — How Josh Curtis fetched Fresh Meat for Breakfast into Camp. — Treed by a Bear. — A Stampede. — "Moighty Poor Luck." — Among the Quicksands. — A Dangerous Crossing. — Bad Luck. — A New Ford. — Hal in more Trouble . . . 188

CHAPTER XXII.

We buy a New Horse. — Mr. Hitchcock. — The Big Trees. — What the Boys thought. — A New England Home. — Hal's Choice. — How he broke his Horse. — Pluck and Grit. — Hal Victorious. — Congratulations. — On the Road once more . 199

CHAPTER XXIII.

Hal's Horse. — A Beautiful Valley. — Ned and I take a Tramp. — The Lion and the Grizzly. — A Terrific Fight. — It continues all the Afternoon. — We take no Note of Time. — Darkness. — What shall we do ? — A Sleep and a Terrible Awaking 211

CHAPTER XXIV.

Wolves. — What we did. — Our Fire gone. — Our Last Resource. — Ned does his Share. — A Very Unpleasant Situation. — A Concert. — Daylight. — I risk a Shot. — Its Effect. — We start for Camp. — A Rifle-shot. — What it said. — Sile. — Camp at Last 224

CHAPTER XXV.

Congratulations. — A Visit to the Scene of our Adventure. — What we found. — More Game. — We return to Camp. — On the Road. — Arrival at New Almaden. — What we saw. — Visit to the Furnaces. — How the Ore is treated. — Something about Quicksilver 234

CHAPTER XXVI.

What we saw. — Description of the Manner of reducing the Ore. — Its Specific Gravity. — Interesting Experiments. — Hal and Ned delighted. — A Fine Entertainment. — Visit to the Mines. — How they are worked. — What we saw Underground. — Return to Camp. — What Sile said 246

CHAPTER XXVII.

Hal and Ned discuss a Point. — The two Indian Chiefs. — A Question. — Shall we go or stay ? — The Decision. — Hal objects. — The Stray Horse. — A Long Tramp. — A Proposition. — Hal apologizes 259

CHAPTER XXVIII.

Early Rising. — Morning the best Time for Game. — The Antelope. — The Boys' Surprise. — Sile tries his Luck. — Speckled Beauties and Red Flannel. — Hal the Doubter. — A Challenge. — The First Shot 268

CONTENTS.

PAGE

CHAPTER XXIX.

Our Game. — We call the Boys. — In Camp. — Lost. — The Effect of a Blunderbuss. — A Sleepless Night. — On the Trail. — The little Lake. — The Camp-Fire. — The Gentleman from Pike. — Hal Discourses. — Found. — "Took Sick." — Why Hal refused to guide us in 280

XXX.

The Proofs. — Hal's Explanation. — How to cook Grouse. — On the Road. — Camp. — Dennis Burke again. — "The Ould Man's in the Hurry." — Old Maverick's Ranch. — The Cattle. — Señor Escarrito. — California as it was. — The Contrast under American Rule. — Ready for a Start at Last . . 294

XXXI.

The Morning after. — On the Road. — Ned's Request. — What came of a Red Blanket. — An exciting Chase. — A wonderful Feat. — Home again. — Old Jerry's Welcome. — A New Project. — What Jerry thinks. — Truth stranger than Fiction. — Adieu 306

CROSSING THE QUICKSANDS.

CHAPTER I.

THE RANCH. — BEARS. — THE TRAP. — HOW WE MADE IT. — A BEE-TREE. — "BURNT HONEY AND BARS." — OLD JERRY EXPLAINS. — THE DEAD LOG.

"HERE we are at last, youngsters, settled on as pretty a ranch as any man ever seed," said old Jerry one beautiful morning in March, a few days after we were fairly established in our new home on the Pacific Slope; "pretty as a picter, and no mistake," continued the old man, as his eyes fondly lingered on the beautiful hills and valleys and forests that stretched far away towards the distant line of blue mountains that reared their lofty heads to the north and east: "'tain't half stocked though; and if we run it as we ought to, some of us hev got ter start out and buy five or six hundred head. Who's the one to go?"

"Let's all go!" exclaimed Hal and Ned in the same breath.

"I shall have something to say about that," interrupted I: "some one must stay behind to look after the stock we have now, or we sha'n't have that long. I found the remains of two calves this morning out near the woods, that had evidently been killed by bears last night; if they are plenty in this vicinity, we must devise some means of getting rid of them before we venture to bring more stock on to the ranch."

"Let's go for the bears, then," shouted Hal: "that'll be rare fun."

"Did you see many tracks 'bout?" inquired Jerry.

"Plenty of them, and the largest I ever saw," was my reply.

"I reckon I'd better saddle up and ride down and take a look at 'em. You left every thing just as you found it, didn't yer?"

I replied that I disturbed nothing; and in a short time we were all on our way to a distant part of the ranch, where I had that morning discovered the traces of our unwelcome visitors.

"We ought to get the stock that belongs to the ranch together, and see if it's properly branded, the very first thing we do; because, in this country, the brand is the only evidence of ownership recognized," said I as we rode along.

"Of course the young critters ain't marked; but they'll keep with their mothers, and we kin tell 'em that way," suggested Jerry; "and, as you say, we must have 'em hunted up, and driven into the coral and branded, the very first thing we do. I reckon we'll start the *vaqueros* out to-morrow."

"I'll go with 'em," declared Hal: "I can help drive 'em up."

"You!" exclaimed Jerry. "What kind of a show do you s'pose you'd make among a lot of them fellers? You couldn't stan' it ter ride a day with 'em, much less four or five. You'd better stay to home and take care of yourself, instead of runnin' over the country with a lot of harum-scarum riders, huntin' cattle."

"You never think we boys can do any thing," replied Hal; "but I want you to understand that I'm not afraid to ride with any of 'em."

"I don't s'pose you be," replied Jerry; "but, if you knowed more, yer would be: them fellers jest live in the saddle, and ain't comfer'ble out of it. You've got a mighty sight to larn afore you kin hunt cattle, or jack-rabbits fer that matter."

"Halloa! what's this?" said Ned, reining in his pony, and pointing to a deep impression in the soft earth.

"That!" exclaimed Jerry. "Why, it's a bar's track; and, as sure as you're a livin' boy, it's a grizzly's; nothin' on this airth but a grizzly ever made thet track. Did the ones you see this mornin' look like that?"

"I should say they were the same," was my reply.

"Then we've got somethin' ter do afore we buy any more stock," replied Jerry; "for if grizzlies is 'round we must git shet of 'em, or we sha'n't hev any stock."

"But ain't grizzlies very dangerous?" inquired Ned.

"The most so of any critter in the mountains," replied Jerry: "they don't hev no kin' er sense, and hed jest as soon tackle a buffalo or a man as a calf, specially if they're wounded: they git desprit then."

"Well, here we are!" exclaimed I. "You can soon tell, for there's one of the carcasses, and the other's just beyond it."

Upon reaching the spot, Jerry at once declared that we had had a visit from "old Ephraim, sure."

"Who's old Ephraim?" inquired Hal.

"It's the name that old trappers hev giv' to ther grizzly," explained Jerry.

"There's no question about their being grizzly tracks, is there, Jerry?" inquired I.

"The size on 'em would settle that, if nothin' else did. Why, this one's a foot and a half long if it's an inch. Yes, and there's bin more'n one here too," declared Jerry, as he slowly followed the track for some distance into the forest.

He soon returned, however, saying, "I reckon the best thing for us ter do is to set a trap for these fellers. We can't spend the time ter go on a hunt for 'em, and we shall be more likely to ketch 'em in a trap any way. What d'ye say, youngsters? shall we trap 'em, or resk a hunt?"

"Oh, let's trap 'em! that'll be real fun," exclaimed Ned.

THE TRAP. 15

"But I say hunt 'em; it'll be just splendid to see one of the great creatures coming right towards you, and when you fire see him drop, and then have every one say, 'That's the boy that killed a grizzly.' It's mean to talk about trapping 'em," said Hal.

"Wal, mean or not, I ain't a-goin' to run any resk huntin' grizzlies with sich hunters as we've got on this ranch: that's sartin," replied Jerry. "I'd ruther trap a grizzly than resk a shot at one, any time. So we'll build a trap, and if you boys'll ride back to the ranch, and fetch a couple of axes and a spade, the judge and me 'll make the trap; and if you want ter hunt, why, you kin hunt a bee-tree while we're doin' it."

"What do you want of a bee-tree?" inquired Hal.

"Why, we want the honey to bait our trap with. Thar ain't nothin'll ketch bars like burnt honey."

"I wish you'd let us help you build the trap," remarked Ned.

"Well, don't stan' there talkin' all day: go and git the axes, and be as quick as you kin, and you may help when you git back, if you want ter."

While the boys were gone for the tools, Jerry selected a suitable place for the trap, and immediately upon their return set them to work cutting a number of straight poles about three inches in diameter: these were driven firmly into the ground side by side, and when we had finished we had a pen three feet in width, six feet in length, and five feet high: we then covered the top with cross-pieces, to prevent the bait from being stolen from above.

Cutting a large log about nine inches in diameter, we rolled it up against the front of the pen, confining it directly on a line with the end of the enclosure by two upright posts, firmly set in the ground, upon each side of it.

We next procured the trunk of a tree of the same diameter, about twenty feet in length; and after getting it in place upon the log, Jerry declared that we could do no more until we had discovered a bee-tree, and procured a quantity of honeycomb for bait.

Upon our return to the ranch, the boys, under Jerry's instruction, placed some slightly moistened sugar upon plates, a little distance from the house: this in a short time attracted the attention of two or three bees, who, after greedily sipping the sweets so generously provided for them, rose into the air, and flew away.

That these were explorers was evident; for in a short time hundreds of their companions made their appearance, and very soon a regular line of communication through the air was established between the ranch and their hive.

This soon became a highway, so clearly defined that we were able to mount our horses, and with but slight inconvenience follow it to their hive in the trunk of a decayed redwood near the edge of the forest.

Axes were sent for, and the tree felled; when it struck the ground the trunk split, displaying an immense quantity of splendid honey in the comb, as clear and limpid as water.

Hal and Ned at first were unwilling to approach the treasure, for fear of being stung by the bees, who crawled and flew about their ruined home in a dazed and lazy manner, as though vainly trying to realize the misfortune that had so suddenly overtaken their once busy hive.

A messenger was despatched to the ranch, and in a very short time every one that could be spared was on the ground with pails, pans, tubs, and jars, in fact, with any thing that would hold the limpid sweetness. These were soon filled; and then Jerry selected a suitable piece of the comb, and, having partially roasted it, proceeded to smear a piece of meat with it: this he fastened to a pole at the back of the pen, so arranged that, in order to reach it, "Ephraim" must step upon a piece of board so contrived that the pressure of his foot would dislodge the stick that supported the heavy log, precipitating it upon the creature's back in such a manner as to crush him to the earth, thus dislocating his spine.

After weighting the "dead-log" by placing heavy timbers against the elevated end, the trap was pronounced ready for any visitor.

CHAPTER II.

HAL DISCOURSES ON BEARS. — JERRY'S STORY ABOUT GRIZZLIES. — THE TRAP IS SPRUNG: WHO CAN TELL WHAT'S IN IT?

"DO you suppose any bear will deliberately walk into that thing?" inquired Hal in a tone of ill-disguised contempt, after surveying for a moment the rather clumsy-looking structure. "Why, any creature would know it was some kind of a trap, and steer clear of it, instead of going into it."

"P'raps bars ain't so smart as you be," remarked Jerry.

"Well, if they have half the sense they have credit for, one 'll never risk himself in such a thing as that; besides, I don't see how on earth it's going to kill one, if he should walk into it."

"The proof of the puddin' is the eatin' of it," said Jerry. "I've know'd many a bar ketched in sich a trap as that; and it's a fact, that one on em'll resk his life any time for a little burnt honey: the scent of it'll bring him a long ways; and after he's got whar 'tis, he can't git it onless he walks under that log; and when he puts his foot on ter that board, it nat'rally sinks, and that raises up the pole with the bait on at the other end er the trap. That forces this stick outer that notch, and lets the heavy log on to him; and it stan's ter reason, sich a weight as that'll break any critter's back."

"But, supposing it shouldn't work as you expect it to," suggested Ned: "what shall we do then?"

"It will work," confidently asserted Jerry; "but, if it shouldn't, we'll rig a gun-trap: that'll do it, sartin."

As there was nothing further to be done, we returned to the ranch, to find the men all feasting on the bountiful supply of sweets secured from the bee-tree.

During the evening the conversation naturally enough turned upon grizzlies; and Ned inquired of Jerry, why he so much dreaded a hunt after them.

"'Cause they're the ugliest critters in the world, 'specially if you git 'em riled. 'Tain't every man that kin hit a grizzly in jest the right place; and if you don't, the chances are nine out er ten, he'll git yer, sure."

"Have you ever had much experience hunting them, Jerry?" inquired I.

"No, sir; and I don't want much, either," replied he. "When I first come out inter this country, in '53, me'n Dave Woodman set out for the diggin's together. We bought a couple of mules, loaded 'em with provisions, and started on a prospectin' tour. We made putty good wages washin' for a time; but got sick er that, and allowed to go up inter the mountains looking for quartz-leads. One day, while we was workin' along the side of a steep hill, we come suddenly on to the sign of a grizzly, as fresh as that 'ere one we see this mornin.'

" Well, Dave was for huntin' him at once. He said he never could let sich a chance to git a shot at a grizzly go by, as that was; so I went with him, of course.

" The sign led us right into the thick underbrush; for a bar not only gits the shade thar, but he gits his berries as well."

" Do grizzlies eat berries?" inquired Ned in a tone of astonishment.

" Certing they do; it's their reg'lar food. They're mighty fond of wild currants, choke-berries, *piñon* nuts, and sich like. I've seed where they've broke off limbs er cherry-trees as big as my leg, for the sake er gittin' the cherries. But, as I was sayin', the sign led right inter the thick underbrush, and we follered in arter it.

" Dave was in the lead; and pretty soon arter we got in, I heerd a crash and a sort of wheezy growl, and then Dave fired. I took a look, and seed somethin' as big as a ox, standin' on his hind-legs, with his mouth open like a thirsty dog, and workin' hisself up and down just like he'd got the colic."

" What made him do that?" inquired Hal.

" Why, I s'pose he didn't like the pill Dave had just giv' him," chuckled Jerry.

"The next minit he dropped onto all fours again, and made a rush for Dave, who was reloadin' his rifle."

"Why didn't you fire at him? That would have been the first thing I should have done," remarked Hal.

"I s'pose so," sneered Jerry; "but you see *I* was scart, and didn't even remember that I hed a rifle; and before I know'd it Dave was down, and the blood runnin' a stream. One blow from old Ephraim's paw hed cleaned the flesh all off er one side of the poor feller's face, besides breakin' his jaw.

"Jest then I happened to think, and fired at him; that started him arter me, but I shinned up a little tree, and got out er his way; and putty soon he disappeared in the underbrush again.

"Yer see, a grizzly'll always leave his game, for any thing else that disturbs him. I didn't know that then, or I should 'a' took care not to hev got so near the critter afore I fired."

"Can't grizzlies climb?" inquired Ned.

"Not arter they're growed," replied Jerry: "they're too clumsy."

"Do you suppose you hit him when you fired?" asked Hal.

"I reckon so. I aimed at his head, for I didn't know then that the bones of a grizzly's head are sort of roundin', and the ball is mighty apt to glance off. There ain't but three places ter aim at in huntin' grizzlies: one's just back of the ear, and his spine, and the heart; and if yer don't hit him in one on 'em, you'll have trouble with him, sartin."

"What became of Dave?" inquired Hal.

"Dave? Why, I carried him down to the nearest settlement, and he finally got well; but he was terribly disfigred, besides losin' an eye in the scrimmage.

"Yer see, boys, my first introduction to old Ephraim wasn't kalculated to encourage me in huntin' 'em much; and of late years my hand's got pretty well out with shootin', so I'd a heap rather take my chances at trappin' than huntin'.

"Now, if you're goin' out to the trap with me in the mornin', boys, you'd better go to bed now, and let me hev a smoke in peace; and send Juan in, 'cause I want to see him 'bout havin' the cattle brought up for brandin'."

Thus dismissed, the boys left us, declaring, however, that they should be out to the trap long before either Jerry or myself were stirring in the morning. Nor had the sun shown himself above the horizon the following day, when I heard them discussing, while saddling their ponies for a visit to it, the chances of finding the trap occupied.

They soon returned at full speed, each endeavoring to be the first one in, and could hardly find breath to inform us that we had "caught something," though both agreed that it looked more like an ox than a bear.

"How near'd yer go to it, youngster?" inquired Jerry of Hal.

"Oh! only near enough to see it," was the reply.

"You didn't go near enuff ter see what 'twas though, did yer?"

"No: because we didn't know but it might be alive."

"Ha, ha, ha!" laughed Jerry. "You're a nice one ter hunt grizzlies, you are. I reckon you'd nat'rally take to trappin' like myself, arter all. It's a heap safer."

"But I wasn't afraid," declared Hal; "only I didn't want to go any nearer before you came out."

"Oh! I see," was the reply: "well, we'll git some breakfast, and then ride out and find what we have got."

CHAPTER III.

EPHRAIM CAUGHT. — PATSEY'S TIP-OUT. — A RODEO IN CONTEMPLATION. — THE VAQUERO AND HIS DRESS. — SPLENDID RIDERS. — THE GATHERING. — BRANDING CATTLE. — A FANDANGO. — THE RESULT.

BREAKFAST over, we immediately set out to examine the game, which proved to be an enormous grizzly quite dead; the log having fallen across his back in such a manner as to completely separate the vertebræ of the spine.

After removing the log, it required our joint exertions to draw old Ephraim from out the trap; nor was it until he lay stretched upon the grass before us, that we realized the size of the enormous creature.

He was nearly eight feet in length, and girt more than six around the body, which was covered with a thick coat of a dirty brown color, specked with gray, the legs being much darker than the other portions; his feet were quite sixteen inches in length, and armed with claws nearly five inches long. Even old Jerry was forced to admit that he had seldom seen a larger one; and turning to Hal, with ill-concealed triumph in his voice he said, —

"Wal, youngster, what d'ye think 'bout trappin' bars now? Yer see they ain't so smart as you be, arter all: they're fond of burnt honey though, and *will* venter arter it. You'd better ride back, and have Patsey hitch a pair of mules afore the wagon, and come after the critter; and stay and come with him, or he'll never git here without some outrageous cuttin'-up of some kind."

Hal at once mounted his pony, and was off, while Ned, seating himself upon the carcass of the bear, said, —

"I'd like to see this old fellow weighed. Why, he's as big as my pony, and must weigh nearly a thousand pounds. See what immense paws he's got. I believe a blow from one of 'em would kill a man."

"Yes, or a ox either," declared Jerry. "I've often knowd of their attackin' and killin' a buffalo on the plains. But while we are waitin' here, I reckon we may as well set the trap again. Maybe we shall get another, one of these fine nights, 'cause there ain't nothin' like burnt honey for ketchin' bars."

The trap had been set some time, and we were waiting patiently for Patsey and Hal to make their appearance, when our attention was arrested by the sight of a pair of mules, with the front wheels of a wagon, dashing wildly over the plains.

"There! I told you that feller Patsey'd git into

some kind of a scrape : there goes them mules," said Jerry. "If them boys hev broke their necks I sha'n't care much;" and the next moment he was in the saddle, scouring away over the plains in search of the missing boys, whom he found after a time, with the overturned wagon-body, in the midst of a dense mesquite chaparral, but little the worse for their tip-out, save a few scratches and torn clothes.

It appeared that shortly after leaving the ranch, a dispute had arisen between them, as to which should have the honor of driving the wagon-load of bear-meat to the house ; and, while Hal was attempting to deprive Patsey of the reins, the mules became frightened, and overturned the wagon, making off with the fore-wheels.

The animals secured, they were once more put before the wagon ; and by the exercise of our united strength the carcass was loaded and driven home, escorted by Jerry, Ned, and myself, on horseback.

It weighed nearly eight hundred pounds; and the flesh lasted us many days, enabling us to thoroughly test the somewhat toothsome frontier viand of "bear-meat and honey."

During the afternoon Juan was despatched to visit the neighboring ranches, to ascertain how many proprietors would join us in hunting up the cattle, and driving them in to be branded. This is done once in every year, when the ranch-owners assemble at the coral,[1] each selecting his own cattle from the herds driven in.

[1] Called by the old Spaniards a *rodeo*.

Before night more than a dozen young fellows, well mounted and equipped, had volunteered for the sport. Although these men necessarily are obliged to undergo great hardships and fatigue in the chase, it is regarded as sport, since it not only enables them to display their superior horsemanship, but at the same time their dexterity with the lasso as well as the quality of their favorite steeds.

The dress of the *vaquero* generally consists of a stiff broad-brimmed hat, securely fastened under the chin; a loose short jacket, with pants of buckskin; around the knee is fastened a square piece of stout leather which protects the leg as well from the attacks of cattle as from the falls sometimes received in pursuing them; in one of these leggings he always carries his knife, which with his spurs, *serape* or blanket, and lasso, complete his equipment.

The lasso is generally made of carefully twisted rawhide or hair, and in the hands of an experienced person is a very formidable weapon.

As we had bought with the ranch some three hundred head of horses and cattle, all except the yearlings being branded thus — BV, Jerry was quite anxious to have the herd driven in and examined before more stock was purchased.

It required all the authority that Jerry and myself possessed to prevent the boys from accompanying the party that started so gallantly out upon the cattle-hunt the next morning; but we finally persuaded them of the dangers they must necessarily encounter upon the expedition, and induced them to remain at home, although Hal persisted in declaring that he could ride as well and as long as any *vaquero*.

No sight connected with life upon the frontier ever impressed me more forcibly than did the first *rodeo* I ever witnessed.

Let me describe it. The cattle collected and confined in the coral, the *vaqueros* proceed to ornament themselves and their horses with all the finery they possess.

Large fires, in which the branding-irons are kept continually heated, are then kindled in close proximity to the enclosure. The gate having been removed, and a broad bar substituted in its place, several of the *vaqueros*, mounted upon their favorite steeds, enter the enclosure.

The first lasso is thrown over the horns of a steer, then, the bar being withdrawn, the animal is coaxed out, the *vaquero* at his side. As he emerges from the coral, a second lasso is dexterously cast so as to catch him by one of his hind-feet; and the next instant the astonished creature is hurled violently to the ground, where he is securely held upon his side, by means of the lassos, strained to their utmost tension by the admirably trained horses, who throw their whole weight upon the ropes. Before the steer fairly comprehends the situation, a Mexican applies the hot brand to the flank or shoulder; a violent struggle, a hiss of the brand, and a little puff of blue smoke, announces that the iron has done its work;

a shake of the lasso then disengages it; the steer struggles to his feet, gives a wild, bewildered look about him, and with an angry bellow rushes off towards the plain as fast as he can run, smarting with pain, and furious at the treatment he has received.

The larger and wilder animals are invariably kept until the last; and as the numbers in the coral gradually become thinned, those left behind, maddened by the rapid driving and loud yells of the *vaqueros*, combined with the heat and dust, begin to show fight from every quarter.

The men and horses become each moment more excited; cattle are falling in all directions, and the shouts of the *vaqueros*, accompanied by the angry bellowings of the cattle, the neighing of horses, the thick clouds of dust and smoke, the hissing of the brands as they ruthlessly descend upon the flesh of the fallen creatures, all conspire to create a scene of the wildest confusion and excitement; one that must be witnessed to be properly appreciated.

Occasionally a young bull, after having been branded and cast loose, instead of hurrying away towards the mountains, turns, and, tail in air, makes a rush at the crowd of spectators, who of course scatter in every direction. These attempts at revenge, however, only serve to increase the excitement, for they always end in subjecting the maddened brute to further indignities, so that when again released he rarely fails to seek the company of his equally unfortunate companions who have found a refuge in the mountains.

The cattle branded, the men are expected to partake of supper; and then the sweet tones of the guitar and mandolin summon all hands to the fandango, which invariably crowns the day's sport.

From early morning the boys had been perfectly wild with excitement; hurrying hither and thither, ordering here and there, one moment scurrying rapidly away on their ponies over the plain in pursuit of some stray steer, again perched upon the wall of the coral, and devouring a huge piece of honeycomb with all the *gusto* of old frontier-men; nor was it until after the crowd had separated, the music ceased, the dancers gone home, and the cold gray light of early morning was struggling with the darkness of night, that they could be induced to retire to their beds, worn out with the excitement, and the (to them) novel experiences of the day and night.

The result of the day's work showed us to be the owners of three hundred and sixty-three head of cattle young and old; but, as Jerry insisted that there ought to be at least a thousand head upon the ranch, I finally decided that the required number should be added as soon as they could be purchased.

It was nearly noon before the boys made their appearance; and the first question asked was if we had been to the trap.

Neither of us had given it a thought; but at Jerry's suggestion, we concluded to ride out immediately after we had partaken of dinner.

"I AT ONCE INVITED THE NEW-COMER TO ALIGHT." Page 31.

CHAPTER IV.

A NEW ACQUAINTANCE. — SILE CARTER AND JERRY. — A VISIT TO THE TRAP. — THE WILD BULLS. — HAL AND NED TURN VAQUEROS. — THE CHASE AND A FALL. — A PONY GORED. — A SUGGESTION, AND WHAT CAME OF IT.

WHILE engaged in eating dinner, our ears were saluted with an unmistakable Yankee "Halloo, the house there!" — which had the effect of bringing us to the door, where we discovered a stranger sitting upon his horse, and regarding with a somewhat rueful countenance the yelping dogs that surrounded him. Leaving the boys to silence the dogs, I at once invited the new-comer to alight.

"Heow on airth do ye 'spect a man tew 'light with such a pack of yelpin' curs about him as you've got here?" was the response to my invitation.

The boys by this time having driven away the dogs, the stranger straightened himself in his California saddle, and, first removing from the pommel his long Kentucky rifle, slowly swung himself to the ground.

He was a man apparently forty years of age, tall

and thin, with a pleasant face, browned by long exposure to the weather, and nearly covered with a long flowing beard.

Upon his head was a broad-brimmed felt hat that served to partially conceal his features, which, however, lighted up with such an expression of surprise and pleasure at the sight of old Jerry standing in the door, that I involuntary glanced at the old man to ascertain if he responded to the recognition.

The horseman was clothed in a short jacket of buckskin, with pants of the same material, the whole suit being heavily fringed and ornamented. Upon his feet were heavy American riding-boots, adorned with a pair of enormous Spanish spurs; and from his belt protruded the handle of a Colt's revolver and a Spanish hunting-knife. Upon the pommel of his saddle was neatly coiled a finely braided rawhide *reita*, or lasso, which, with the Mexican blanket tied to the back of the tree, completed his outfit.

As he stood beside his horse, partially leaning upon his rifle, he said in a pleasant voice, but with a strong nasal twang,—

"They told me deown tew the Bay that I should find a Yankee ranch eout here; and as I was raised deown on the Kennebec, in the State of Maine, I thought I'd ride eout and take a look at yer, for the sake of old times; but if that ain't Jerry Vance's face in that 'ere door, why, consarn it, it's his picter or his ghost, I dunno which."

Upon hearing himself thus alluded to, Jerry came

forward; and no sooner did he get a good sight at the stranger's face, than he exclaimed, " Sile Carter, as I'm alive!" and the two grasped hands with a warmth that betokened an unmistakable but most agreeable surprise.

"You bet I'm glad to see yer, Sile," said old Jerry. "You see, I didn't git a right good look at the ugly mug under that big hat o' yourn, or I'd knowed yer in a minute, if 'tis nily ten year since I seen you last; but come in, Sile, come in; I want ter introduce you. — Here, boys, this is Sile Carter, an old friend, a hunter, trapper, miner, and forty-niner, that I've summered and wintered, and found to be as true a man as ever eat a corn-pone. — Here, Patsey, lead this hoss round to the coral; and you, Sile, come in, and hev sumthin' to eat. You bet I'm glad ter see yer though! why, I hain't seen a face that I ever seed afore sence I struck the country this spring. Whar' yer been this long time, and what yer doin' down ter the Bay? Tell us all about it."

Calling the boys to me, I suggested that we leave Jerry and his friend to enjoy their visit together, while we rode out and made an inspection of the trap; and in a few minutes we were off for the woods.

As we were slowly galloping over the plain, my attention was arrested by the appearance of a small herd of wild cattle grazing in the distance; whereupon I suggested to Hal that here was a fine opportunity to show his skill as a rider, as well as to gratify any taste he possessed for a *vaquero's* life.

I had hardly spoken, ere both the boys started in pursuit of the herd, which consisted of five black bulls, one of them evidently a young one.

They were splendid beasts, with sleek, glossy coats, short horns, thin flanks, and broad chests; evidently as wild and fierce as the most daring *vaquero* would have desired to meet. The instant they caught sight of the boys, they evinced considerable uneasiness, staring wildly at them, sniffing the air and pawing the ground in a frantic manner, and then starting at a round gallop for the mountains.

The boys pursued them for some time without gaining on them in the least; when, seeing that it would be impossible to overtake them, Ned raised his rifle, and, just as the young one presented his broadside to him, fired, bringing the bull to his knees, while the rest of the herd, tail on end, trotted briskly away over the plain.

As Ned had been obliged to rein in his pony before shooting, the halt had given Hal a decided advantage, and he was now some distance in the advance; seeing the bull fall, he spurred towards him, reaching him, as it proved, altogether too soon for his own good; for he rode so close to him, that the bull by a sudden exertion rose, and plunged at him.

So quick and unexpected was the effort that before Hal could get out of his way, the creature struck his horns into the pony's shoulder, badly goring it, and unseating Hal, who was violently hurled to the ground by the shock. Jumping to his feet, he ran towards us yelling, "Shoot him! shoot him! why don't you shoot him?" as badly demoralized a *vaquero* as I ever remember to have seen at a cattle-hunt.

The last effort of the bull proved too much for his strength; for the gallant fellow immediately fell upon his knees once more, and then rolled over upon his side, dead, while Hal's pony started for home as fast as he could go.

As soon as we were satisfied that Hal was "more scared than hurt," we could not resist the inclination we felt to laugh at the woe-begone, disconsolate appearance of the young man, who stood trying to brush the dirt from his clothing, occasionally pausing to survey his pony now fast disappearing in the distance, and then glancing towards the cause of his discomfiture, who lay lifeless before him.

Up to this time neither of us had spoken. Hal was the first to blurt out,—

"I was a-going to bleed him, just as the *vaquero* told me they always did, and he got right up and come at me;" then turning to Ned, he angrily exclaimed, "I never knew you to half kill any thing anyhow."

"You had the same chance to fire that I did: why didn't you shoot him?" laughingly inquired Ned.

"You should have approached him more carefully, Hal," said I: "you'll never become a *vaquero* until you learn to exercise more caution as well as presence of mind; these are indispensable."

"I don't care: nobody could have got out of his way," declared the boy. "And I've had enough of hunting cattle. If you want any more hunted, you may hunt 'em yourself."

This ebullition of temper caused both Ned and myself to burst into a loud laugh, in the midst of which Hal started limping away in the direction of the house.

"Where's your rifle?" shouted Ned. "You'd better take it with you;" but Hal limped on, nor would he accept of Ned's offer to go after his pony.

"Let him go, Ned," said I: "perhaps it will learn him a lesson, or, at all events, teach him to be more cautious in the future. We'll ride on, and examine the trap, and then have Patsey come out for your game.

The trap was found to contain a good-sized cub; and after removing it, and finding ourselves unable to reset it, we rode back towards the ranch, where we found Hal entertaining Jerry and his friend with a recital of the wrongs he had experienced at the hands of Ned and myself.

Patsey and a couple of the Mexicans were despatched with the wagon for the game, and then the pony examined. The wound proved to be a slight one; old Jerry assuring us that in ten days "he'd be jest as good as ever," declaring that in the mean time "Hal ought ter be made ter go afoot, ter pay for his cussed careless way of talkin'."

During the remainder of the afternoon and evening, I had a fine opportunity of becoming acquainted with Sile, who proved to be thoroughly conversant with all portions of the country as an experienced guide, as well as miner and trapper. Indeed, without Jerry's assertion " that he'd summered and wintered him, and knowed him to be as white as any man that ever wore buckskin," his appearance alone would have prepossessed us in his favor; for we found him modest and unassuming in his bearing, and with a pleasant, genial manner that spoke loudly in his favor.

So well pleased was I with his appearance, that, before I retired that night, I ventured to unfold to Jerry a plan that I had for some time been maturing; which was, to visit the more northern and eastern portions of the State in company with the boys, who like myself were entirely unacquainted with the country, and while there purchase such stock as we required for the ranch.

The fact that I did not care to go unless accompanied by an experienced guide, and had no suitable person to leave in charge at home, had alone deterred me from starting before; now I proposed to secure the services of Sile Carter, and leave Jerry behind to take charge of and superintend the affairs on the ranch.

The plan pleased Jerry, who immediately declared it was just the thing, saying " there warn't another man in Californy he'd as soon trust as Sile Carter; because he not only know'd the country so well, but was honest, had real grit, was brave, and had jest as soon fight his weight in wild-cats or grizzlies as not: besides, he wouldn't let nobody impose on the boys 'cause they was young."

I requested Jerry to say nothing of the plan until it had been more fully considered, and went to bed to dream over it; for I had lived long enough in the world to learn that any step worth taking was worth thinking of beforehand.

CHAPTER V.

A TRIP SUGGESTED. — A HUNT. — THE RESULT. — HOW WE JERKED OUR MEAT. — ORGANIZING A PACK-TRAIN. — A STAMPEDE. — ON THE ROAD. — HAL AND NED IN A FIX. — CROSSING THE QUICKSANDS.

EARLY on the following morning I despatched Hal and Ned upon a tour of inspection to the trap, taking advantage of their absence to mention the subject of the contemplated trip to Sile, who at once declared his readiness to accompany us, and do all in his power to make it a pleasant as well as successful and profitable one; suggesting, however, the advantage of transporting our stores with pack animals instead of wagons, as originally intended.

Upon consulting with Jerry, he assured me that we already had every thing needed for our personal outfit, but expressed the opinion that we might find some difficulty in breaking our mules to the pack-saddle, especially as since our arrival they had been permitted to run wild with the herd of horses.

Sile suggested that himself and the boys should take a day for hunting; hoping thereby to secure enough venison for "jerking," which was to be carried along for use, provided game should be found scarce upon any part of the route.

While we were discussing this subject, the boys returned, and forthwith began to ply us with so many questions relative to the trip, its object, destination, &c., that we were obliged in self-defence to fully explain the project.

The preliminaries arranged, Sile and the boys made ready for their hunting expedition the following day, while Jerry and myself were to visit San Diego, and purchase a tent and the necessary outfit for our *atajo*, or pack-train.

Upon our return the following night, we found the hunters had arrived with a fine supply of venison, in addition to which they reported another large grizzly in the trap.

Old Jerry was in high glee at this unexpected good fortune, and could not forbear reminding Hal that "thar wasn't nothin' like burnt honey for ketchin' bars, if they warn't quite so smart 's some folks."

It was hardly daybreak the next morning, ere Jerry and a couple of the Mexicans, with the wagon, were on their way to procure the bear's carcass, which we decided to "jerk" with the venison.

Upon its arrival, we all went to work with a will, cutting the meat free from the bones into small thin strips. These pieces were then laid upon the inside of the hide of the animal, and completely covered with salt: they were then carefully wrapped in the skin, and suffered to remain about four hours, when they were ready to be "jerked."

HOW WE JERKED OUR MEAT.   41

Under Sile's direction the boys produced four strong, forked sticks, which were driven firmly into the ground about six feet apart, in the form of a square. Two stout, firm poles were then laid across the forks, upon opposite sides of the square, about four feet above the ground; the space between being filled with smaller poles about two inches apart, thus forming a huge gridiron upon which the strips of flesh were spread.

A fire was then kindled beneath it, which was carefully fed with clean, fresh wood; and at the end of twenty-four hours the meat had shrunk to about one-half in size, the salt had been thoroughly dried in, and Sile declared we had provisions enough to carry us through, even though we failed to find any game upon the route.

In the mean time a couple of the *vaqueros*, who had been sent out to the ranch to select and bring up the animals for the pack-train, returned with eight fine strong mules, who followed the old bell-mare[1] so placidly and sedately that we all enjoyed a laugh at Jerry's expense for entertaining the idea that we should find them in the least intractable. Indeed, so well-behaved and quiet were they that we deemed it unnecessary to give them even a trial before the time of starting.

After securing a half-breed for our cook, and a

---

[1] Mules entertain such a peculiar affection for an old white mare, with a bell around her neck, that an animal of this kind is generally driven with every herd, to prevent the mules from straying.

couple of Mexicans to act as *arrieros*, or muleteers, we decided to leave the following day, travelling as far north as the valley of the San José, where we knew we should find such stock as we desired to purchase.

When the mules were brought out from the coral, preparatory to being packed, Jerry suggested, as a simple matter of precaution, that they should be blinded by tying cloths about their heads, so as to prevent them from using their eyes. They submitted so quietly to the operation of having the clumsy pack-saddle adjusted, as well as to that of loading, that we all voted them models of patience and good-temper; but when brought into line, and the blinders removed from their eyes, it was altogether another story.

The meek, submissive creatures that had been so "roundly abused" by the muleteers for being no better than dead mules, became suddenly endowed with life and motion, and began to assert their independence in such a manner as to astonish not only ourselves, but the bell-mare as well, who seemed to be quite at a loss to account for their unseemly behavior; for away they went, helter-skelter over the plain, in the most reckless manner imaginable, — kicking, braying, and indulging in all the ridiculous antics that mules were ever known to indulge in.

In less time than I have taken to tell of it, the *cargas* became loosened, and then such a scene as we witnessed cannot be properly described upon paper.

Camp-kettles, coffee-pots, Dutch-ovens, tin cups, hams, sacks of flour, boxes, in fact, our entire stock of commissariat stores, were scattered over the plain in the utmost confusion; while the animal that carried the tent deliberately walked into a small lake near the house, and lay down.

I was disposed to be angry at first, but a moment's reflection convinced me that no one was really to blame for the mishap; and then the ludicrous appearance we all presented, standing with mouths, ears, and eyes wide open, without making the least exertion to overtake and stop the runaways, caused me to burst into a hearty laugh, in which the rest speedily joined; and then, hurriedly mounting, all set out in pursuit of the flying fugitives.

It was nearly sunset before the animals were caught, the scattered stores collected, and order restored: altogether too late to think of starting that day. We were therefore obliged to postpone our departure until the following morning, when old Jerry announced his intention of accompanying us on our first day's travel, which was to be as far as the old mission of San Diego.

Once upon the road the boys manifested their delight in the most extravagant manner, declaring their intention of riding ahead and selecting a camping-place for the party; and before I had time to remonstrate with them, their ponies were scampering madly over the plain, as though for dear life.

A couple of hours later we came to a small stream,

where, owing to the steep bank, we found some difficulty in persuading our animals to cross: after a short delay we got them safely over, Jerry and myself following up the bank. After riding a mile or more we came unexpectedly to Hal and Ned lying upon the grass, and looking as dejected and disconsolate as two boys could well look.

They appeared to have been in the water nearly up to their necks, and were quite covered with sand and dirt; their ponies, which were quietly feeding near them, having evidently shared the fate of their masters.

"What's the trouble, boys?" inquired I, riding towards them.

"Got into the quicksand," sententiously answered Ned.

"Whar on airth did yer find quicksand?" inquired Jerry.

"In the stream there," was the answer.

"Of course if there was a spot anywhere within ten miles you youngsters would hev got inter it: that's sartin. You must er hed a lively time findin' it: who diskivered it?"

"Hal got into it first, and then I went in to help him out," was the reply.

"I might 'a' know'd it without axin' sich a question. He'd find any thing like that a heap quicker than he'd find a pot er gold.

"How come you ter git inter sich a muss?" continued Jerry, turning towards Hal.

"I didn't think about quicksand," replied Hal. "I rode my pony into the stream, and stopped a minute to let him drink, and the first thing I saw he began to sink, and before I knew it I found he couldn't pull his feet out of the sand; so I called to Ned and he rode in: but when he found what the trouble was he spurred his pony across as fast as he could, and then waded in to help me, and we both got wet getting my pony out."

"Wal, you was lucky ter git him out, anyhow; 'cause it's mighty dangerous crossin' quicksand, specially for boys that don't know nothin' 'bout it," said Jerry.

"Boys sometimes know as much as those that are a good deal older," replied Hal.

"So I've heern tell," remarked Jerry, "though I hain't seed none er that sort 'bout here. Now, if you'd bin one er that kind, you'd 'a' built a fire and dried them clothes er yourn afore this time, instead of settin' on the grass talkin' about it."

"We should have done it a long time ago, only we had nothing to light a fire with; for our matches all got wet, and wouldn't burn," said Ned by way of apology.

"Matches all got wet!" repeated Jerry in a contemptuous tone. "What er that?"

"Why, of course we couldn't light a fire with wet matches," somewhat impatiently interrupted Hal. "I should think any fool'd know that."

"I've lighted many a fire when there weren't a

match, wet or dry, within a dozen miles, youngster; and kin do it again too."

"I know the Apaches do it by rubbing two dry sticks together," continued Hal; "but it can't be done any other way."

"Don't be too sartin of that, youngster. There's a good many ways er doin' it. I'll wager a good fat buck agin a coyote, that Sile Carter never'd be put ter his stumps ter start a fire any time, without matches or rubbin' two dry sticks together either, for that matter."

"Well, I'd like to see him do it," replied Hal; "and when I do, I'll believe it, and not before."

"Jes so, youngster. You've got a heap ter larn afore you know much; but that ain't no reason why we mayn't as well ride on ter camp, for I see Sile's got his fire started while we've been talkin' here," said the old man, pointing to a column of light-blue smoke gracefully ascending upon the still evening air, some distance to our left.

CHAPTER VI.

THE OLD MISSION OF SAN DIEGO. — OLIVE-TREES. — HOW WE MADE WATERPROOF MATCHES. — HOW SILE "GOT KETCHED," AND HOW THE GRIZZLY WARMED HIM. — INDIANS COMING.

WE were soon galloping towards camp, which we found pleasantly located near a fine grove of olive-trees in close proximity to the walls of the old mission of San Diego; the last of the California missions to be abandoned.

The boys at once set out upon a tour of exploration; and it was not until we had finished our supper, that they returned, full of astonishment at the extent and magnificence of the ruins about us.

No sooner were we gathered around the camp-fire that evening, than Hal commenced questioning Sile, as to how he would start a fire if his matches were wet and wouldn't burn.

"I shouldn't let 'em git wet in the fust place; but if they did, 'twouldn't make no difference, 'cause they're fixed so that they'll light anyhow, wet or dry."

"How is that done?" inquired Ned.

"By dissolving a little shellac in alcohol, and dippin' the match into it; then you kin soak it in water for hours, and it will burn just ez well," replied Sile.

"Yes," interrupted Hal; "but suppose you were out in the woods, and had no matches, how would you light a fire?"

"Wal, there's a number er ways that would dew, on a pinch. I've lit one afore now, by pourin' a little powder on tew a rock, and puttin' a percussion-cap in it, and then kiverin' the hull thing with dry leaves, and explodin' the cap with a stone; by pilin' on dry leaves and twigs, yew kin very soon start a big blaze. Then, again, I 'most always carry a sunglass, and when the sun's out, it's easy enuff tew dew it."

"But suppose you had no sun-glass, or powder, or caps, or matches," persisted Hal: "what would you do then?"

"If I hadn't no sun-glass, nor powder, nor matches, nor caps, nor nothin' tew make a fire with, what would I dew?" repeated Sile slowly. "Why, then, I should scrape some lint off er my shirt, or git some dry spunk-wood, and put it on a rock, and, by strikin' a skippin' sort of a blow with a stone, I should be putty sure tew bring fire; and if a spark teched it, it'd ketch sartin; and by fannin' it with my hat, I'd soon git a blaze out of it, you bet, youngster. There's a good many ways tew dew it.

I never was afraid of starvin' or freezin' yet for want of a fire; 'cause if a man's got any sorter sense, he'll find some way tew git out of sich a scrape, ef he gits inter it."

"But it isn't everybody that would be able to think in such a case," said Ned.

"Then he hain't got no bizness ter be trav'lin' on the plains; 'cause he's liable ter be ketched in a onsartin predicament any time," remarked Jerry.

"I'll tell you a predicament I once got ketched in, youngster," said Sile. "I was a-minin' up in Yuba, and hed jist come in from the sluice, when I see a wolf rite in the edge of the clearin' whar my cabin was. I ketched up my rifle that stood by the door, and started fer him. I followed him up the mountain fer quite a ways, and all of a sudden it begun tew grow cold, and a blindin' snow-storm come on. I know'd' twan't no use tew try tew find my way back in that storm; and I know'd putty well, that if somethin' didn't happen afore a great while, Sile Carter'd freeze tew death, sartin'. Well, while I was a-thinkin', I seed a big grizzly come tearin' right by me as though he was in a thunderin' hurry tew git hum. So I up and fired, and, as good luck would hev it, hit him rite behind the left fore-shoulder; and I'll be switched if 'old Ephraim' didn't jest keel over, as dead as Obed Rollins's ghost. I couldn't hardly believe it at fust, but he was dead, sartin as I was 'enamost froze tew death myself; so I jist took out my knife, ripped the old feller open, pulled his in-

'ards out, and got rite in tew that air carcass, butes and all. And I tell you, I laid thar all night as snug as ever a feller laid in his life; and in the mornin' I crawled out, and went hum. I told the boys how 'twas, and they went up and fetched the carcass down; and if we didn't hev a high old time over that grizzly, my name ain't Sile Carter, that's all. I tell yer what 'tis, boys, I never see no stove that kept me so warm as that old grizzly did that night; 'twas as good as a oven."

"I should rather have slept cold, than in such a place as that, even if I'd 'a' thought of it," remarked Ned.

"Some folks would; but it's different from me," said Sile.

"I'm sure Sile did just what I should have done if I'd been caught in the same scrape," remarked Hal.

"If I hadn't done it I'd bin a stiff froze corpse before mornin', sartin," continued Sile. "I've allers allowed 'twas a mighty big streak er luck that fetched that old grizzly along jest then. Yer see, I didn't hev another charge er powder, nor a cap, nor nothin'; b'sides, 'tain't one time in a hundred that a feller'll kill a grizzly on the fust shot: yer see, if I'd missed the critter, why, I was a plaguy sight wus off than I was afore; 'cause I should er hed the bar tew fite as well as the cold, and 'twixt the two on 'em they'd 'a' got Sile, sartin. But his carcass saved me, and I'm willin tew give the credit rite whar it b'longs: suthin' er other sent the critter along jist then, right in the nick of time ; fer thar hain't ben a grizzly seed within ten mile er that place sence ; and never was afore, thet I heerd of."

"It was a rale risky thing ter do," remarked Jerry; "but there ain't many men would have knowed enough to hev took the advantage you did, if they hed thought of it. They'd hev friz all the same, bar or no bar."

"I don't know about that," interrupted Hal: "'twould have been the first thing I should have thought of. A man must always have his wits about him on the plains."

"Jes' like you did the other day, when you was chasin' that steer ; but then, you see, you'n' Sile hev hed sich a mighty sight of 'sperience on the plains, its likely *yew* would hev thought of it. Thar ain't nothin' that brings a feller out like 'sperience."

"Excepting burnt honey," remarked Hal, in a tone not intended for Jerry's ear.

"That's ekally good for cubs," continued the old man. "I reckon it would fetch you; but it's nigh about time ter turn in, 'cause we shall want ter git a airly start in the mornin'. I must git back ter the ranch by ten o'clock, sartin."

"Well, Jerry, you must keep things straight there, and you may look for us back in about thirty days. We shall see you in the morning, however, and say good-by," said I.

"I don't b'leve in sayin' good-by: yer won't ketch me that way; 'tain't good luck. I reckon though you'll hev a nice trip; and if ever you get lonesome like, hev Sile spin one er his yarns for ye; he's a mighty good hand at that sort er business. If ye find a lot er cattle that suit yer, be keerful 'bout hevin' the brand vented afore yer start with 'em, cause anybody kin take 'em if yer don't; and don't buy nothin' over three year old nor under two."

The next morning we parted from old Jerry, and just at sun-up were once more on the road.

"I'm glad Jerry ain't going with us. He's forever snubbing me, but never says a word to Ned," remarked Hal, just after the old man bade us "God speed."

"Jerry rarely talks without an object," remarked I: "if therefore he talks to you, he unquestionably does it for your good."

"No, he don't. The fact is, he's jealous because I learn so fast: he's afraid I'll know more about travelling on the plains than he does; and I mean to get Sile to teach me all he knows about it, before we get back. I'll make Jerry sick."

"That's all nonsense, Hal. If you were to live a hundred years, you could never acquire the knowledge of the frontier that Jerry possesses. It would require closer observation, and more thought than you ever bestow upon any one subject, to give you even a smattering of Jerry's information."

"There's a sage-rabbit!" exclaimed the boy, as a large hare started up almost from beneath our very feet. For a single instant we caught sight of a pair of immense ears overtopping a bit of silvery gray fur, and then Hal darted off on his pony in pursuit of the timid creature, calling loudly upon Ned to follow him. But Ned only laughed, declaring that Hal might chase lightning if he cared to, but he believed he would reserve his pony's surplus strength until he could find a deer to follow.

Hardly had the words been spoken, ere Sile rode up, and, pointing to a dark mass far out upon the prairie, remarked that there was a herd of deer feeding there, the next moment declaring that there was also a party of Indians in sight.

"What do you suppose they are?" asked I.

"Pai Yutes, I guess: them's 'bout the only ones we'd see along here," was the reply.

"Harmless, ain't they?" asked Ned.

"As far as killin's consarned; but they're the meanest, dirtiest, laziest Injuns that was ever let loose tew plague a white man. All they're good for is tew ketch grasshoppers and wasps and such like vermin. We'll see enuff of 'em afore we've ben out a great while."

"Halloo, here comes Hal!" shouted Ned. "I wonder did he get the rabbit?"

"What! has he bin runnin' one o' them sage-rabbits on that pony er his'n? He might chase him till the crack of doom: he couldn't ketch him. Yew've got tew hev a dog for that sort o' huntin'. Why, one on 'em'll jump twenty foot, git 'em scart."

The next moment Hal came riding furiously up,

his face pale with suppressed excitement, and his pony covered with sweat and foam. As soon as he could speak he burst out with, "You're a nice set of frontiersmen, riding right into a whole nest of Apaches. I'd like to know whose business 'tis to keep a lookout. We shall every one of us be scalped: there's two to our one."

"Why, how you talk!" replied Sile. "Yew don't tell me them's 'Paches. When I seen 'em, I thought they was Diggers. Be they 'Paches, though?"

"I wouldn't worry about the safety of the train, Hal," remarked I. "Better trust that to Sile, and attend to your own concerns. Where's your game?"

"Confound it! I couldn't catch him: he run like the wind."

"And if these was Apaches, and we had tew depend on our hosses tew git us away, what kind of a chance d'ye think yew'd stand on that pony?" inquired Sile, pointing to the panting, reeking animal, thoroughly blown by his hard ride.

Hal looked exceedingly foolish, but, instead of answering, only protested that he didn't think of that.

"A man's got tew have his thoughts about him trav'lin' on the plains," continued Sile. "He don't never want tew run his hoss foolishly, 'cause he can't tell how soon he may be obleeged tew dew it. Thar ain't no use o' chasin' them rabbits, 'cause yew can't catch 'em without a dog: so I'd be a little more careful in future, sonny, if I was in your place.

Them Injins ain't nothin' but Diggers; yew needn't be afeard of them;" and Sile returned to the train quite unconscious of the fact that he had unwittingly offended Hal by the patronizing tone he employed in addressing him; while Hal, almost bursting with rage, rode sullenly beside us, muttering to himself in a manner that plainly showed no very great appreciation of Sile's well-meant counsel.

CHAPTER VII.

INDIAN VISITORS. — DIGGER MANNERS. — A GRASSHOPPER-HUNT. — A LAME MULE. — A VISIT TO A PAI UTE CAMP. — CAGED RATTLESNAKES. — POISONED ARROWS. —COOKING IN A BASKET.—A DIET OF WASPS.—FISHING.

WE had hardly made our camp that night, ere, as Sile had predicted, it was filled with some twenty of the most degraded, vilest-looking Indians we had ever encountered.

"Now, boys," said Sile, as he saw them approaching, "these fellers won't hurt hurt nobody; but they'll steal the terbacca out er your pipes, or the butes off er your feet: so keep both eyes on 'em, and don't let 'em come near the *cargas*, or inter the tent; and, if they don't mind what yew tell 'em, fetch 'em a crack over the head with a club. Yew needn't be afeard of 'em;" then turning towards Hal, he slyly remarked, "Them's your 'Paches, ain't they, sonny? Don't yew be afeard: they sha'n't hurt you."

"I'm not afraid of Indians, I'd have you understand. I've lived among them," replied Hal in his most dignified and freezing manner.

"Dew tell!" replied Sile, instantly comprehending that his well-intended assurances had caused offence to the boy; then assuming a more confidential manner he remarked, —

"Dew yeou know, I never should'v'e 'spected it from the way yeou looked when you rid up this forenoon. I kinder thought yeou was scart then; but I see now yeou was only poking fun at us;" and Sile gave Hal a most knowing wink, facetiously nudging him with his elbow, as he continued, "As my old mother deown in Maine used tew say, you can't most allers tell from the looks of a critter heow fur he'll jump, hey?"

By this time the Indians were fairly in camp; and, after shaking hands with each member of our party, they squatted upon their haunches around our fire, taking such complete possession of it as to seriously interfere with the cook's labors. One of the filthiest of the party, without the least ceremony, removed the cover from one of the kettles, and, plunging his hand into it, drew out a portion of the contents, which he conveyed to his mouth, and devoured with all the *gusto* of an epicure.

This act so incensed Sile, that, seizing a heavy quirk[1] from one of the Mexicans, he commenced belaboring the naked backs and shoulders of the intruders so vigorously,[1] he soon cleared them out

[1] A short-handled whip.

of camp, when, withdrawing a short distance, they stood regarding us with scowling countenances and any thing but friendly demeanor.

I was fearful that such a summary expulsion would bring trouble upon us; seeing from my face that I was somewhat apprehensive of the consequences that might follow such treatment, Sile hastened to dispel my alarm by saying, —

"Don't you be scart, squire. I know them fellers, an' as long as thar's two on us together, thar ain't no sort o' danger: if they was tew ketch any one alone though, they'd go for him, sartin. I wonder if some on 'em don't speak Mexican," and, turning towards them, he made the inquiry.

Instantly two or three of the party approached, one of whom in horrible Spanish began an explanation to the effect that they were friendly. "Utes," who were out upon a grand hunt, and having found no game, were nearly starved, and had visited our camp only for the purpose of obtaining something to eat.

"Of course they're hungry," said Sile: "nobody ever seen a Digger that wasn't. But 'tain't no use tew feed 'em, 'cause two on 'em 'd eat all the pervisions in camp, and starve for a month arter it."

"I wonder what sort of game they're after?" inquired Ned.

"Grasshoppers, I presume," said I.

"Grasshoppers! what on earth are they hunting them for?"

"For food, of course: they are esteemed a great luxury."

"Grasshoppers a luxury!" repeated the boy in a very incredulous tone. "Well, if they're a luxury, what's their principal diet composed of?"

"Wasps, mice, acorns, and roots. It was Gen. Fremont who gave them the name of Diggers, because they were continually digging through the snow to get at the roots and grubs in the earth, which furnish their only food in the winter."

"I should think it would be fun to go on a grasshopper-hunt," said Hal. "I wish we could have a chance to see how they hunt 'em. How do they do it, I wonder?"

"They first dig a hole deep enough to prevent the insects from jumping out after they are once in. The Indians then arm themselves with brush, and forming a circle beat the grasshoppers towards the pit. When in the hole they are crushed, and either eaten fresh or made into small cakes, which are preserved for future use by being dried in the sun. During the wasp season the ground is sometimes burned over, thus answering the double purpose of disabling the grasshopper and consuming the wasp-nests from which they obtain the young ones, which are said to be very delicious."

"I don't think I should care for such delicacies," said Ned. "Come, Hal, let's go out and see them;" and the two boys started for the place where the Indians seemed to be engaged in having a consultation as to the cause of the harsh and unpleasant treatment they had received.

At this moment Sile came up to inform me that one of the pack-mules had gone "dead lame," caused by stepping on a cactus-spine, and ought really to be permitted to lie still for a day or two; a piece of information I in no manner regretted to hear, since the delay would give us an opportunity to visit the Ute camp, and enable the boys to see something of the peculiar manners, habits, and customs of this most remarkable of the Indian tribes inhabiting the State of California.

Early on the following morning Hal and Ned, with Sile and myself, rode over to the Ute encampment, about five miles distant.

We found it composed of some thirty huts, or rude shelters, made of sticks or boughs interwoven together, and located upon the edge of a small *laguna*, or lake. Most of the men were entirely naked, the women having pieces of blankets or strips of bark fastened about the loins and hanging nearly to the knee: all, taken as a whole, were about the filthiest looking Indians I had ever seen. They were armed with bows and spears, but welcomed us to the camp with every expression of good-will. We had hardly entered it, however, when we were somewhat surprised to have one of their number, an old gray-haired man, approach, and, extending an exceedingly dirty hand, hear him say in pretty good English, "How d'ye do? Me speak 'Merican putty good. How's Gen'l Fremont?"

Inquiry revealed the fact that he had been employed as a guide by the general many years before; and during the time he was with him he learned to speak the language, an acquirement of which he was justly proud.

The boys soon started on an exploring tour about the camp; shortly returning with a really astonishing account of what they had seen in their peregrinations, the most wonderful of which were two caged rattlesnakes, and squaws cooking in baskets.

The old man (whose name I have forgotten) smiled at their enthusiasm, and explained, as nearly as we could understand, as follows:—

"There are many kinds of game in the country so wild we cannot get near enough to kill it outright with our arrows unless they are poisoned: this is done by placing the liver of some animal in a box or cage in which two or three rattlesnakes are confined. By constantly irritating the reptiles, they are made to repeatedly strike their fangs into the liver, which soon becomes saturated with poison, into which the warriors dip their arrow-heads, thereby rendering the slightest wound with them fatal."

The baskets are made of "sedge-grass," by the women, and are woven so closely that they are perfectly water-tight. The food to be cooked is placed in water in these baskets; hot stones are then dropped in, which as fast as they cool are removed, fresh ones substituted, and the water thus kept at the boiling-point until the food is cooked.

The old man was quite anxious that we should taste of their bread made from acorns, assuring us that Gen. Fremont had himself eaten it many times.

We watched the preparation of this dish, and found that when free from dirt and sand, it did not appear to be a very unpalatable article of diet.

The acorns were first pounded between two stones; water was allowed to percolate through the meal thus obtained, until the bitter taste of the acorn was in a measure removed; after which it was wrapped in leaves, and covered with hot stones until baked.

Although the boys partook of the bread readily enough, nothing would induce them to give the grasshopper-cake a trial; nor would they consent to taste of the old man's somewhat scanty supply of young wasps, notwithstanding his assurances that "dey was bery good, like white man's honey."

Sile, who during our conversation had been strolling about the camp, here put in an appearance, and inquired of the old man what the braves were building at the lower end of the camp.

After some hesitation, we were informed that the tribe were to celebrate the mysteries of the wolf-dance that evening, a rite that no stranger was permitted to witness.

This information only made us the more anxious to see it; and it required all the persuasive power of Sile and myself, backed by the promise of a new hunting-knife for himself, and plenty of brass wire for his squaw, before he would agree to intercede with the "medicine" who had the dance in charge, to allow us to witness it; finally, upon our promising to present the "medicine-man" with a pair of bright red blankets, he started off to obtain the necessary permission if possible.

While he was absent, we strolled down to the bank of the lake, and became much interested in watching one of the natives engaged in fishing. Turning over a sod, and picking therefrom a few grubs, he selected some light, dry reeds; he then tied the grubs to one end of the reeds with hair that he pulled from his own head, surrounding the bait with loops of the same material; then sticking the grubs in the mud and shallow water at the edge of the lake, he squatted upon his haunches, carefully watching them. Presently one of the reeds trembled slightly at the top; seizing it, he immediately tossed lightly out upon the bank, apparently without the slightest effort, a very large fish. This operation was repeated several times, after which he lighted a small fire, and heated some stones; then enveloping the fish in green leaves, he covered them with the heated stones, and, burying the whole under a mass of hot ashes and earth, left them to cook at their leisure.

It was nearly two hours before our messenger returned announcing that he had finally prevailed with the medicine, and obtained the necessary consent to our being present unseen, at the celebration of the wolf-dance.

Before describing it I will give you the old man's account of its origin, which, in connection with the events that followed, you will not find uninteresting.

Imagine yourself seated with us beneath the spreading branches of an acacia-tree, near the margin of the pretty little lake, listening to the old man's story, which he told as follows: —

CHAPTER VIII.

THE STORY OF THE WOLVES. — THE UTE MEDICINE-MAN. — THE INCANTATION. — THE DANCE-HOUSE. — THE BLACK WOLF DIGS, AND WHAT HE FOUND. — A SURPRISE. — INDIAN JUGGLERY. — A WONDERFUL FEAT. — SPIRITUAL MEDIUMS.

THE wolves were a tribe of Indians, whom the Great Spirit turned into their present form on account of their evil deeds.

The chiefs of the tribe, who were cruel and bloodthirsty, became the fierce black or timber wolf, whose home is in the mountains; the braves took the shape of the gaunt and hungry gray, and made their homes in the dense forests; while the squaws took the form of the more timid and harmless *coyote*, or prairie-wolf, whose home is upon the great plains.

Instead, however, of this transformation annihilating the bad and treacherous tribe, as was intended by the Great Spirit, they were immediately taken under the protection of Haelse, or the evil spirit, who cherished them so carefully that they soon began to thrive and to increase so rapidly that they were able to go out into all parts of the earth.

Once upon a time a young Ute hunter, who was desirous of becoming a great warrior, went out into the woods, as was the custom of the braves of his tribe, to seek and consult his " medicine."

For many days he travelled over mountain and plain, without finding him whom he sought. At night he laid himself down upon the bosom of the earth, and slept without dreaming where he should find him. Still he persevered, for he was determined to become a great warrior, or perish without returning to his tribe.

One night, as he was about to lay himself down to his dreamless sleep as usual, he saw far above him upon the side of the mountain, a great light which he determined to visit; approaching it he found a camp-fire surrounded by wolves who were recounting to each other their exploits of the day. Concealing himself close by, he remained and listened, becoming so charmed with what he heard, that he determined to continue with them, notwithstanding the Great Spirit solemnly warned him of the evil consequences attendant upon such a decision. So infatuated did the young brave become with the easy, pleasant life led by the band, that the following morning he joined their number, and from that time abode with them, neglecting not alone his tribe, but his dearest friends, who grieved to think him dead, and sincerely mourned his loss.

One day one of the hunters of his tribe, who was out in pursuit of game, came suddenly upon this band of wolves travelling along the mountain-side, and immediately recognized the friend for whom he had so long mourned.

He watched him for a long time, and saw that he oftentimes walked erect upon two legs, but more frequently ran upon all fours, and that his face even had become shaped like that of a wolf, and bore so fierce and savage an expression that he really feared to speak to him: he therefore hastened back to his friends, and reported what he had seen.

Many of the tribe who heard the report doubted his statement, and scouted the idea of their friend being found in such bad company; but the hunter insisted so earnestly upon the truth of his story, the chiefs finally decided to send out and attempt to induce the renegade to return to his home.

They therefore called upon their hunters to make strong snares of deer's sinews which they set in many places upon the side of the mountain, in one of which they finally succeeded in entrapping the wanderer, hoping thereby to restore him to his tribe.

But, alas! every effort was fruitless, every kind intention thwarted; for the warrior not only refused to recognize or speak to his friends, but snapped and snarled and bit at them furiously, as though he were indeed the savage creature he pretended to be.

Upon seeing this, the old men called a council, and, after considering the matter a long time, decided that, as the young hunter's nature and habits had become so changed by association with the outcast wolves, it was far better for the tribe as well as himself, that he should be forced to return to his new friends, and be forever debarred from his home and those who had loved him so well.

When the young man heard this terrible sentence, he realized for the first time the frightful consequences that this punishment must entail, and most piteously besought the council that they would restore him to his forfeited heritage; but they were inexorable, declaring that he should immediately depart from among them, and return no more, lest his example should be followed by other young men of the tribe.

The renegade departed, bowed down with sorrow and grief, and was nevermore seen by any of his tribe, who rejoiced greatly at his absence, since they had seen for themselves that "evil communications corrupt good manners."

Once in each year the "Utes" celebrate this expulsion of the renegade by a dance under the auspices of the "medicine" of the tribe, which we were to be permitted to witness that evening, stranger eyes being rarely allowed to view the solemn ceremonies, and only under circumstances that would prevent their presence being known to the performers.

After it began to grow dark, the boys and myself (Sile having returned to camp) were quietly conducted to the rear of a large hut situated a little distance from the encampment near the edge of the plain.

It was composed of brush and reeds ingeniously wattled together, but securely covered all around on the inside with mats, and was much larger than any other lodge in the encampment. A small opening in the rear, well shielded by leaves, had been left in the mats, through which we could obtain a good view of every thing that transpired within, without being seen ourselves.

After we were fairly ensconced in our hiding-place the old man left us, with many injunctions in no case to discover ourselves, whatever we might see; saying that the braves were gone out to prepare for the celebration: after leaving us, he stopped for a moment to light a fire before the entrance to the hut, and then departed.

It was a beautiful night: the rising moon cast a pale, weird light over the emerald-green plain that stretched out before us into illimitable space; over the dark, sombre forest behind us, from out which the smoke from a dozen camp-fires lazily ascended, settling over the tree-tops, and resembling a bank of beautiful blue clouds; over the placid surface of the little lake, which was undisturbed by a single ripple, and looked like a beautiful mirror, silvered by God's own hand, and set in Nature's chaste frame; while the lurid glare of the fire, now burning brightly, lighted up our more immediate surrounding with a ruddy glow that brought into bold relief the shadow cast by every branch and twig in the structure before us.

No sound disturbed the stillness that reigned about us, save the crackling of the burning wood, and the shrill note of some cuckoo from out the depths of the forest.

Suddenly the boys called my attention to a number of dark, half-developed objects moving slowly over the plain; while we were lost in conjecture as to what they were, we saw them approaching the hut; and in a short time the light of the fire revealed about thirty warriors clad from top to toe in wolf-skins, who sneaked into the hut in single file upon all fours, howling, growling, snapping, snarling, and biting at one another, imitating the movements of the animal itself so perfectly that we had hard work to persuade ourselves that the scene was not a reality.

After passing several times around the enclosure with their noses to the ground, sniffing and smelling in every direction, we observed one very large black wolf[1] quietly enter, and, after passing once or twice around the circle, suddenly give a quick sharp yelp, and with his hands commence scratching a hole in the earth.

The next moment the entire pack were fighting one another, growling, yelping, and uttering the shrillest cries; apparently all anxious to join the

---

[1] The medicine-man of the tribe.

black wolf in digging, yet by their very anxiety depriving themselves of the coveted task.

While this was going on, the black wolf kept steadily at his work, and finally, to our amazement, succeeded in exhuming a full-grown naked Indian, who, upon being dragged to the surface, soon gave unmistakable signs of life.

And now commenced a scene, the like of which I never before witnessed. The wolves commenced sniffing and smelling of the new-comer's person, elevating their noses in the air, uttering shrill cries, snarling and snapping, pawing the fresh earth, and indulging the grossest and most obscene gestures, until, under the protection of the black wolf, the Indian was conducted outside the hut.

The next moment the "medicine-man" re-appeared; silence was instantly restored, the wolves seating themselves upon their haunches in a circle about the hut, while he, taking a position in the centre, seated himself in like manner, and, elevating his nose high in the air, uttered a most piercing and prolonged howl; soon two Indians entered, bringing with them a tall covered basket, made of sedge or coarse lake grass, out of which stepped the Indian previously exhumed. A short snarling yelp was now uttered in chorus. When the man again retired to the basket, the cover was adjusted; and, after a lapse of a few moments, the basket was turned bottom upwards and lifted, when, to our amazement, nothing but a pile of feathers was visible, which by a dexterous movement of the medicine-man's hands were sent flying in all directions.

And now commenced one of those peculiar concerts often heard by the traveller upon the plains, where seemingly a hundred wolves have assembled together for the purpose of making the night hideous; chattering, barking, snarling, howling, yelling, screeching, and growling, — in the midst of which the medicine-man and his basket disappeared; and shortly the entire pack, one by one, sneaked out of the hut as though they were thoroughly ashamed of the part they had borne in the celebration; but it was only to meet one another around the bright fires that were now burning upon the plain, when the tribe were all to join in the festivities of the dance.

CHAPTER IX.

THE MYSTIC RITE. — THE WOLF-DANCE. — A PICTURE. — OUR RETURN TO CAMP. — HAL AND NED. — SILE EXPLAINS MEDICINE-MEN, — WHO AND WHAT THEY ARE. — INDIAN SKILL IN SHOOTING. — HAL'S OFFER. — WHY HE DIDN'T SET UP HIS HAT.

IT was with difficulty that I persuaded the boys to quietly remain in our place of concealment until the old man returned, so anxious were they to have him explain the meaning of the wonderful sights they had witnessed. When he came, however, he proved to be so deeply impressed with the mystic rites, himself, that he could make neither an impartial nor intelligible interpretation.

They were therefore obliged to wait until our return to camp, when we hoped that Sile would be able to elucidate the mystery to our satisfaction.

Meanwhile the sound of the drums and rattles called all hands to the locality where the entire village had assembled to witness the dance. Immediately upon reaching the place, the old man assigned us seats upon the ground, in a convenient position, at a little distance from the principal fire, around which were gathered the braves, still arrayed in their wolf-skin dress. Here we were to await the beginning of the performance.

I had hardly taken my seat before I missed the boys, who, however, returned in a short time with the information that they had been to see the music, which was made by beating upon dried hides spread upon the ground, and shaking gourds containing pebbles and shells.

These explanations were cut short at this juncture by the appearance of the black wolf, or "medicine-man," who gravely walked upon all fours into the centre of the circle; and then, standing erect, began a slow, dignified dance, consisting more in a wriggling motion of the body, — peering about as though in search of some hidden object, and imitating the movements of a wolf, all the while keeping time to the music, — than any dancing.

One after another the braves joined in, until finally the entire band were jumping about the fire, and shaking their rattles furiously to the time marked by the drums, all the while singing in a low, monotonous tone. As the dance continued, they grew more and more excited, the musicians every moment beating faster and faster time, until the entire party seemed to have become frantic in their exertions to outdo each other.

It was a strange, weird picture: the boundless expanse of plain and forest appeared like a sombre back-ground, bringing into startling prominence the hideous forms, upon which the bright light from the fire cast a lurid glare; revealing with wonderful fidelity the grotesque and extravagant movements of the dancers, over whom the black smoke had settled like a huge funeral-pall, through which the pale face of the full moon dimly shone with an almost unearthly light, creating a scene so uncanny and wild that I could associate it with nothing but Tam O' Shanter's strange dance in "Alloway's auld haunted kirk." It was a sight, when once seen, never to be forgotten.

At midnight the dancing was as vigorous as early in the evening; for, as the performers one after another became exhausted, their places were immediately filled from among the spectators, and the wild orgies thus kept up until daylight ended the scenes the following morning. After we had ridden miles over the broad moonlit prairies, on our way towards camp, the sound of the rude drums could be distinctly heard upon the still evening air; nor was it until we had descended into the little valley where our camp was located, that we no longer heard it.

We found Sile sitting by the smouldering fire, smoking his pipe, and patiently waiting our return. As we rode up, I said, " Well, Sile, you hadn't begun to be alarmed about us, I hope."

"Oh, no! I knowed thar warn't nothin' tew be 'fraid of 'mong them no-'count Injuns," was his reply.

"No-account Injuns," repeated Hal in a most contemptuous tone: "they can do more things than any white man I ever saw. If they're no account, I'd like to know where you find any who are of account. Why, we saw them dig a live Injun out of the ground, and then turn him into feathers that flew all about the lodge."

"Not really, Hal," interrupted Ned.

"Yes, really," declared Hal. "I saw him do it with my own eyes: there wasn't a bit of humbugging. I'm too smart not to know when I'm sold."

"But you don't really mean that he truly turned the man into feathers?" said Ned in a tone of inquiry: "he only seemed to. It was a trick; wasn't it, Sile?"

"I guess it was, and a pretty 'cute one at that, from your tell; but you boys had better go ter bed now, and in the mornin' I'll hear all about it;" then turning to me, he remarked, "I'm 'feard we sha'n't be able tew git started in the mornin': that ere lame mule ought tew hev another day's rest afore he's fit tew travel."

"All right, Sile. A day more or less don't matter much: so we'll be on the safe side, and let him rest."

"Hurrah, hurrah!" exclaimed the boys in concert. "We can go over to the camp again to-morrow."

"Well, boys, you won't go anywhere to-morrow unless you go to bed now," said I; "so off with you."

"And don't let the moon shine in your faces after yeou git ter sleep," shouted Sile.

"Why not?" inquired Ned.

"'Cause we don't want yer any more lazy than yer be neow," was the reply. The boys hurried to spread their blankets, and were soon fast asleep.

"Now, Sile, we want you to explain the wolf-dance for us," said Ned the following morning when Sile made his appearance for breakfast.

"I dunno what to explain," said Sile, whereupon the boys went on, and gave him a very correct account of all they witnessed the previous evening, ending with, "Now tell us where that Indian came from."

"Out er the airth, of course," responded Sile. "Couldn't yer see that for yourselves?" asked he facetiously.

"There, Ned, that's just what I told you," said Hal. "I knew there couldn't be any trick about it, for I saw him dug out with my own eyes."

"Well, where did he go to, then?" demanded Ned.

"Went intew the basket, and was turned intew feathers, of course," responded Sile.

"There, Ned, I hope that satisfies you. You said 'twas nothing but a trick; but I knew better. That was a genuine live Indian: didn't I see him breathe, with my own eyes?" said Hal.

"Do you think he was really turned into feathers?" asked Ned, appealing to me.

"No, Ned: it was a mere trick," was my reply, "a simple sleight-of-hand performance, such as Indian jugglers have frequently been known to do before."

"Sile don't think it was a trick, do you?" asked Hal.

"'Twa'n't nothin' else but a trick, of course. I didn't 'spose yeou was in airnest when you was askin' 'bout it afore," responded Sile.

"But they didn't get up the thing for our benefit, and I don't see what object the man had in fooling his own people," persisted Hal.

"Listen, Hal," said I. "These Indians are the most superstitious people in the world. All the Western tribes believe in medicine-men; i.e., men who are supposed to possess some kind of supernatural power, but who are generally the most unprincipled and sharpest fellows in the tribe, who, imposing upon the credulity of the superstitious, manage to be supported in idleness. You saw an instance last night, when the 'medicine' permitted us to witness the ceremony, or wolf-dance, contrary to the rules of the tribe: the promise of a pair of red blankets won his permission to be present, and nothing else."

"Yes, and here comes the old man for his pay," said Sile, pointing to three Indians approaching in the distance.

"That's bully!" cried Ned. "Now we'll make him tell us all about it, before he gets it."

"Scarcely, Ned. We promised him certain things, if he would obtain permission for us to remain and see the dance. He did that, consequently is honestly entitled to the articles promised, without further conditions; so go and get them for him."

"That's right, squire. I've allus found that if yeou treat them fellers as yeou agree tew, they ain't half so likely tew make yeou trouble. A man don't lose nothin' in this world by bein' honest, yeou bet! Them fellers hev got their bows with 'em: we'll hev some shootin' p'r'aps."

"I'll shoot with 'em," cried Hal. "I'm almost as good a shot with a bow as I am with a rifle."

"By the way, Sile, speaking of shooting reminds me that we have never seen you shoot yet. Are you a pretty good shot?" said I.

"I ain't nothin' tew brag on, though I gin'rally manage to git the game I shoot at," was the reply.

"Why can't we shoot at a mark some day?" inquired Hal. "I'd like to try Sile a whack with my revolver."

"All right, sonny. I'll shoot with yer any time yeou want tew try it."

By this time the Indians were in camp; and, after shaking hands all around, Ned presented them with the promised articles, adding thereto a string of blue beads for his squaw.

Our guests were evidently delighted; and, after a thorough examination of the different things, the old man announced that we were "berry good; white man heap," — a decision to which his companions grunted a seeming approval.

"Now you're here," said Ned to the old man, "we want to see you shoot some," placing his hands upon the bow, and making a motion as of drawing it. "Do you understand?"

"Umph! you want see shoot, eh?" And, turning to one of his companions, he spoke a few words in his native tongue.

The Indian laughed, and, selecting an arrow from his wolf-skin quiver, carelessly fitted it to the bow-string, and held it pointing to the ground, while the old man said, —

"What for shoot, eh?"

"I guess he wants some one tew set up a mark for him," remarked Sile. "Hev yeou got a old envelope, squire?"

While I was hunting in my pocket for one, Hal shouted, "I'll set up my hat; I ain't afraid of his hitting it at sixty-yards."

"All right, Hal: go and set it up," said I. "You take the risk, will you?"

"I'll risk it," was the reply. "I don't believe he can hit it."

Hal started to measure off the requisite distance; but just before he reached the point a large-eared rabbit[1] sprang up almost from beneath the boy's feet, and with a tremendous leap darted away over the plain, as though shod with the wings of the wind.

[1] More commonly known as the "mule" rabbit, so called on account of its enormous ears.

"It went clear through it." Page 81.

At the same instant I heard the twang of the bow-string, and, turning, saw that the Indian had fired. Before I fully realized that he had shot at the rabbit, Hal picked it up, and holding it by its great ears shouted, "It went clear through it: I ain't going to set up my hat."

While we were laughing at this sudden change of opinion, the Indian had fitted another arrow to his string, and again sent it clear through the rabbit's body which Hal was holding out at arm's-length for us to examine.

As the arrow struck it, Hal as suddenly dropped it, and in a bewildered sort of way looked first at us and then at the rabbit, finally exclaiming, —

"What did that, I'd like to know?"

"He s'posed yeow was a-holdin' it out for him tew shoot again," said Sile. "Pick it up and bring it in."

"Not much!" replied the boy. "If you want it brought in, bring it yourself: *I* don't touch it again." And Hal hastily strode towards us, with a face as white as a sheet.

CHAPTER X.

DANGEROUS SHOOTING. — REVOLVERS *vs.* ARROWS. — HAL'S TRIAL OF SKILL. — COMANCHE SHOOTING. — WHAT THE GREAT SPIRIT DID. — OUR VISITORS' DEPARTURE. — VAMOSE. — GETTING READY FOR A START.

"I TELL you what it is, Sile Carter, I don't like such jokes as that," exclaimed Hal angrily. "He might have hit me instead of the rabbit. Such shooting is dangerous."

"Dangerous? Why, he didn't shoot at you," replied Sile.

"He might have hit me though, if he didn't: the arrow passed within two inches of my face."

"Then I don't see how he hit the rabbit; for you was holding it at arm's-length," said Sile.

"Well, it might not have been two inches; but it was pretty near, any way," said Hal.

"Well, Hal, the question is, do you want a trial of skill with either of these Indians?" said I, taking one of the bows in my hand.

"No, sir. I won't shoot against them with their own weapons; of course they'd beat me: but I'll shoot my revolver with 'em."

"They never fired a revolver in their lives; and I heard you say you could shoot a bow almost as well as you could your pistol. Now, if this is so, your proposition is not a fair one."

"Well, I won't shoot with their bows, any way," declared Hal.

"Won't you let me see the bow a minute, please?" asked Ned. "What is it made of?"

"This one appears to be made of cypress, wound about the middle with sinew," said I. "The string is also sinew, and the arrows are made of reeds pointed with obsidian."

"What is obsidian?" inquired Ned; "and where does it come from?"

"It is a kind of native glass, or lava, and is found in all those parts of the country that are of volcanic formation. It has been used by the Indians of this region for more than three hundred years for arrow-heads."

"How does any one know that for a fact?" queried Hal.

"All the old Spanish explorers, including Coronado, who visited this country in 1540, speak of its use."

"Do you suppose those Indians could shoot as well as these do?" asked Ned.

"I know of no reason to doubt the fact," said I.

"Pshaw! That fellow's shooting was more than half luck. I'll bet he couldn't do it again," remarked Hal.

"I wouldn't like to bet that he couldn't, would you, Sile?" inquired Ned.

"I guess, if I was a-goin' to bet, 'twould be on your side, sonny," answered Sile. "I've seed some of them Injuns that would shoot 'stonishin'."

"I'm not afraid to shoot my pistol against his bow and arrow, at sixty-five yards," declared Hal.

"Oh! won't that be jolly?" cried Ned. "Let's have a shoot! let's have a shoot! I'll back Hal."

"No: there shall be no backing about it," interrupted I. "If the Indian with his bow beats Hal with the pistol, Hal shall give him a new pair of blankets; and, if Hal beats, he shall have the Indian's bow, arrows, and wolf-skin quiver — each one to have three shots."

The preliminaries agreed to, Sile and Ned proceeded to measure off sixty-five yards. Sile then cut a stick about an inch in diameter, and, after peeling it, set it firmly in the ground about two feet in front of the trunk of a large live-oak, which served as an admirable background to bring the mark out into bold relief.

Sile then tossed up for the choice of shots, which Hal won, selecting the last; whereupon the Indian, without the least hesitation, took his position, and, fitting an arrow to the string, discharged it with but apparently little effort: we saw the stick quiver; and the next instant, with a grunt of dissatisfaction, he again shot. This time the arrow struck the mark in the centre, splitting the stick, passing handsomely through it, and remaining imbedded in the trunk of the tree.

Before we had time to express our admiration at the excellence of the shot, the twang of the bow-string announced the third shot: an arrow once more cleft the stick in twain, and again imbedded itself in the trunk of the oak, about two inches above the other.

It was wonderful shooting: we all acknowledged that, and Hal freely declared that he could neither expect nor hope to beat it; still he took his position, and, slowly bringing his navy revolver up to the required level, fired. The bark flew from the trunk of the tree, but the mark was untouched. Again and again did the boy repeat the shot, without touching the stick; and the Indian was finally declared to have honestly earned his blankets, which were forthwith handed to him.

"I don't care if he did beat me," said Hal: "I did the best I could; but no one at that distance could beat one of these fellows with a bow and arrow."

"That's true, Hal; but it was your own proposition to shoot at that distance and in that manner. You asserted that you could beat him even then," said I. "You've had a fair trial, and been badly beaten; now, don't let us hear you brag about your shooting again. There's nothing that so be-littles a young man, as to hear him boast of being competent to do that which, upon a test, he shows himself unable to perform."

"I think Hal shot first-rate," said Ned. "He can beat me all to pieces."

"Hal shoots very well," was my reply; "but that is not the question: he asserted that he could do a certain thing, without reflecting that he knew nothing about it."

"Yeou did some purty good shootin', sonny, but 'twa'n't good enuff, was it? These Injuns are at home with the bow and arrow. I've seen some of 'em that would beat these fellers all tew pieces, 'specially among the Comanches down in Texas," remarked Sile.

"Pooh! the Comanches can't begin to shoot with these fellows," asserted Hal. "I know all about their shooting."

"I once seed a party of twenty on 'em on hossback," continued Sile, without heeding Hal's interruption, "a-shootin' at a target about eighteen inches in diameter, made of dressed buffalo-hide stretched on a rim of wood, and fastened tew a lance that was stuck in the ground. They passed within about fifty paces of it, their hosses on the keen run; and as each one on 'em rid by, he let off an arrow from under his hoss's neck, and then they turned quicker'n lightnin', and, shiftin' over to t'other side of their hosses, fired agin' at long range. When they got threw, I counted seventeen arrer-holes in the target out of the twenty that had bin fired at it. I called that good shootin'."

"It certainly beats any thing that I've ever seen done with the bow and arrow; but I suppose Hal would not call it very good shooting," said I.

"Well, I never saw them shoot any thing like as well as that," declared Hal.

"You've seen but very little as yet, Hal, and, before you're many years older, you will think so yourself. But come, these Indians are getting ready to go back to their camp: if you want to ride over with them, now's your chance."

"I believe I don't want to go," remarked Ned.

"Nor I either," said Hal: "only I'd like to know where that Indian they dug up, came from."

"Well, ask the old man," said I: "perhaps he can tell you."

"Where did the medicine-man get the Indian he dug out of the ground?" inquired the boy of the old Indian.

"Great Spirit bring him: tell medicine where find him," was the answer. "Medicine big Injun, heap;" and the old man turned away with the air of a person thoroughly convinced that there could be no further question as to the medicine-man's power.

"That's 'bout as much satisfaction as anybody ever gets out er one of them fellers: they all on 'em think their own medicine kin dew any thing in this world, and yew can't beat 'em out of it either. I guess they've got all they come for, and, as we sha'n't be likely tew want any thing out er them, they may as well go back tew their own camp;" and, taking one of them by the shoulder, Sile led him a short distance, and then, pointing towards their camp, uttered the single word "*vamose*," and the three visitors departed without further adieu.

"There," said Sile, as soon as they were fairly off, "we sha'n't see any more of them fellers ter-day, so I'll begin and git ready for a start in the mornin'; we ought tew make twenty miles ter-morrow, sartin."

"Where'll that bring us?" inquired Ned.

"Well, if nothin' happens, I mean tew stop at old Berella's cattle-ranch ter-morrow night: you'll see a genuine old Spanish ranch then; the old man owns nigh about twenty thousand acres of land, and has lots of cattle and Injuns."

"He don't own the Indians, does he?" inquired Hal.

"Not exactly, but he might as well: they're just like the *peons* in Mexico; he gives 'em four or five dollars a month, an' they trade at his store; an' as long as they owe him any thing they can't leave his employ; that's nigh 'bout as good as ownin' 'em, cause they're so lazy and shiftless, they never pay out er debt."

"How many Indians has he got?" asked Ned.

"I 'spose fifty or seventy-five," was the reply. "You'll see for yourselves when you git thar; but I want you boys ter come and look over the pack-saddles with me now. I don't want ter start agin till they've bin overhauled."

CHAPTER XI.

AN OLD CALIFORNIA RANCH. — THE PROPRIETOR AND HIS PEOPLE. — HIS HOUSE. — HIS POSSESSIONS. — A MOST WONDERFUL EXHIBITION OF SKILL WITH THE LASSO. — SUPERIOR HORSEMANSHIP. — THE DON SAYS IT IS NOTHING. — ONCE MORE ON THE ROAD. — OUR TRAIL FORKS. — NO-ACCOUNT PEOPLE. — ADDIOS.

SUNRISE on the following morning found us once again on the road, and after a somewhat tedious ride of twenty miles we came in sight of the cattle-ranch of Don Anastacio Berella, a wealthy New Mexican, who had been in California nearly thirty years, and was the owner of several thousand horses, ten thousand sheep, and as many more cattle; to say nothing of the twenty thousand acres of land claimed to have been granted by some emperor of old Spain to the ancestors of some other Don two hundred years before.

As we rode towards the ranch, we had a fine view of it and its surroundings.

The house was of *adobe*,[1] i.e., of sun-dried brick,

[1] *Adobes* are made of mud in which cut straw has been mixed: this material is pressed into moulds eighteen inches long by about ten wide, and four thick; they are then dried in the sun.

and, like most houses of that kind, was of one story. It was built in the form of a hollow square, into which the rooms all opened. There were but two windows visible, and these were protected on the outside by horizontal iron bars, and from the inside by stout wooden shutters; the only entrance from the front being through large double doors, of sufficient size to permit the ingress and egress of the Don's carriage and horses.

Just behind the house was a long range of *adobe* buildings in which his Indians lived; near to these was a large Mexican oven, conical in shape, and elevated upon posts about three feet above the ground, looking not unlike a huge bee-hive; while in close proximity was the coral, its walls, about eight feet in height, being also constructed of *adobe*.

As we drew near, Sile pointed out Don Anastacio, who was standing near the entrance to the coral, conversing with some of " his people " as he termed them.

He was a man about fifty years of age, very portly and tall, and, like all native New Mexicans, with a very dark complexion, and long jet-black hair: he was dressed in a light pink calico shirt, with pants of blue jean, heavily ornamented upon the outside of the leg with little silver buttons; around his waist was a scarlet silk sash; upon his feet, boots with a pair of enormous Spanish spurs; and upon his head, a broad-brimmed, low-crowned, stiff hat, of Mexican manufacture.

A STOCK-RANCH.

As we rode up, he bid us a courteous *Buenas tardes*;[1] to which Sile responded in English; briefly asking permission for our party to encamp near the ranch. He at once yielded a ready assent, adding that he should be pleased to consider us his guests as long as we could be content to accept his poor hospitality.

Our animals were soon unfastened, and sent to the coral, the muleteers to the Indian quarters, and ourselves invited into the house. One of the rooms was occupied as a store, in which was kept a general assortment of dry-goods, groceries, liquor, and such articles as were of universal demand among " his people;" the other rooms, of which there were twelve, being occupied by the Don's family and the house-servants. We were shown into a long narrow apartment, in which there was neither table nor chairs, but three very inviting-looking beds; while arranged upon the clay floor, beside the walls, were cushions to serve as seats.

An hour later supper was served. This consisted of a mutton stew, in which garlic formed a prominent ingredient, splendid wheat bread, stewed beans, *chile verde* or green peppers, and a cup of strong coffee without milk; after this we partook of *caso*, or cheese, — made of goat's milk, — with *dulce*, or sirup.

Supper over, the Don joined us outside, when an Indian boy appeared, bearing a small silver brasier upon which were coals of fire. We then lighted our

[1] Good-evening.

cigarettes, and, while enjoying our evening smoke, discoursed with our host, upon cattle-raising, farming, hunting, and California life in general.

We found him, on the whole, genial and intelligent, and passed a very pleasant evening in conversation with him, during which he informed us that he was the owner of about twenty thousand head of cattle all told, and had in his employ more than a hundred native Indians, " who were no-account people, but, on the whole, did very well."

He seemed to take particular pride in his ranch and the dexterity of his *vaqueros*, promising to show us a sample of their skill in the morning.

As the boys were very tired, we all went to bed early, and, after enjoying a splendid night's rest, arose to find, that, although barely light, the Don was out before us. He greeted us very pleasantly, and said he had been down picking out a few of his people to show us what they could do with the lasso; and in a short time a dozen sleepy, dirty-looking fellows appeared, mounted upon stout Californian horses raised upon the ranch. In the right hand of each was held the slip-noose of a lasso, the coil swinging from the pommel of his saddle.

At a word from Don Anastacio, one of the number, striking his spurs into his animal's flanks, darted away from the others as if for dear life.

The next instant the balance were in pursuit. Away they went over the plain like the wind, he in the advance, apparently half dead with terror. As

SKILL WITH THE LASSO.

his pursuers approached, he threw up both hands as if appealing for mercy; the next instant a lasso went whirling through the air, and caught him by the shoulder and one of his arms. We involuntarily shut our eyes; for we expected to see the poor fellow dragged from his horse, and dashed to pieces upon the hard ground.

Not so, however. The instant the captor checked his horse, the captive did likewise, the rope hanging slack between them: then came a moment's pause, and on they rushed, the one endeavoring to drag the other from his horse, while he, with the most wonderful dexterity, not only thwarted every effort, but really turned the tables upon his captor, almost forcing him from the saddle.

One moment it seemed that one had a decided advantage, and the next, his adversary would appear to have gained it. Now they dragged each other around in a circle with astonishing velocity; and then, as if pausing for breath, each would watch the movements of the other with a wary watchfulness that boded any thing but success to his opponent's efforts.

Both manifested the most extraordinary prowess; for if for a single instant either had succeeded in tightening the lasso so as to check the movements of the other's horse, the rider must have inevitably been hurled to the ground.

Whenever the captive seemed about to effect his escape, another of the party would spur forward, and cast his lasso. One caught him by the foot, and another by the right hand, thus rendering him almost powerless; but he still continued to regulate the movements of his horse with wonderful dexterity, evidently by the pressure of his knees against the animal's sides.

The balance of the party now dashed forward, and hurling their lassos over the heads of the captors, they fell around the body of the captive, and about his horse's neck.

It seemed now as though nothing could save him, as though it were absolutely impossible for him to avoid the terrible fate that stared him in the face. We held our breaths in our anxiety, and nerved ourselves to see him torn from his horse, and dragged, a mutilated corpse, over the rough ground.

But no: the moment his animal felt the rope, it stopped as suddenly as did those of his pursuers; and the next instant, with a movement like lightning, he rid himself of the lassos, and bounded away from his pursuers — free.

Sile and myself involuntarily uttered a shout of joy, while the boys swung their hats in the air, and fairly yelled with delight; Don Anastacio himself being evidently as much pleased at the result as ourselves, although his proprietary dignity forbade his showing it.

But this most wonderful exhibition of horsemanship was not yet finished; for, as the *vaqueros* wheeled their horses to return, one of their number spurred

SKILL WITH THE LASSO. 95

forward some distance in the advance, apparently with the lassos of his comrades coiled upon his right arm, and, adopting a zigzag course, dropped them one after the other upon the grass behind him.

The others followed at a furious pace; and as each one reached his own lasso, he swung himself over upon the side of his horse, hanging by the left heel to the animal's back, and, sweeping the ground with his hand, recovered the rope; and then, resuming his seat in the saddle, proceeded to recoil it neatly, riding up to us as unconcernedly as if the centaur-like feats just performed, had been of the most ordinary character.

A word from Don Anastacio sent the horsemen to the coral to unsaddle their animals, and then we proceeded towards the house for breakfast.

So astonished had I been at seeing the marvellous adroitness and dexterity of these men, that I had quite forgotten to properly express the admiration we all felt at the sight so unexpectedly witnessed.

Sile declared he had never seen it equalled; while the boys were almost wild with excitement, and before I knew it were down at the coral, gazing in stupid wonder at the performers, who, seated upon the ground about a little fire in front of their quarters, were already devouring their simple breakfast of *carne seco*, or dried meat, bread, and coffee, with a relish noways diminished by their morning's exercise.

As we were walking towards the house, I expressd our thanks for the pleasure he had given by enabling us to witness such an unparalleled exhibition of fine horsemanship; but he cut short my little speech with a pompous wave of the hand, saying, "It is nothing! it is nothing! they are no-account fellows any way, the very poorest I have;" notwithstanding which statement, I fancied I could detect a feeling of conscionable pride in his manner, which said quite as plainly as words could have done, —

"These are my people, — good horsemen, if they are no-account fellows: how those Yankee eyes did open though!"

At any rate, something appeared to have put the Don into an exceedingly amiable mood, for immediately upon reaching the house he sent a servant for a bottle of grape brandy; "And let it be the oldest," he cried. Then turning to us, he assured us he was pleased to think he had been able to give us an hour's entertainment before breakfast, of which we should partake as soon as the servant returned with the brandy, "manufactured from grapes grown upon my own ranch, where it has been safely kept for more than fifteen years," said he.

Both Sile and myself assured Don Anastacio that we must be excused from partaking of his brandy; and, seeing that no urging would induce us to taste it even, he led the way into the breakfast-room, where we found a bountiful repast to which we did substantial justice.

Near this point our trail forked: one carrying us by what was known as the coast route, passing through the towns of Los Angeles, Santa Barbara, Monterey, &c.; the other following the base of the mountain range. After consulting with Don Anastacio, we decided to take what was known as the "mountain trail," notwithstanding he assured us we should run more risk of meeting with wild animals, than if we took the other more travelled and better path.

It was quite ten o'clock before our train was ready for a start; and, after thanking the Don for his generous hospitality, I once more referred to the wonderful skill of his *vaqueros*. He rather pompously replied that it was a mere nothing, as all his best horsemen were out on the range collecting cattle for the annual *rodeo*, a gathering which was to come off in a few days; that those we had seen were no-account fellows, but were all there were on the ranch at this time; adding, that, if we would do him the honor to stop at his poor house on our return, he would show us horsemanship that would put to shame any thing we had as yet witnessed.

Shaking hands with him, we mounted our horses; and bidding him a *bueno dias*, or good-day, we again started on the trail.

CHAPTER XII.

HAL DISCUSSES THE SITUATION. — THE MISSION INDIANS. — THEIR PROBABLE NUMBER. — HAL DISCOURSES ON GRIZZLIES. — SILE'S ADVICE. — HAL BOASTS. — SILE'S HUNT. — HIS SKILL IN SHOOTING. — THREE BULLETS IN ONE HOLE. — THE SPLIT SHOT. — OUR DOUBTS. — SILE'S SUCCESS. — HIS PROMISE.

WE had hardly left the ranch, ere Hal blurted out, —

"I wish I could speak Spanish."

"Why so?" inquired I.

"Because then I could have talked with those Indians. I don't believe that the best horsemen were all on the range. I don't believe there could be any better than them; do you, Sile?"

"Wall, 'twould be putty hard work to find 'em. I never seed any better ridin'," was the reply.

"And the Don was always trying to make us think it was nothing, it was nothing. If he said it once, he said it a dozen times, but always as though he knew it was a good deal. I hate anybody that's always bragging like that."

"It is not very pleasant to hear any person constantly reminding you of what they possess or what they can do," remarked I. "And yet it's only a few days ago, that I heard a certain young man declare that he could ride as well as any *vaquero*. Now, what chance do you think you would stand among a lot of horsemen like those, Hal?" inquired I.

"Not much," was the answer. "But then, there's very few can ride like them."

"Now you are trying to explain a very foolish speech; one that you can't, by any kind of excuse, reconcile with the truth."

"I didn't exactly mean that I could ride as well as any *vaquero*; but I meant that I would be willing to ride with them, and take the chance of holding my own."

"You wouldn't take much of a chance, and what yeou did take, wouldn't last more'n a minit," remarked Sile.

"How comes it that these Indians speak Spanish, and those we saw the other day could speak hardly a word?" inquired Ned.

"They're altogether different Indians. Those we saw the other day were Pai Yutes; these are Mission Indians," was my answer.

"What are they?" inquired the boy.

"They are the remnant of those Indians who were Christianized by the Catholic priests, who founded the old California missions," was my reply.

"How many are there of them?" asked Hal.

"At the time the missions were abandoned, there

were about fifteen thousand; but it is hardly possible to estimate their number at the present time, as they are scattered all over Southern California."

"Don't the Pai Yutes belong in California?" inquired Hal.

"No; properly they belong to the country lying to the east and south of California: those that we saw were only out upon a hunt."

Here our conversation was interrupted by Sile, who rode up to say that we had nearly reached the fork of the trail; and in a few minutes more we came to the point of divergence, and, taking the one leading to the right, passed on. As we approached the base of the mountains, the appearance of the country changed for the better, being more rolling and heavily timbered.

We frequently caught sight of large herds of cattle, flocks of sheep, and droves of horses.

"We sha'n't see no game till we get off the sheep range," said Sile.

"Why not?" inquired I.

"'Cause deer won't stay nigh 'em: there's nothin' that'll drive deer out of a country so quick as sheep, and they won't come back tew it either till the scent is gone; leastways it's so with black-tailed deer, and them's the kind we ought tew see hereabouts."

"They're curious creatures, are they not?" asked I.

"Yes, awful," was the reply. "They want tew

know just what's goin' on, and all about it. It's putty nigh time for the bucks to take tew the mountains now, to grow their horns."

" To what ? " inquired Hal.

" Tew grow their horns : they shed 'em in February, and gen'ly start for the mountains in April. We ought tew begin tew see does though, as soon as we git off 'er this range, 'cause they herd tewgether 'bout this time."

" I hope we shall see a grizzly," said Hal. " Those are the fellows for my money. It must be terribly exciting to see a wounded grizzly making right for you. I wouldn't give the snap of my finger to kill a deer; but just let me get sight at a full-grown grizzly, and I shall be satisfied."

" I guess yeou would, sonny. I kinder think the sight will be all yeou'll want," replied Sile.

" Do you think I'd run ? " inquired Hal.

" Not onless you had a good chance," was the reply ; " but in case you did, we shouldn't see yer, from the dust yeou'd raise. No, no, sonny: yeou take Sile Carter's advice, and keep out 'er the way of grizzlies."

" Well, I'll show you, if I ever have the chance," replied Hal, as Sile fell back to look after the train.

" How often do you want to be reminded that you're indulging in your favorite pastime of boasting, Hal ? " inquired I.

" Boasting ! why, I wasn't boasting : I was only saying what I should do in case I saw a grizzly."

"Well, how do you know what you should do under such circumstances?" was my question.

"Know? Why, of course I don't know, but think I should do as I say."

"Then why not say 'think,' if you must say any thing? it sounds much less like boasting."

"I'd as soon say 'think' as any thing else, only I can't understand why everybody wants to snub me."

"No one wants to snub you, Hal; but it would be much pleasanter for all, if you were less inclined to boast of what you can or would do, under such and such circumstances. Try and avoid it in the future: it may be, that you will have an opportunity to show what you will do in case you meet a grizzly."

"Do you really think we may see one?" inquired Ned.

"Of course I can't tell; but Sile tells me that they sometimes come down to the plains at this season of the year, when the winter has been unusually severe in the mountains."

"Well, if I see one, I know what I shall do," said Hal.

"There you are again, Hal," said I.

Hal laughed, and, correcting himself, said, "I mean, I think I know what I should do."

"That is better, Hal; now don't say what you think, but wait until we have a chance to see what you will do."

"All right," said he. "I'll go back and talk with

Sile for a time;" and, wheeling his horse, the boy rode back and joined Sile, who in a short time came forward, and suggested camping upon the bank of a pretty little stream we were about to cross.

"Isn't it early to camp, Sile?" inquired I.

"Wal, we give the mules a putty tough drive yesterday, and I thought we'd better make a short one tew-day," was the answer, " 'cause, you see, a pack-train ought not tew average more'n twelve or fifteen miles, at the outside."

"Very well, Sile: arrange it as you think best," was my reply; and Sile rode ahead to select a suitable camping-place.

In a short time we came up to him; and it required but a very few minutes to unpack our animals, and commence preparations for supper.

While these were being made, Sile borrowed a shot-gun from one of the *arrieros*, and started up the stream upon an exploring expedition, returning in less than an hour with a fine lot of grouse, which made us a most delicious meal.

Supper over, I said, "Come, Sile, I've never yet seen you shoot: I want you to show these boys what can be done with a rifle."

"Wal, squire, I ain't in practice neow, an' I'm afeard I shall make a poor show; however I'm willin' tew try 'Jenny,' if yeou want tew see me."

"Very well. Hal, let's go and set up a mark: how far shall we make it, Sile?"

Finding a suitable tree, we chipped off a place in

the bark about six inches square, in the centre of which, with a piece of coal, we made a spot about an inch and a half in diameter; we then paced off three hundred feet, and Sile took his position. Bringing his rifle to his face he fired, apparently without stopping to take aim: this was done three times, and then the boys started to examine the mark.

Reaching it, they shouted, "Only one, Sile," and, after examining the bark of the tree, declared that there was no other mark to be found.

"I know'd I was consid'ble out'er practice," said Sile, after the result of his shots had been announced; "but, I declare, I'd 'a' bet I hit somewhar 'beout the place, sartin."

"Well, Sile, while you are reloading, I'll go and see for myself; perhaps the boys are mistaken."

"You needn't come," shouted they, as they saw me starting towards them: "there was only one bullet hit, and that's right in the centre of the bull's-eye."

"But I propose to examine for myself," said I, continuing my way towards the tree.

The boys looked on while I made a careful examination of the bark, upon which no mark of a bullet could be seen. I then made a more critical examination of the target, and observed that the bullet-hole was more of an oblong than round shape.

I called the attention of the boys to this fact, but they only laughed, while to satisfy myself, I cut into

"Bringing his Rifle to his Face, he fired." Page 104.

the wood of the tree, from which I soon succeeded in extracting not only one, but the three bullets. Sile's aim had been so accurate that he had literally piled the bullets one upon the other.

"There, boys," said I, after picking out the third bullet, "when you can shoot as well as that, I'll trust you to hunt grizzlies single-handed and alone."

"I don't believe he could do it again," said Hal.

"Nonsense," replied Ned, "of course he can. You don't suppose that was mere luck; you can't be so foolish as that, Hal. It's what I call good shooting."

"It's splendid shooting, and no mistake; but we won't say a word to Sile about it until we hear what he says of your first report," said I.

Our plan was useless, however, for looking up we saw Sile approaching: before he reached us, Ned shouted out, "Hurrah for you, Sile! you've beat yourself this time. Three bullets and one hole is doing pretty well."

"You've found 'em, then. I kinder guessed they must be somewheres 'bout, 'cause I don't often make so much of a miss," said Sile.

"I reckon that's so, Sile, for we found that every bullet had plugged the centre of the bull's-eye: there wasn't the variation of the sixteenth of an inch in three shots; they were so near it, that the boys thought but one had struck it," said I.

"I used tew be able tew split a bullet at three hundred feet with old Jane; but it's so long sence

I've tried it, I reckon 'tain't any use now," was Sile's only reply.

"How split a bullet?" inquired Ned.

"Why, set my knife with the edge of the blade out, like this," explained Sile, drawing his sheath-knife " and, striking the edge, split the bullet intew halves."

"I'd rather see that done than hear any one tell of it," remarked Hal: "the fact is, no man could see the edge of that blade at three hundred feet."

"If I hed any way of fastenin' my knife agin the tree, I'd try it; though it's likely I might not be able tew do it the fust time," said Sile.

"Run over to camp, Hal, and bring my lasso," said I. "Sile will soon show you what he can do."

"Why can't Ned go?" asked the boy.

"Because it's for your benefit that we propose to have the trial made. If you can't go, Sile won't shoot," said I.

Hal immediately started, and in a few moments returned with the rope; taking Sile's hunting-knife, we soon had it lashed securely to the trunk of the tree, with the edge facing us. Sile then took his position, and, carelessly raising his rifle, fired.

Away went the boys, who after a hasty examination of the tree called out, "No bullet here."

"Of course thar ain't; but if you'll look about a little, you'll find the pieces," shouted Sile; then turning towards me he said, "I never knowed the old gal tew miss on a shot like that: 'tain't her natur."

"There's no pieces here," cried Ned. "At least, we can't find any."

"Wal, stan' tew one side, and watch for these, then," said Sile.

The boys withdrew a short distance, and Sile once more fired.

Ned bounded to the right of the tree, and the next moment held up something in his hand, shouting, "I've got it, I've got part of it, Sile! it's cut right into two pieces. Bully for you!" cried the excited boy, fairly jumping up and down; as soon as Hal, who was busily hunting for the other half, had found it, the two came running up with the pieces, declaring that they didn't believe there was another man in the State could make a shot like that, twice running.

"There's many a man in Californy can beat me shootin'," modestly replied Sile. "Which of you boys is goin' to run back and bring me my knife?"

"I will, I will!" cried both in the same breath as they started.

"Don't forget the lasso," shouted I.

Then turning towards me, Sile said, "We'll try it over agin some time when the light's a leetle stronger. I find my old eyes ain't as good as they used tew be."

The boys soon returned with the articles sent for, and during the remainder of the evening could talk of nothing but shooting; but before Hal retired, he went to Sile of his own accord, and said,—

"I didn't mean to doubt your word to-day, when I said I'd rather see than hear a man tell of splitting a bullet at three hundred feet. It was a foolish thing to say."

"Never mind, sonny, that's all right. I knowed well enuff what yeou meant tew say. I've talked that way myself afore now; but I larnt my lesson when I warn't much older than you be; and, when I hear a man sayin' what he kin do, I don't never contradict him now."

"What was the lesson, Sile? Tell us about it, please," said Ned.

"It's too late tew spin yarns ter-night, but p'r'aps ter-morrer night; we'll see: anyhow, you boys had better turn in now, or you won't turn out in very good season in the mornin';" and Sile chuckled to himself as he slowly tucked a live coal into the bowl of his pipe, preparatory to his late smoke.

CHAPTER XIII.

SILE GOES DEER-HUNTING. — FRESH MEAT FOR SUPPER. — THE PROMISE. — SILE'S STORY. — DOWN IN MAINE. — ON THE MISSISSIPPI. — TRAPPING IN THE ROCKY MOUNTAINS. — PETER A. SARPY. — "EARLY TO BED, AND EARLY TO RISE." — THE PANTHER'S CRY. — TO BED.

WE had barely reached camp the next afternoon ere the boys began asking Sile to tell them the promised story; but he only laughed, and said, —

"What, now? Who ever heerd of settlin' down tew story-tellin' at four o'clock in the afternoon, and no fresh meat in camp for supper? You'll hev tew wait, boys, till I've hed my supper, afore I kin tell stories. I'm goin' out to earn it, too, afore I eat it. Don't one of you want to come with me?"

"What are you going for, Sile?" inquired I.

"I guess I shall take Jenny along, and look for a deer; for I've been kinder hankerin' for a venison steak for the last two or three days."

"Well and good, I'll go with you," said I.

"So'll I," "And I," shouted both boys.

"One'll be enuff," said Sile; "and as the squire spoke first, why, he must go. Yeou boys stay about camp, and keep an eye on the mules; and be sure and hev a good fire, with plenty of coals for br'ilin', ready ag'in we git back."

"Any one would think you expected to bring in a deer, from the directions you give," exclaimed Hal.

"Likely enuff, likely enuff, sonny: a feller can't allers tell what'll happen afore he starts out, as well as he kin arter he gits back."

"You don't expect to see a black-tail, do you?" inquired I while loading.

"No: I guess we're too near the sheep-range for that yet;" adding in a lower tone, "I ketched sight of a red deer a little ways back, and whar thar's one, thar's gen'rally three or four at this time er year; so I thought we might as well camp here, and have a shot at 'em. Now, as we go 'long, yeou want tew keep an eye on these thickets about here, 'cause as likely as not we might start one up, and then, yeou know, a quick eye and steady hand'll bring him, sure."

We had proceeded not more than half a mile from camp, when I saw Sile suddenly raise his hand, as if warning me to be cautious, while he peered carefully through the thick undergrowth that separated us from an open space I could see a short distance ahead.

The next instant he brought his rifle to his shoulder, and fired.

We both rushed forward, and, upon reaching the edge of the clearing, saw, about two hundred yards from us, a fine fat doe lying upon its side, evidently in the agonies of death; and, in the distance, half a dozen more speeding gracefully over the prairie. Altogether too far away for me to fire, they were still near enough to challenge my admiration; but the magnificent bounds that seemed to combine so much strength and lightness, with speed and grace, soon carried them into the woods and out of sight. Turning towards Sile, I saw that he had just ended the poor creature's struggles by cutting its throat; and, with a half-sigh at the necessity that caused the slaughter of a creature a moment before so full of strength and beauty, I said,—

"Is it fat, Sile?"

"I never seed a fatter one," was the reply, as he disembowelled the carcass: then tying the legs together, we slung it about his neck, and slowly made our way back to camp, where we were warmly welcomed by the boys, who loudly expressed their satisfaction at our quick return and lucky find.

In less time than I have taken to tell of it, each of us had a fat, juicy steak broiling upon sticks over the coals; the savory fumes of which, caused us to consign the stew provided by the cook for our supper, to the tender mercies of the muleteers, while we ourselves feasted upon a dish fit for a king.

"Now for the story," said Ned, as, sucking the gravy from his fingers, he strutted about the fire, not unlike a well-gorged turkey-gobbler.

"Yes, Sile, we want the story now," urged Hal, as, in a condition very similar to Ned's, he stretched himself before the fire, declaring that he believed he'd eaten too much supper.

"Well, boys," remarked Sile, "if you'll wait till I've got my pipe lit, and taken the kink out 'er this left leg o' mine, I'll tell you the story, such as 'tis." In a few minutes he commenced as follows:—

"When I was a boy I hed a pretty hard time of it. My mother was a widow with four children, and I the oldest one. Arter I was twelve year old, I begun to go as cabin-boy in a coaster that traded between the Kennebec and Bosting, and once or twice durin' them years I went down New York.

"When I was fifteen I shipped as cabin-boy on board a vessel loaded with staves, for New Orleans, for a hundred dollars the season, and my board. I was paid off in New Orleans; and thinkin' I should like up country better, I bought a ticket for St. Louis, and started up river on one of the Mississippi steamboats.

"Wal, arter I got my ticket, I hed jest a hundred dollars; and I allowed that when I got tew St. Louis and found something tew do, I'd send mother that money. Thar was a good many passengers aboard, and I was jest old enough to think I knowed as much as any one on 'em: so I mixed in pretty lively.

"One day we got tew talkin' about shootin.' I heerd one and another say what he could do; and putty soon a rough-lookin' old man, who'd been sittin' round but hadn't said much, begun tew tell what he'd seed; and, among other things, said he'd seed a man tie a empty bottle tew the end of a line two hundred feet long, and throw it over inter the wake of the boat, and break the bottle with a bullet.

"Some of the young fellers aboard had been saying they would bet they could do so and so, and I felt as though I'd like tew have 'em know that I hed money to bet, as well as they; and, when the old man said what he did, I thought 'twas a good chance for me to say somethin', cause you see I knowed how hard 'twas tew hit any thing bobbin' about on the water, for I'd tried it a hundred times. So I said I didn't b'lieve anybody could do that.

"'Do you doubt my word?' said the old man, lookin' pleasantly at me.

"I said no, but I didn't believe it could be done.

"'Well, as tew that,' said he, 'I kin do it myself.'

"Now, by this time putty nigh everybody was a-lookin' at me; and thinkin' tew rather s'prise 'em, more'n any thing else, I said, —

"'I'll bet a hundred dollars there ain't a man on the boat can do it.'

"You see, at that time, everybody used tew bet in that country; and I'd heerd so much talk about bettin,' that it slipped out without my knowin' it; but the old man looked at me a minit, and takin' out a roll o' bills, said, 'I don't want tew win your money, young man, but I can do as I said I could.'

"Thinkin' he meant tew back down, and that he only wanted to show his money, I said, 'If you think yew can do it, put yeour money right up.'

"He did put his money inter the captain's hands, and then went inter the cabin tew git his rifle, while I handed my money tew the captain. The mate brought out a line, and then measured off six hundred feet; and we tied a empty junk-bottle to the end, and throwed it overboard.

"When I see it bobbin' about in the wake of the boat, long arter the line all run out, I thought tew myself, 'Sile Carter, you'll hev two hundred dollars to send home instead of one hundred, as sure as you're a livin' boy.'

"Arter the line was all played out, we couldn't hardly see the bottle 'cept as it once in a while skipped in the water; but the old man brought his rifle to his face, and, watchin' his chance, fired.

"I was so excited while they was haulin' in the line, that I could hardly breathe; and when it come in — well, boys, there warn't nothin' but the neck of the bottle on the end of the line.

"I couldn't believe it for a minit, and then I heard 'em hollerin', and see the captain pay my money over; and — well, I didn't know nothin' for a while. I felt dizzy, sick, and weak as a cat. Then I begun tew think how much good that money'd done mother, and how I'd just throwed it away, and I declare tew gracious, boys, Sile Carter come putty nigh jumpin' overboard then and there. Everybody was a-praisin' the man who'd won my money, but nobody hed a kind word for me. I slipped away and went inter my stateroom, and laid down and cried. I never went out er my room agin that day; I laid thar and thought it all over, and wished I was dead.

"Jest afore dark, somebody knocked on the door, and come right in. I looked up, and thar was the old man. He sot down on a stool, and said,—

"'I feel sorry for yer, my boy. I didn't want tew win your money, and don't want it now; but I did want to larn yer a lesson. When yew hear a person older'n yourself assert that he can do a certain thing, don't contradict him. It's not only impolite, but very foolish.

"'Now remember this, my boy, and never bet again in this way. Here's your money; and I hope it may do yew much good.'

"I thanked him, and made a vow then and there, that I'd remember the lesson I'd larnt that day, as long as I lived; and I hain't forgot it yet."

"What became of the old man?" inquired Ned.

"He was gone in the mornin'; got off at his plantation in the night, the cap'n said. I've never seed him sence."

"What did you do, Sile?" asked Hal.

"I came up to St. Louis, where I fell in with an old Missouri-river trader, Col. Peter A. Sarpy. Every one on the river knowed him; and he hired me tew go on a huntin' and trappin' expedition tew the Rocky Mountains that fall. I staid with him two year, and then found my way over into California, where I've bin ever sence."

"You must have had lots of adventures, Sile," said

Ned. "I wish you'd tell us some of them, and about the Indians you trapped among. I sha'n't forget your story, Sile. It was a real good one."

"So I think," rejoined Hal. "I know I shall remember it; but I wish you'd tell us about those Indians. I always did like to hear Indian stories, especially if they are true ones."

"All right, boys: yeou shall have stories enuff afore yeou git home; but yeou know 'Early tew bed and early tew rise, makes a man healthy, wealthy, and wise;' leastways, that's what my old mother used tew tell us boys at home. I ain't so sartin about the 'wealthy and wise' part of it, but I've allers bin mighty healthy sence I've bin out on the plains. So we'll all turn in for a good night's sleep."

"Hark! what's that noise?" said Ned, suddenly stopping on his way for his blankets.

We all listened. The stillness of death prevailed. Suddenly a long, low cry, as of some person in sore distress, trembled upon the night air for a moment, and then all was still again.

Never before had I heard such a wail. It seemed to me to be just such a cry as I should imagine some lost spirit would utter, when for the first time it fully realized that it was bereft of all hope.

The boys stood with pale faces, listening for a repetition of the sound, when Sile somewhat rudely ended our surmises by exclaiming, "What are you waitin' for, boys? You don't want tew go out at this time er night arter that painter, do yer? 'cause 'tain't worth while, if yer do."

"Is that a panther, Sile?" I asked.

"Why, of course 'tis: what else did yer think it could be?"

"I never heard any thing like that before," said I.

"I've heerd 'em a hundred times. It sounds skeery at first, but when yer remember it's a painter yer don't mind it so much: leastways I don't. So ye may as well go on tew bed, boys."

After they were fairly gone I remarked to Sile that I had heard many panthers screech before, but never such a peculiar heart-rending wail as this one made.

"I guess it's a female a-callin' her mate," was the reply. "If you've got any curosity 'bout it, we'll slip out and see."

Just at that moment I chanced to remember a certain night adventure with old Jerry on the banks of the Nueces in Texas, some months before, and I respectfully but firmly declined the invitation: thus the subject was summarily dropped for the night.

CHAPTER XIV.

A SUGGESTION. — HAL WANTS A GRIZZLY-HUNT. — A SUR-
PRISE. — NED SHOOTS A CUB. — HAL'S EXPLANATIONS.
— WE ARE ATTACKED BY A GRIZZLY. — THE BOYS
RETURN. — WHY THEY LEFT. — SILE'S QUERY. — TWO
CUBS.

SOON after starting the following morning, Sile rode up beside me, and said, " Where be yeou expectin' tew buy your cattle, squire ? "

" I have supposed, from what you and Jerry said, that the best place would be in the San José Valley."

" That's my way of thinkin' ; and I didn't know, as long as you was goin' so near, but you'd like tew take a look at them quicksilver-mines up in the mountains ; they ain't more'n a dozen miles out of our way, and are worth seein', sure."

" I'd like nothing so well," said I: " we'd better visit them before we buy our cattle, had we not, Sile ? "

" That would be my way of thinking, and I guess I'll strike for them mines instead 'er the town."

" All right, Sile : I'm glad you spoke of it," said I.

When the boys, who had been dawdling behind,

came up, I asked them how they would like such a visit. Ned at once declared he would like it above all things; but Hal believed he would a great deal rather have a grizzly-hunt.

"Maybe we kin have both," remarked Sile: "there's grizzlies all through these mountains, and we're likely ter meet one most any day."

"That's what I want to meet more than any thing else," shouted Hal. "It must be bully to see a real live grizzly out in the woods: I sha'n't ever be satisfied till I've seen one."

"One'll be plenty, sonny: you won't ever want ter see another," remarked Sile.

"As for me, I'd a great deal rather hear Sile tell us about the Indians that he trapped among, than to see all the grizzlies in the mountains," said Ned.

"So had I, Ned; and I reckon we must get him to do it," was my reply.

"What do you say, Sile? While we are riding along can't you begin?" inquired Hal.

"I'd rather do it arter we git inter camp at night. Yer see, talkin' allus takes a man's mind away from his bizness; and a feller wants his eyes and ears both wide open when he's trav'lin' through any new country."

"I can see that you are right about that, Sile," said I: "suppose we ride ahead, boys, and let Sile attend to the team."

Our trail led through a section of country more heavily timbered than any we had yet seen: dense forests of pine, spruce, fir, and cedar, with but little underbrush, surrounded us upon all sides. Occasionally we would come to an opening comprising many acres, as smooth and beautiful as any gentleman's well-kept lawn, and dotted here and there with a large live-oak, that added greatly to the picturesque beauty of the scene.

After riding in silence for some time, admiring the many beauties of the landscape, Hal rather unexpectedly said, —

"I'm going back. I'd a heap rather be with the mules than riding along as stupidly as we are;" and, wheeling his pony, he galloped towards the train, while Ned and myself continued on.

Suddenly the boy, who was a little in advance, stopped his horse, and said, —

"What is that down there?"

I looked, but seeing nothing replied, "Probably a stump or rock."

"No, it's some kind of an animal: it looks like a bear."

This instantly aroused me; and, looking in the direction indicated, I soon discovered a young bear, about as large as a calf, rolling over and over upon the pine-cones with which the ground was thickly strewn, and evidently having a jolly time all by itself.

"It's a cub," said I: "shoot it, Ned; take careful aim, just behind the left fore-shoulder; don't be in a hurry, take your" —

Before I had time to finish the sentence, the boy

NED SHOOTS A CUB. 121

fired; and with a convulsive leap the little fellow rolled over upon his side, dead.

"That's a young grizzly, Ned, as sure's you're born;" said I, as we dismounted. "Hold on! you haven't reloaded yet; and that's the first thing a good hunter always does after he fires."

"But I ain't a good hunter," cried the boy, so excited and nervous that he could hardly speak intelligibly; hastily setting his rifle against the nearest tree, he dashed down the hill to inspect his game.

At this moment I heard the sound of horses' feet, and looking up saw Sile and Hal, whom the report of the rifle had evidently caused to hurry forward.

"What is it?" anxiously inquired Hal, who was a little in the advance.

"Ned's shot a grizzly," was my answer.

"Shot a granny, I guess," shouted he in return. "You can't play that on me. What is it, though?"

At this moment he caught sight of Ned in the bushes; and, springing from his horse, started to join him, leaving his rifle swinging in its loop, attached to the pommel of his saddle.

"Stop, Hal! that's no way to leave your horse," said I; but paying no heed to my remonstrance, in his anxiety to see Ned's game, he dashed away into the bushes: the next instant we heard a loud "hough, hough," a noise between a wheeze, a grunt, and a roar, and about the most frightful one I ever heard, for it caused my hair to almost stand on end.

What it was I could not imagine, until I saw Sile throw himself out of his saddle, and heard him exclaim, —

"Good God! it's a grizzly, sartin."

I grasped my rifle, and, leaving the horses, started after Sile, who was hurrying towards the place from whence the noise had come, and was just in time to see the boys rushing through the bushes, followed by a large bear. Sile instantly fired: this drew the attention of the bear towards us, and with an angry roar she turned.

I shall never forget my sensations when I saw the huge beast, with open mouth and lolling tongue, waddling towards us. My heart fairly ceased to beat for a moment. Every story that I had heard about the ferocity of grizzlies flashed like lightning through my mind; and I stood there, without attempting to fire, while Sile discharged chamber after chamber of his revolver at her, apparently without the least effect.

On she came, directly towards him. I could see her long white teeth and great red tongue, and I remember wondering if he was going to use his knife; and then she partly raised herself upon her hind-legs as if to embrace him.

The next instant I comprehended the situation perfectly, and, raising my rifle as coolly as though about to fire at a mark, took deliberate, careful aim, and fired at a point in her belly, about four inches below her left fore-leg.

"WITH AN ANGRY ROAR SHE TURNED." Page 122.

She appeared to stagger a little, but, recovering herself, turned her attention directly towards me. Drawing my revolver, I gave her the contents of three chambers; then I saw her stop, and with a kind of wheezy growl she settled back upon her haunches, and finally rolled over upon her side, dead.

The next instant I felt as though something within me had given way. I heard Sile say something: what it was, I did not know; but trembling with excitement, and so weak that I could with difficulty stand, I walked towards the huge lifeless carcass.

Sile, who was already beside it, said, —

"Wal, squire, she's a whopper."

My reply was, "Where are the boys?"

"Gone arter the hosses, I guess: leastways the hosses hev gone, and so's the boys," was his answer.

Then bursting into a loud laugh I said, "Well, Sile, I thought we were both done for."

"Wal, I kinder thought Ephraim and us'd come tew clus quarters, 'cause yeou was so long about firin' at him."

"Did I hesitate?" inquired I.

"Wal, it seemed tew me 'bout half an hour arter I fired my last charge, afore I heerd the crack er your rifle. Yer see, I didn't dar'st tew turn my head, cause I hed tew look the critter'n the face, and I didn't know what yeou was a-doin'; but it seemed a awful while afore yeou fired. I knowed though when I see your ball strike, what yeou'd bin a-waiting for, and that yeou'd saved me from a all-fired huggin'."

"Did you?" said I in an incredulous tone.

At this moment we heard the train coming; and I said, "I wonder if the boys are with them, Sile. I wish you'd see."

He started to intercept the train; and I was glad of an opportunity to seat myself upon the carcass, and await his return. He came back presently, and said, —

"They've got the hosses, but hain't seen nothing er the boys."

"I wonder where they can have gone to?" said I. "We must find 'em."

"I guess likely Hal's started for home now he's seen a live grizzly, and p'r'aps Ned's gone tew keep him company," was Sile's reply. "'Twon't do tew let them mules stop, or they'll be lyin' down: so I'll just tell José tew keep on till he finds water and grass, and then camp, and bring a couple on 'em back for these 'ere carcasses. The boys'll come 'round when they've got threw runnin'; they was a-heelin' of it lively, when I seed 'em last;" and Sile went to give the necessary orders to the train, and secure our horses, soon returning with Ned's rifle, which he found standing by the tree where it had been left.

"By thunder, squire! but she's a whopper though," said Sile, as we stood looking at the huge carcass stretched out before us, "an' as fat as butter too.

Yer see, tacklin' that cub's what raised the mischief with her: they'll fight like Satan for their young ones any time. Who shot that?"

"Ned," answered I.

"Did he though? wal, that's a good one. Ha, ha, ha! how t'other one will squirm when he sees it, and he all the time wantin' tew see a live grizzly, wild in the woods! Wal, wal!" continued he in a reflective tone, "arter all, that's the way with human natur'."

"What is, Sile?" inquired I.

"Why, here he's bin wishin' he might see one of these critters, ever sence we started; and, the first time he got his wish, he wouldn't stop tew look at it. She was a tough one though: 'leven balls in her old skin as sartin as yeou're a live man."

"Perhaps some of them missed her," suggested I.

"We'll see when we come tew take off her jacket for her," was the answer, as he stooped over to measure her. "Six feet nine inches long and six feet 'round, if she's a inch. She'll do, she'll do. Halloo! I hear them boys a-comin'," continued he, just as one of the ponies whinnied. "Yer see, the critters know 'em, if they did run away."

"I don't blame 'em for running," said I. "I felt as though I wanted to myself."

"If all on us hed run, some of us wouldn't hev got very fur with them things arter us," said Sile, calling my attention to the creature's enormous claws. "One of them would have knocked the life out of us as easy as a streak er chain-lightnin', and just about as quick too."

"Halloo, sonny!" shouted he, as the boys appeared looking decidedly foolish. "Where on airth yer bin?"

"I got scart and legged it," promptly answered Ned. "I tell you, I never want to see another grizzly as long as I live."

"I wasn't scared," said Hal, "but was surprised: you see, the old fellow come upon me so suddenly, with that 'hough, hough!' of his, that I felt kind of bewildered."

"How do yeou spell that word, sonny?" inquired Sile. "When I was a boy we used tew spell it s-c-a-r-t. I don't s'pose yeou spell it so now, eh?"

"You don't think I was scared, I hope," demanded Hal.

"N-o-o," replied Sile: "only me an' the squire was a-wonderin', when yeou've been wantin' tew see a grizzly so bad ever sence we started, why on airth yer didn't stop tew look at him when yer hed such a stavin' good chance."

"I did get a good look at him," said the boy.

"Did yer? Wal, yer found one look was enuff, as I told yer 'twould be; didn't yer?"

"If I'd had my rifle"—began Hal.

"You'd have done just what you did without it, —turn tail and run, frightened half out of your wits," interrupted I. "Whose fault was it that you didn't have your rifle? Where is it now? Who ever before heard of a hunter's leaving his rifle swinging at his saddle-bow while he went into the woods to see a grizzly? We've had enough of this kind of talk, Hal: don't let us hear you mention the word 'grizzly' again while on the trip. You did just what we all knew you'd do if you ever met a grizzly, and have settled the matter for all time. Now, don't let me remind you of this again."

Seeing that I was thoroughly in earnest, neither of the boys replied; but Sile, who was busily engaged removing the skin from the carcass, looked up with a sly wink, and said,—

"Hadn't he better be gettin' that cub inter camp? we shall want some steaks out er that, for supper; an' then, we ought tew kind 'er get the two together, I s'pose.

"The two what?" asked Hal, looking very fierce.

"Tew cubs," responded Sile very quietly.

"No," said I: "Ned's able to get his own game into camp;" then turning to Hal I remarked, "You'd better go and find your rifle."

"Where is it?" inquired the boy.

"How should I know? go and find it;" and Hal started slowly toward the horses.

CHAPTER XV.

OUR CONCLUSIONS. — NED'S STATEMENT. — A GRIZZLY'S A GRIZZLY, BIG OR LITTLE. — HOW TO DRESS SKINS. — THE PROCESS. — WHOSE BRAINS. — WHICH SHALL IT BE? — SILE'S OPINION. — HE THINKS HAL IGNORANT OF THE SUBJECT OF TANNING.

BY dint of much questioning after Hal's departure, Sile and myself arrived at the following conclusions relative to the boy's disappearance: —

The old bear was probably lying asleep in some thicket, close by the spot where Ned shot the cub. Hal, in his anxiety to ascertain what Ned had shot, dashed into the thicket so abruptly that he startled her into uttering that peculiarly frightful noise, between a grunt and roar, that the grizzly always makes when suddenly disturbed.

Hal, catching sight of the bear, and frightened by the really terrific noise, started off pell-mell through the bushes; and Ned, knowing about the cub, suspected the noise came from its dam, and, seeing the bushes violently agitated as the bear forced her way through them, started after Hal, whom he saw in the distance.

It is a peculiarity of the grizzly, that it will always leave any object it is pursuing, for a fresh subject: and Sile's shot not only diverted her attention from the boys to him, but wounded her as well. Turning in her rage towards Sile, the boys were enabled to make good their escape, which they could never have done by running, for a grizzly will travel as fast as a good horse; their only other possible chance being to climb a tree, a feat impossible for a grizzly to perform.

Hearing our shots, and concluding that we must have been successful in overcoming him, they concluded to return.

"It wasn't a very brave thing to do; but I declare I don't believe any thing could have kept me from running, I was so frightened," said Ned. "Hal was scared too: he needn't say he wasn't, because, when he heard me following him, he thought it was the bear; he told me so, and if he hadn't been some scared he'd never take me for a bear, would he?"

"I've found ten o' the bullets, and the other one's somewhere 'round," said Sile, looking up from his work with an amused expression upon his face. "Somebody ought tew be skinnin' that 'ere cub." Then pausing, he added, "'cause that meat'll make better steak than this 'ere: 'tain't so tuff for them as likes bar-meat; I don't care nothin' about it 'ceptin' with honey, and we hain't got none er that."

"Well, Sile, I think I can manage to take that little fellow's jacket off: I'll start it anyhow," said I.

"No, yer needn't; here comes José with the mules: he'll take it off mighty quick. — Here, José," called he, "get this little shaver ready for camp."

"*Esta bueno, señor*,"[1] was the reply, as the Mexican went to work in a manner that convinced us that Sile's estimate of his ability had been entirely correct.

"Now, sonny, you'd better watch and see how José does it: 'cause maybe sometime, when yeou git tew be a lucky hunter, yeou may hev tew do the job yourself. Thar ain't many boys of your age that kin say they've killed a grizzly."

"It wasn't a grizzly, it was only a cub," replied Ned.

"A grizzly's a grizzly, whether it's big or little," responded Sile. "You've done a big thing for a boy of your size — and without braggin' too; that's what Sile Carter likes about it. There," continued he, holding up the creature's heart, "what'd I tell you? thar's the place where your ball went plumb through her heart: that was a good shot, squire. But jest see the rolls er fat: it's currus how these critters keep so fat, ain't it?"

Just at this moment Hal came up with his rifle on his shoulder; and I said to him, "You found it, I see."

"Yes, sir," was his reply.

"Well, Hal, never, under any circumstances, leave your rifle again, as you left it this afternoon: you're

[1] Very good, sir.

a lucky fellow to find it at all. Now take hold here, and help Sile."

"I believe I've got about through," said Sile. "We sha'n't want tew take this whole carcass inter camp: so I'll pick out the best parts, and leave the rest."

"What are you going to do with all that fat?" inquired Hal.

"Eat it," was the answer: "it's just as sweet as good fresh butter."

"You won't catch me eating it," replied the boy.

"Then there'll be all the more for the rest of us," said Sile. "Eatin' ain't nothin' but a notion anyhow: thar's many a thing that I've found tew be first-rate, that I wouldn't have touched when I was a boy; but it's only because we ain't brought up to it."

"What are you going to do with this skin?" inquired Hal.

"Dress it, same as the Injuns do, and have it tew sleep on."

"How do the Indians dress their skins?" inquired Ned.

"Pooh! I can tell you that," interrupted Hal. "When I was with the Apaches I used to see 'em dress"—

"I asked Sile," said Ned; "and if you'll let him answer, I'll be obliged to you."

"I know just as much about it as Sile does," responded Hal.

"Now, Hal, what nonsense! how can you know as much about it as Sile?"

"Why, don't you know some folks have a knack of seeing a thing once, and knowing all about it?"

"Same as yeou see'd this old feller here, and know'd all about him in less'n a minit, eh?" said Sile; then turning to Ned he replied,—

"One thing at a time, sonny: I can't talk and work too. Yeou wait till we git intew camp ternight, and I'll tell yer 'bout dressin' skins."

Having by this time loaded the carcasses upon the mules, we mounted our horses, and after half an hour's brisk gallop reached camp, which we found located upon the banks of a beautiful stream, in the midst of a grove of magnificent pines whose dark tops interlacing, formed a perfect roof, far above our heads.

Although weary and worn with the excitement of the day, I found myself making a hearty supper of the juicy steaks furnished from Ned's cub; and after I had finished, and lighted my pipe, I listened to Sile's account of the Indians' manner of dressing skins with as much interest as did Hal and Ned.

Immediately after supper was over, Sile had gone into the woods; when he returned he had with him four stout straight poles, about an inch and a half in diameter by seven feet in length.

"What are you going to do with those?" inquired Hal, as Sile seated himself by the fire.

"Set down, boys, and I'll show ye," was the reply.

"I'm goin' tew make a stretcher tew dry this skin. Yer see, the first thing the Injuns do in dressin' a skin is tew stretch it; this is gen'rally done by peggin' it tew the ground, hair side down, and lettin' it dry in the sun; but as we're on the road, and can't spend the time for that, I'm goin' tew stretch this one, on that frame, and dry it as well as I can, afore the fire ter-night."

"Will it dry enough in one night?" inquired Ned.

"I guess so: leastways by gittin' up two or three times, and turnin' the frame, and keepin' up a good fire, I reckon I shel be able tew work it. There ain't nothin' like tryin' in this world, boys: nobody kin tell what they kin do afore they try.

"Arter the skin gits stretched, the next thing tew do is to scrape every mite of flesh off of the inside of it. This is done with a little tool made of bone: it looks like a little adze, only the edge of it's more like a saw.

"Arter the skin dries a little, it's scraped with another bone tool, and then smeared all over with the brains of the critter itself, and rolled up, flesh side in, and left for two or three days. Arter the brains has kinder soaked intew the pores of the skin like, and it gits soft, they wet it, and then rub it till it gits dry; this they do half a dozen times, sometimes with pumice-stone, and sometimes by drawin' it back and forth over a small rope, slack stretched, between two poles, till it's as soft as a piece of cloth."

"But suppose they want to dress it for clothing, and want the hair all off," said Ned.

"Then they soak the skin in some creek or pond, till the hair begins to get loose, when they pull it out with their hands, and treat the skin as they allers do. So yer see, boys, it's all in knowin' how. Thar ain't no skin that you can't dress that way.

"Now, I hain't told you this, expectin' yeou boys are goin' tew set up a tan-yard as soon as yer git hum; 'cause yeou hain't got squaws enuff to make a profitable bizness of it."

"Do the squaws dress all the skins?" inquired Ned.

"Of course they do; besides carryin' wood, makin' fires, skinnin' and dressin' meat, cookin' the food, herdin', drivin', and saddlin' the horses, pitchin' and strikin' the lodges, packin' baggage, and every thing else 'ceptin' huntin' and fightin'; them two things the bucks 'tend to."

"Who make the moccasons and leather petticoats?" inquired Hal.

"The squaws, of course: they do every bit of work that's done about the camp, whatever 'tis."

"Well, they must have a pretty hard time of it," said Ned.

"So they do," was the reply: "but they're used to it; and, arter we git used to a thing, we don't mind it so much, you know."

"Have you got the grizzly's brains, Sile?" asked Hal.

"Got the grizzly's brains?" repeated Sile in a tone of inquiry. "No, sir'ee, I've got my own: the grizzly's are in her own head; but I brought the head along, and, if yeou're up airly enough, yeou kin see me take 'em out."

"I mean to dress the skin of every animal I shoot, after this," said Ned. "I'd no idea it was such easy work."

"It does look kinder easy, but it took me a good many years to larn it," replied Sile.

"Can't you tell us something about trapping, Sile?" asked Ned.

"First it's Injuns, and then it's trappin'. I never seed sich boys: yeou want ter larn all a feller knows, and want ter do it in a minit too."

"Come, Ned, let's go," said Hal: "there's no use of talking to any one as cross as he is. I can tell you as much about Indians and trapping as Sile Carter can, and in half the time too."

Ned only laughed, and remained with Sile, who shook his head slowly, and turned towards me saying, —

"If that Hal don't beat every thing I ever seed in the shape of a boy, I'll be switched. He may know somethin' 'bout Injuns and trappin'; but he don't know half so much 'bout *tannin'* as he would 'a' done if I'd bin his father."

"Oh, well, Sile!" said I, "Hal's but a boy yet: he'll learn as he grows older."

"Larn? he don't think he can larn any thing: he knows it all now, and kin tell it in a minit too, though he thinks he couldn't in a year;" and Sile walked away as though his opinion fully settled it.

CHAPTER XVI.

TRAPPERS AND TRAPPING. — IKE MCKENZIE AND THE SILVER FOX. — HOW TO SET A FOX-TRAP. — SMOKE AND LYE. — THE VALUE OF SKINS. — HOW TO MANAGE A PACK-TRAIN. — " 'TEND TO YER OWN BIZNESS IF YER WANT IT TENDED TO." — HAL DOUBTS FOX AND GEESE.

THE next morning, when we resumed our journey, Sile had evidently recovered his good humor; Ned was in the best of spirits; and Hal had quite forgotten his little wordy encounter with Sile the night previous.

It was a glorious day, even for California; and every one seemed to appreciate the clear dry air and magnificent sunshine.

As we rode carelessly along, Sile appeared to forget his usual aversion to talking on the road, and went into a dissertation upon trappers and trapping in the Rocky Mountains, that proved very interesting to the boys, enlightening them upon the most valuable skins, and how to obtain them with the least trouble, until his listeners, deeply impressed with his descriptions of the wild, careless life of the trapper, declared their settled intention to take to that manner of life immediately upon their return home.

Indeed, Hal applied for permission to visit San Francisco, and purchase a quantity of traps, declaring that they " could pay for them with two silver-fox skins."

" Yes, but where do you expect to find the silver-fox skins?" inquired I.

" Oh! up in the mountains, back of the ranch," replied the excited boy.

" But there are no silver-foxes there: they are only found in the much more northern portions of the country, and are exceedingly rare even there," said I. " Ask Sile to tell you how many of these little animals he ever trapped, and whether they were easily caught or not."

Spurring my horse forward by the side of Sile's, I listened for his answer.

" Wal, I've ketched three in all, and they was the hardest critters to trap I ever ketched: one on 'em'll make a feller more trouble than all the others, martens or minks, that he'd ketch in a hull winter."

" Can't you tell us how you trapped 'em?" inquired Ned.

" Silver-foxes ain't nothin' but a streak any how," said Sile.

" Streak!" repeated the boy,—" streak of what?"

" Luck," sententiously answered Sile. " A man might trap ten years, and not git one. They're the slyest critters on this airth, I do b'leve. One day my pard, Ike McKenzie, came in at night, and told me he'd seed a white fox that day. We was a-trappin' then way up on the North Fork of Clark's River, right on tew the line; so him and me agreed we'd set a trap for him. We took a reg'lar fox-trap, and washed it in some weak lye, and then greased it, and smoked it with duck-feathers, and went out and found the critter's track just where Ike seed it, and set it."

"What did you wash it in lye and do all that for?" inquired Hal.

"So's tew destroy the scent," replied Sile. "Yeou might as well try tew ketch a streak of chain-lightnin' with a tow string, as to ketch one of 'em if yeou tetch the trap with your bare hand: they'll smell it half a mile away."

"Arter we got the bed made"—

"How'd you do that?" asked Ned.

"Why, we made a bed of moss and wood-ashes, about two feet and a half across, and two inches deep. We hitched the trap to a chunk of wood, and buried the hull thing under this bed, and then strewed some pieces of raw meat, cheese, and sich like, on top. Wal, ev'ry morning that bait would be gone, but the trap wouldn't be sprung: finally we took it up and scented it with musk, but 'twa'n't no go; he wouldn't tetch it. Wal, we tried buryin' a dead rabbit, and a bird, and everything we could think of; and the critter never failed tew git the bait, but we never seen the color of his fur.

"At last we tried a new game. We sot a trap under water, in the edge of a little brook, whar we see he was in the habit of comin'. We sot the trap about a foot from shore, and over beyond, say a foot and a half, driv a stake into the bottom of the stream, with a dead bird tied, so's it would float on the water.

"Ike cut a piece of sod just large enuff tew fit in atween the jaws of the trap, and come above the top of the water, and laid it over the pan, for the critter tew step on when he reached for the bird. Then we sprinkled a few drops of musk on the bait, and kivered up our tracks as well as we could, and went hum. The next mornin' Mr. Whitey was in the trap, and as putty a feller he was, too, as I ever see ketched; but I tell yeou, boys, we had a heap o' trouble tew git him."

"How much did you get for his skin?" inquired practical Ned.

"Eighty-five dollars, in St. Louis," was Sile's answer, "and 'twas sold cheap at that, for silver-foxes is awful scarce."

"What would you think of the project of catching them in the mountains back of the Buena Vista ranch, Sile?" inquired I.

"Ha, ha, ha!" roared Sile: "that's a good one;" but, noticing that I did not smile, he added, "Excuse me, squire: I thought you was a-jokin'. Them critters are only ketched in the very coldest countries. Why, I should jest as soon think of ketchin' a white bar in San Diego Harbor, as a white fox in the mountains down thar."

"Master Hal had a project of"—

"Oh! I was only joking," interrupted Hal. "I hope you didn't think I was in earnest. I knew enough to know that those animals didn't live as far south as that."

"Thar, I told yer that a man hed no bizness tew be talkin' on the road: while I've been yarnin' it, we've got clar out o' sight er the train."

"Well, suppose we have: it's all right, I know," said Hal. "I'll ride back and see," and, wheeling his pony, he started on the back track, while we rode slowly on.

In about half an hour he overtook us, saying that the train was all right, but had been detained by a couple of the mules lying down.

"That's it," said Sile: "if a man don't 'tend tew his bizness, he needn't expect any one'll do it for him; yer see, my place was with them mules. They never'd laid down if I'd bin along."

"What harm does it do 'em, if they do lie down?" queried Hal.

"Harm!" repeated Sile: "why, nine times out 'er ten, if a pack-mule lays down with his *carga* on, the muleteers 'll make him git up without onpackin' him; and that 'll spile the best critter that ever walked in in a train."

"How spoil him?" asked Hal.

"It strains 'em through the loins, and they ain't wuth a cent after it. I've knowed many a hundred dollars throw'd away by havin' lazy muleteers; and all them Mexicans be lazy, nat'rally. Yer see, if a train is allowed tew stop on the road a minit, some o' the mules'll be sure tew lay down; and then they ought tew be onpacked afore they're made tew git up. There ain't no way for a man tew do, but to 'tend tew his bizness, if he wants it 'tended tew; so I'll ride along back, and 'tend tew mine;" and Sile wheeled his horse, and started to join the train.

We rode along for some distance, enjoying the beauties of the day and landscape in silence, which was finally broken by Hal's exclaiming, —

"Do you know, I don't more than half believe Sile's yarn about that fox?"

"Why not?" inquired Ned.

"Anybody might know that a fox couldn't steal that bait, as Sile says he did, if the trap was set as it ought to be. He tried to make it out that a fox is an awful cunning creature; but the fact is, Sile ain't a very good trapper, and so he laid it on to the fox."

"Now, I've always heard that the fox is the slyest and most cunning of all animals," rejoined Ned; "and I believe every word Sile told us."

"What do you know about foxes?" asked Hal.

"I never saw one; but I've read about 'em in books. I know as much as you do, any way," was the reply.

"Know as much as I do!" retorted Hal. "Have you ever lived among the Apaches?"

"What did you learn about foxes during the two

or three weeks you were with the Apaches?" inquired I.

"Well, I don't know as" —

"That won't do, Hal: give me a direct answer to my question."

"I didn't say I learned any thing," was the boy's reply.

"Nor did you, Hal: yet you endeavored to convey the impression that you did; this was nothing more nor less than an attempt to deceive us into the belief that you possessed a knowledge of the habits of the fox, when, in reality, you know nothing at all of them."

"Oh, yes, I do!" replied the boy; "because I've read about them in fables."

"What is a fable, Hal?" inquired I.

"A fable is a st-o-ry about" —

"Of fiction, told to enforce some moral truth," said I, finishing the sentence for him. "Now, I don't think you ever read a fable in which a fox was not represented as a sly, cunning fellow, always ready to save himself at the expense of others."

"Yes, Hal. I think you was a little foxy on that Apache business," said Ned, interrupting our conversation.

"I wasn't a bit foxy, as you call it," replied Hal angrily.

"Then you must have thought me, on the goose order," retorted Ned.

"You're as much on the goose order as I was on the fox," replied Hal.

"That may be; but I'll tell you one thing, Hal Hyde: there'll have to be a smarter fox and bigger goose about here, before any one'll be caught by your Apache experience."

"There, boys," interrupted I, laughing, "that will do: don't let me hear any more talk like this; it's neither pleasant nor profitable. Hal sees as plainly as anybody, that he's constantly getting himself into trouble by endeavoring to impress others with a false idea of his own knowledge. Now, Hal, I hope that I sha'n't have occasion to refer to this subject again. Suppose we stop here, and let our horses have a taste of this fresh grass, and wait the arrival of the train. Perhaps Sile will conclude to camp here."

CHAPTER XVII.

SILE SHOOTS A DEER. — TRAPPING. — HOW INDIAN BRAVES BECOME WARRIORS. — DESCRIPTION OF THE INITIATION, BY AN EYE-WITNESS. — A TERRIBLE SCENE. — THE BUFFALO BULL DANCE. — THE MEDICINE-MAN. — "IT DOES A FELLOW GOOD TEW HOLLER WHEN HE FEELS LIKE IT."

THROWING myself upon the beautiful greensward, I fell asleep, and was awakened an hour later by Sile's cheery voice saying, "Halloo! just the spot I'd have picked for a camp, if there's any water hereabouts."

"There's a splendid spring only a little way in the woods," said Ned. "Hal and I have been down to it."

"All right, then, my boy! here we stop till mornin'," replied Sile, dismounting. His feet had hardly touched the ground, ere he brought his rifle to his face, and the next instant the report echoed through the woods.

The boys and myself sprang to our feet, while Sile made his way into the forest as fast as he could go.

We had neither of us seen any thing; nevertheless each asked the other the question, "What was it?"

A moment later, we heard Sile shout; and then the boys bounded away in the direction of the sound, while I followed more leisurely, and soon found them all standing over the prostrate form of a fine fat doe.

"Well, Sile, don't ever complain of poor eyesight again," said I, after I had taken a look at the carcass.

"I ketched sight of her just as I was a-getting off er my hoss; but I didn't have no time to explain, for she was on the go then," remarked Sile.

"No explanations necessary, Sile," replied I. "Suppose you let the boys help dress it: they may as well begin to learn now, as any time."

"Help?" repeated Hal, with rather a contemptuous intonation of voice: "as if I didn't know enough to skin a deer!"

"All right, sonny: there's the train comin', and while I'm gone ter look arter that, you dress it," said Sile, hurrying away towards the animals.

"Well, Ned, if Hal's going to dress the deer, we may as well go and take care of the horses. Be as quick as you can, Hal, for we want some steaks for supper;" and Ned and myself started for camp, leaving Hal standing alone by the carcass in rather a surprised and bewildered attitude. Before we had taken five steps, he shouted after us, —

"You don't expect me to dress this deer alone, do you? Can't Ned stop and help me?"

"Certainly he can," replied I.

"I don't know a thing about it," said Ned, "but I'll stop if I can help him any;" and Ned turned back, while I continued on.

After the mules had been unpacked, the horses all picketed, a fire built, and supper under way, I thought I would walk back and see how the boys progressed in their task.

Some time before I reached them, I heard the sound of their voices, evidently in an argument relative to the proper manner of commencing the flaying process; after listening a moment, I made my appearance upon the scene saying, —

"Well, boys, have you got it all nicely dressed?"

"Dressed!" responded Ned: "why, we haven't touched it yet."

"Haven't touched it?" said I in tones of astonishment; "why, we are all ready to cook the steaks: what's the trouble?"

"Hal isn't exactly sure how he ought to commence, and I don't know enough to tell him," was Ned's answer.

"My knife's so dull, I can't do a thing with it," said Hal, by way of explanation.

"I guess that's what the matter with mine," responded Ned, laughing.

At this instant we heard Sile shout, "Fetch on your steaks: we are all ready for 'em."

"Come, come, Hal, this won't do: we shall all starve to death if you don't work faster than you have been doing," said I. "You've had time enough to dress half a dozen deer, while you have been standing there arguing with Ned. Why don't you commence?"

"I can't dress it," frankly owned the boy, looking exceedingly foolish and very much mortified at thus being obliged to confess the truth.

"Then go at once, and ask Sile to be kind enough to come and dress the deer: tell him you don't know how to do it," said I.

"Must I go?" inquiringly asked the boy: "I'd rather not."

"Yes, Hal, of course you must go; and don't ever again profess to be able to do that which you know you can't perform, for it will always be a source of mortification to you in the end. Now go at once."

Hal started, considerably crestfallen, returning in a few moments, however, with Sile, who pleasantly went to work; and in a very short time the carcass was nicely dressed, the hind-quarters were in camp, and we in a fair way to make a hearty supper of venison-steak, which proved to be exceedingly nice.

The meal over, Sile brought forward his bear-skin, which he had packed upon one of the mules, as also the poles that composed the drying-frame, which he put together, intending to finish drying the skin by the fire that night.

Lighting his pipe, he began setting up the frame,

when Ned inquired if he wasn't going to tell us something more about trapping that night.

Before he had time to answer the question, Hal protested, saying, —

"Oh, no, Sile! please tell us about Indians."

Sile regarded each with a puzzled look, saying, —

"There ye be again. One wants trappin', and t'other wants Injuns. I guess I'll have to tell 'bout both, tew suit. So I'll tell ye how the Injuns make warriors out of the braves, and then how they hunt buffaloes: how'll that suit?"

"First-rate, Sile," exclaimed I. "I've always wanted to hear some one who has been an eye-witness of the initiation of a brave into the list of warriors, describe the ceremony; for, in all my journeyings in Indian countries, I've never happened to witness it."

"There's mighty few white men that have, squire," was Sile's reply; "and 'tain't no easy thing tew do; but I'll try it, 'cause I want these boys tew know what all youngsters hev tew go threw afore they kin be counted warriors."

"Do all tribes have the same ceremonies?" inquired I.

"That's what I can't answer," replied Sile: "they all have some ceremony; I never seen it done but once."

"I didn't know that there had to be a regular initiation before a brave could become a warrior," said Hal.

"Then there's one pint that ye didn't larn when you was amongst the Apaches, eh?" said Sile with a sly wink, continuing as follows: —

"The second year I was out trappin', me and my pard Ike, got ahead of the rest of the party in the fall somehow, and had to wait nearly a month for 'em; so we took up in a encampment of Cheyennes, that was out on their annual buffalo-hunt: they were mighty friendly, and glad tew have us with 'em, 'cause we hed our rifles and fixins; and, as they didn't have any weapons then but bows and spears, they thought our guns was 'big medicine,' and would bring 'em luck.

"You see, Ike had been trappin' seven year, and he'd got so he could talk the Injun lingo pretty fair; and he come in one day, and said they was a-goin' tew have their great buffalo-bull dance, which would last several days, for the purpose of inducin' the Great Spirit tew send 'em a big drove of buffalo, and good luck in the hunt; and we should hev a chance tew see it.

"The next day we seed that matters was a-goin' on lively in the camp; for the squaws were all tew work cleanin' off the ground in front of the chief's lodge, where the ceremonies was tew take place; the bucks were a-flyin' 'round, gittin' their selves fixed up for the dance, which was ter last four days, the performers havin' tew fast the hull time.

"The next mornin', the 'medicine-man' come intew camp. He was a dried-up old feller, about sixty year old, and as naked as he was born, 'ceptin' a white wolf-skin slung over one shoulder, some bands of the same kind about his ankles, and a pair of moccasins from which the tails of two wolves dragged behind; he had on a cap er white buffalo-skin, stuck full er eagle's feathers."

"I never heard of a white buffalo. Is there any such animal?" inquired Ned.

"Sartin there is, or how could he hev got the skin? They're mighty scarce, and the skin is always used for 'medicine' by the Injuns. There's about the same proportion er white buffaloes that there is er black sheep. But I can't have you boys interruptin' me ter-night by askin' questions: yeou must wait till I git threw.

"Wal, the old feller's body, legs and all, was painted over with red clay, and he was about as hedeous-lookin' a old cuss as any livin' man ever seed.

"But I can't tell yer all that was done durin' the four days that the dance lasted, 'cause it would take all night, and the 'nitiation didn't come off till the fourth day: so I'll just tell yer 'bout that.

"Early in the mornin' two of the oldest warriors fetched out er the medicine-lodge a couple er young braves, 'bout eighteen year old I should say, and leadin' 'em up to two stout poles sot in the ground, and 'bout twelve foot high, unfastened some cords of raw-hide that hung from the top of 'em.

"One er the braves knelt down at the foot er the pole, restin' his thighs on his heels, and throwed his head back and his breast forreard.

"The warriors then took an old butcher-knife, cut through the skin and flesh on each side er the breast, and stuck some splints of wood under the sinews, and fastened the cords to 'em. Then they served the other brave in the same way, and left 'em alone.

"As soon as the two warriors was gone, the braves rose tew their feet, with the blood streamin' from their breasts, and throwed their hull weight onto the cords, jumpin' back tew the end of the ropes, and swingin' about, tryin' tew break loose from the poles. All the while, neither one on 'em groaned or made the least noise: 'cause, yer see, the hull thing was done tew test 'em, tew see if they had pluck or grit enuff tew make warriors; anyhow they had to stan' it till they could *break* loose, 'cause the splints mus'n't be pulled out, nohow. One on 'em finally managed tew tear the sinews loose, and was carried away to his lodge by his friends. The other one, after hangin' two or three hours, finally succeeded in pullin' himself loose, and then, the hull tribe had a grand feast in honor of their pluck and endurance."[1]

"Can they always contrive to break the sinew, Sile?" inquired I.

"They hev tew: they can't get loose any other way if they want tew become warriors. Sometimes,

[1] The above terrible rite has for many years been practised among the Mandans, the Assiniboines, the Cheyennes, and other Western tribes, and is the only acknowledged ordeal for testing the endurance of the applicant for admission into the brotherhood of warriors.

"'Cause they couldn't even holler." Page 153.

when it's very tuff and strong, they'll hitch on eight or ten buffaloes' heads tew ther rope, and make the brave drag 'em about till the sinews gives way."

"It must cause terrible suffering," remarked I.

"Yes; and the worst of it is, if the brave flinches, or groans, or complains the least particle, he is set loose at once; but he can't never be nothin' but a squaw-man after that."

"What's a squaw-man?" inquired Ned.

"One that ain't allowed ter fight, or hunt, or git married, or own hosses; but has tew stay about the camp with the squaws all the time."

"Well, I'd rather be a squaw-man, you bet!" cried Hal. "They wouldn't catch me submitting to any such nonsense as that, for the sake of being a dirty warrior. I've seen enough of that sort of stock when I was with the " —

"There, there, Hal!" interrupted I. "Don't say any thing more about that."

Even Hal joined in the laugh at his own expense, and Sile continued, —

"Now, boys, I've told yer what a Injun boy has to go threw with afore he kin expect tew be any kind of a man: yeou ought tew be glad yeou ain't Injuns, and kin be considered men without havin' tew undergo sich tortures as them poor braves did. I never pitied anybody so much in all my life, 'cause they couldn't even holler: I think it sometimes does a feller lots of good just tew hev the priv'lege of hollerin' when he feels like it. There," said he, starting to his feet, "I come nigh forgettin' tew turn old Ephraim. I guess he'll be dry enuff tew brain in the mornin'. Yeou git up airly and help me, boys, won't ye?"

"Yes; but you said you'd tell us about an Indian buffalo-hunt, you know," said Ned.

"Good gracious, sonny! you don't want to hear nothin' more ter-night, do yer? I guess I've talked enuff for once: you must wait till 'nother time for the rest."

"But, Sile, we don't want to go to bed. We ain't a bit sleepy; are we, Hal?" persisted Ned.

"No, sir," replied Hal: "I'm as wide awake as an Apache scout."

"I don't s'pose you'd be sleepy if yeou sot there all night. I sha'n't talk any more ter-night, nohow. My throat is as dry as a hot skillet now," said Sile.

"Come, boys, don't ask Sile for any thing more to-night: he's tired, if you aren't," said I. "Go to bed now, and turn out early in the morning, and help him finish his skin: that will be a good way to pay for your evening's entertainment. We ought all to be willing to do what we can for each other's pleasure, even though it entails some little sacrifice for ourselves."

"Well, when will you tell us the rest?" asked Hal.

"Ter-morrer night, perhaps," was Sile's answer; and with it the boys departed, quite as well satisfied as if Sile had talked for another hour.

CHAPTER XVIII.

BRAINED AND PACKED. — SILE'S STEW. — AN UNEXPECTED SIGHT. — THE WHITE HORSE AND ITS RIDER. — WE SHOOT A LION. — A SEARCH AND DISCOVERY. — "WHAR'S ME HOORSE?" — DENNIS BURKE AND HIS SHILLALAH. — A "PUMEL" AND WHAT CAME OF IT. — A SEARCH FOR THE HORSE, AND THEN A SEARCH FOR DENNIS. — CAMP.

SILE was up and at work the next morning before it was fairly light; and when the boys arose, just after sunrise, the skin had been "brained" and packed, ready for transportation; and Sile himself was preparing a cup of coffee.

"Halloo! ain't you going to do the skin this morning?" sleepily inquired Hal, who was the first to put in an appearance at the camp-fire.

"What skin be you talkin' about?" asked Sile, with a most innocent expression upon his face.

"Why, the grizzly's, to be sure," said Hal.

"Oh! that was finished more'n an hour ago," replied Sile.

"I don't care, Sile Carter, I think you're just as mean as you can be; don't you?" said Hal, addressing Ned, who by this time had made his appearance.

"Here he asked us to get up and help him; and, instead of waiting for us, he's been and done it himself. I mean to go back to bed again."

"Then you won't git none er this stew er mine," said Sile, well knowing that if there was one thing the boy liked above another, for breakfast, it was a venison-stew; for Sile's stews were delectable. They were the result of constant practice combined with long experience, concocted with a consummate art that I have never seen equalled in the most celebrated French *cuisine*.

The bare announcement of what was in store for them was sufficient to drive all thoughts of returning to bed from the boys' heads; and they both commenced making amends for harboring such a thought by vigorously attacking the stew, which attack they followed up so energetically and persistently that in a very short space of time it was completely annihilated.

It was quite nine o'clock before we were ready to start; and, fairly getting upon the road, the boys and myself were soon some distance in advance of the train.

Our trail led through quite an extensive forest, containing many gigantic oaks, whose spreading branches and thick foliage formed a magnificent arbor above our heads, completely excluding the sunshine, and rendering our ride an exceedingly pleasant and comfortable one.

As we were carelessly ambling along, enjoying the refreshing shade, suddenly all heard a shout.

AN UNEXPECTED SIGHT.

" Hark, boys! Sile's calling," said I.

We reined in our horses, and listened: the silence for the moment was profound; then came a cry as of some one, or something, in mortal agony, and the next instant we saw a white horse, saddled and bridled, with a full-grown, tawny, Californian lion or puma, upon its back, coming directly towards us.

We were so astounded by this unexpected apparition, that for a moment we sat in stupid wonderment gazing on the sight. The next instant I recollected myself, and, taking deliberate aim at the puma's head, fired, just as the boys also discharged their weapons.

The creature seemed to cling to the affrighted animal a moment tighter than ever, and then dropped suddenly to the ground, where it lay writhing in the agonies of death, while the terrified horse, the blood running in streams down its flanks, dashed past us, and disappeared in the depths of the forest.

Up to this time neither of us had spoken a word; but with one accord we spurred our horses towards the place where the carcass of the now lifeless puma lay stretched upon the ground.

Hal was the first to reach it; dismounting, he cautiously put his hand upon the creature's side, saying, —

" He's settled now for good; but ain't he a beauty? I wish Sile was here."

" So do I," was my reply. " Suppose you remain here, Hal, while Ned and I ride on and see if we can discover the owner of that horse."

"I'd rather go with you. I wish you'd let me," said the boy.

"Very well, you can go; and Ned will stop here until Sile comes. Tell him how it is, Ned, if he gets here before we return. We sha'n't be gone very long."

We had ridden scarcely a quarter of a mile when Hal's keen eyes detected some object stretched upon the ground close by the trail, a little distance ahead.

"I see him, I see him!" shouted he, pointing to the body. Upon reaching it, I dismounted, and proceeded to make an examination of the apparently lifeless form, which proved to be that of a laboring-man about twenty-five years of age.

There was but a little blood visible, and that had come from a slight wound on the shoulder, evidently made with the creature's claws.

After looking at the man, Hal said, rather hastily, —

"He's dead, I reckon: we can't do any thing for him."

"I don't think so," said I, placing my ear to his breast: "his heart beats any way. Get down and help me to raise him until I see."

"I don't like to touch him," replied Hal, dismounting.

"Nonsense! take hold here, and let's see how badly he's hurt," said I.

At this instant the supposed dying man, slightly astonished us by opening his eyes, sitting upright, and gazing about him in evident bewilderment for a moment, and then saying, with an unmistakably strong Hibernian accent,—

"Where's that ould divil gone wid my hoorse?"

This singular question, together with the comical appearance of the man, struck Hal and myself so forcibly that we both burst into a roar of laughter, which appeared to somewhat excite the ire of the wounded man; for assuming an injured tone of voice, with a most lugubrious expression upon his broad Irish face, he said,—

"Yez moight az will larf at a coorpse; but it ain't viry amusin' for the coorpse though."

I endeavored to assure the man that we were not laughing at him, asking if he was badly hurt.

"Is it hurted I am you're axin' me? and I bladin' loike a shtuck pig, wid the whack that ould divil give me wid his shillalah. Sure 'twas enuff to break ivery bone in me body, so it was."

Having by this time become assured that the fellow was actually more scared than hurt, I said, "How did it happen?"

"How did it happen?" said he, repeating the question after me. "It didn't *happen* at all, at all, [strongly emphasizing the word "happen"]: it was just done a purpose, so it was. Some murtherin' ould divil (I didn't see his face at all) cum oop behind me whin I was ridin' along paceably enuff, and knocked me aff me hoorse wid his shillalah, struckin' me in the back sinsible, so he did, and I layin' on the ground intirely spacheless all the toime."

"He evidently thinks somebody struck him on the back," said Hal to me in a very low tone.

"*Thinks* somebody shtruck him, does he?" replied the man, very cleverly imitating Hal's tone and manner. "Bedad, thin, he *knows* somebody shtruck him: Dinnis Burke knows the touch of a shillalah as well as any livin' man in ould Ireland."

"No person struck you," said I, by way of explanation. "It was a wild beast, a puma, that knocked you out of your saddle."

"A pumel, was it? Will, if iver I git hould of him wid a bit of shillalah in me hand, I'll pumel him, till there isn't a bone lift, as big as a gossoon's finger, in his whole body, so I will."

"But you don't understand. Let me explain to you, Dennis: where were you when you were knocked off your horse?"

"Where was I? On his back, to be sure: where else would I bae?"

"Yes," said I, very much amused at the answer, "I understand that; but you were riding beneath a large tree, were you not?"

"Suppose I was, sure: hadn't I a right to ride beneath a trae?"

"Certainly you had; but the animal was concealed among the branches, and, as you passed under them, sprang upon you, and knocked you off your horse."

"He did, sure," replied Dennis, "and then wint off wid me hoorse, and that's wat I want now."

"Well, after we shot him, your horse went off down the trail: if you'll come with us, we'll show you the animal."

"Come wid yez? av coorse I will. I'd go a hunthred miles to sae the pumel that knocked Dennis Burke aff that hoorse."

During this conversation Hal had been so much amused at the odd appearance as well as the quaint expressions of Dennis, that it was with the greatest difficulty he could restrain himself from bursting into a laugh. Noticing this, I suggested that he might as well join Ned; and, glad of an opportunity to escape, he mounted his horse, and, almost bursting with laughter, galloped back.

"What's that b'y laffin' at?" queried Dennis suspiciously.

"I can't tell you," said I. "Where did you come from?"

"Where did I come from? From the ould counthry, av coorse."

"Yes; but you live on some ranch, don't you? To whom does it belong?"

"Muster Maverick, sure; and I'd betther be foindin' that hoorse, so I had, or I'll niver dare to go back, bedad. What was that b'y laffin' at?"

"Why won't you dare to go back?" inquired I, ignoring the last question.

"Ould Maverick'll take the rist of the hide aff me back, for l'avin' his baste, so he will."

"But you couldn't help it: you were knocked off."

"So I was, sure; but ould Maverick niver'll belave it. He'll turn me aff, sure."

At this time we came in sight of the boys, who were standing by the carcass of the puma, laughing immoderately; and when Dennis saw them, he suddenly turned towards me, saying, —

"If thim b'yse is laffin' at me, I'll bate 'em till widin an inch of their lives."

"Oh, no, you won't, Dennis!" said I, as we came upon the carcass of the great tawny creature, stretched at full length upon the ground. Gazing at it in evident consternation, he exclaimed, —

"Howly Mother! what's that, now?"

"That's the puma that knocked you off your horse, Dennis," replied Hal.

"Is that the pumel, now?" inquired he.

"That's the identical chap," said Hal, laughing.

"Where's the hoorse, thin?" querried he.

"We shot the puma, but we couldn't stop the horse," explained Hal.

"I could av done that mesilf," replied Dennis, putting his hand to his belt; then with a bewildered look exclaiming, —

"Where the divil's ould Maverick's pistil gone to?"

"Did you have one?" inquired Ned.

"Did I have one? af coorse I had one, and it's gone wid the hoorse, by me sowle!"

"Perhaps Sile will catch the horse," remarked Ned, by the way of consolation.

"And perhaps he won't. I'll go afther him mesilf. Which way did he go, sure?"

The boys pointed out the course, telling him that he'd better wait till Sile came up; but, paying no heed to their advice, he limped off in the given direction.

"I presume Sile has seen the horse, and caught it, which is the cause of his delay," said I, laughing: "the fellow is an original."

"I thought Hal had gone crazy when he rode up, he was laughing so hard: he kept repeating what the man said, and laughing so much that I couldn't understand a word he said," said Ned. "I hope he'll come back."

"Howly Mother! is that the pumel, now?" exclaimed Hal, imitating the tone and manner of Dennis so perfectly, that Ned and myself fairly shouted at the representation.

"Come, boys, I want to measure this puma," said I.

"Oh let me measure him!" cried Hal, producing his rule: "six feet seven inches from the tip of his nose to the end of his tail," said the boy, stroking the sleek tawny fur, "and not a spot on him. I thought pumas were always spotted."

"They are so when young; but I believe their spots disappear after they attain a certain age."

"See what immensely strong paws he's got," said Ned. "I don't wonder Dennis thought somebody struck him with a shillalah;" and the boys laughed again.

"His claws ain't so very sharp," remarked Hal: "still, I wouldn't want 'em in my back. Do they always jump on to a fellow from a tree?"

"Generally, I believe," replied I: "I have heard old hunters say that one can jump with ease, thirty or forty feet. Sile can tell you more about that though, than I can."

"Halloo! here he comes," shouted Hal. "I hear him;" and a moment later Sile came in sight with the train. "Yes, he's got the white horse, but I don't see Dennis," continued the boy.

Upon seeing us, Sile rode rapidly forward; but stopped at the sight of the puma, evidently greatly surprised, saying, —

"Who shot that critter?"

"We did, Mr. Sile," replied Hal, strongly emphasizing the "we."

"Was the horse badly hurt, Sile?" inquired I.

"The critter has tared him some, but he'll git over it. He was awful scart though, and it took me consid'ble time to ketch him; it's hard work lassoin' a crazy hoss in the woods: but whar's the man that owns him?"

"Haven't you seen him?" asked I.

"I hain't seen a livin' soul but them Mexicans, sence yeou left me, till now," was Sile's answer.

"What can have become of him? He must have wandered off into the woods," said I, proceeding to state, as briefly as possible, the facts above narrated.

Sile's only reply was, "We mustn't let the feller git lost. We ought ter hunt him up."

"Yes, we certainly must do that," said I.

"Wal, I guess we'd better find a campin'-place, and make a day of it, then," suggested Sile: "'cause by the time we git this puma skinned, and the Irishman hunted up, it'll be putty nigh night, if he's like any Irishman I ever seed."

"Correct," shouted Hal. "You'll die laughing, Sile, if ever you do find him, he's so funny."

"Wal, we'll find him, sonny: yeou kin depend upon that. Now let's throw this puma over that hind mule, and go on till we find a good campin' ground; then we'll come back and have a hunt."

After riding a very short distance beyond the spot where Dennis met with his accident, we came to the banks of a beautiful stream, upon which we made our camp. The men had the greatest difficulty in persuading the white horse to pass the spot where he had been attacked; but, while doing so, picked up the revolver dropped by Dennis, which was given into Hal's charge.

The mules unpacked, and camp settled, directions were given as to dressing the puma's carcass; and then Sile, the boys, and myself rode back on our search for Dennis.

CHAPTER XIX.

HUNTING FOR THE LOST. — HE IS FOUND. — PREFERS TO "WALK AFOOT." — HIS HISTORY. — "OULD MAVERICK'S RANCH." — OULD SAM. — "MA'AM AND THE GALS." — WE MOVE CAMP. — "A CALIFORNIA BUCK." — A BOY WITH THE "GENII." — HAL AND NED. — THE DISPUTE. — "YOU HEAR ME NOW."

"I DON'T suppose you've any idee which way ther feller went, or how much he knows 'bout ther country," said Sile, addressing me, as we galloped along.

"Not the least," was my reply; "but, if he's as ignorant of that, as he appeared to be on other subjects, he certainly can't know very much about it. He was evidently badly frightened and somewhat bewildered, by the unceremonious treatment he received from the puma, which may in a measure account for his singular manner."

"I wish you could have seen him, Sile, when he was telling us how it happened. It was as good as a play. Now, here's where we shot the puma; and when Dennis left us, he started in that direction," said Hal, pointing.

"Well, you hold my hoss a minit, and I'll see if I can find his trail," said Sile, dismounting.

In a short time he shouted that he'd found it, and then we made our way towards him, and in a few minutes were following on the trail: occasionally we would shout aloud, or fire our revolvers, and then stop and listen for a reply.

After doing this several times, Hal said,—

"I don't believe the fellow knows enough to answer; as likely as any way he'll think it's the ould fellow that knocked him off the hoorse wid his shillalah," imitating Dennis so perfectly, that, in spite of our best endeavors, we could not restrain our laughter.

"I reckon we shall find him before a great while," said I; and sure enough, after searching nearly an hour, we heard him call out loudly,—

"Say, yez, have yez seen the hoorse?"

At first we could not tell from what direction the voice came; but Hal's roving eyes shortly discovered him sitting upon a log, in the midst of a clump of firs.

As we came up to him, Sile answered his question by informing him that we not only had found the horse, but his pistol as well.

The look of despondency and weariness upon the man's face instantly gave way to one of joy and pleasure: he appeared like a new man, as gay and merry as a boy of sixteen, jumping to his feet and snapping his fingers, while he exclaimed,—

"Thin ould Maverick may go to the divil wid his hoorse, if ever I git the crayther back to him safe and sound. Is he hurted much?" asked he.

Sile assured him that the horse was only scratched a little by the puma's claws, and would soon be as good as ever.

"Will he, now?" exclaimed he, attempting to execute an Irish jig: "thin, by the powers, I don't care a cint for ould Maverick. He kin take it out of my boord and clothes, but divil a rag'll I have lift afther it."

"Where does Mr. Maverick live?" inquired I.

"On his ranch, to be sure," was the reply.

"Where is that, Dennis?" I asked.

"You'll go down to the crassin' beyant there, and foller up the straem till yez comes to it."

"How far is it from the trail?" inquired Hal.

"Risin' of two mile," answered the man.

"Wal," said Sile, "you git up behind me here, and ride down tew camp, and then we'll go over tew the ranch with yer."

"Will yez, now?" said Dennis, "but I'll walk by mesilf. Where's me pistil?"

"Hal's got it down ter camp. Why on airth don't ye git up and ride?" said Sile.

"And be knocked off wid another pumel? No, surr: az long az Dinnis Burke's got two ligs he'll walk bedad, that he will. I'll foind the way back mesilf," and Dennis started for our camp.

As he walked along beside us, both Sile and myself

endeavored to ascertain what the fellow was doing on the ranch, and where he was going at the time he encountered the puma.

At first he was disinclined to talk, but after a time became more communicative, informing us that he had been in California about two months; that immediately after landing in San Francisco, he had been employed by Mr. Maverick, and brought down to the ranch to superintend the " pigs," of which there were several hundred upon the place; and that, when he was knocked off his horse, he was on his way to Señor Escarrito's ranch, with a letter from his master, — in proof of which statement, he produced it from some secret depository in the waistband of his pants, where it had been placed for safe keeping.

It was about three o'clock in the afternoon when we reached our camp; and, after partaking of dinner, we set off for the ranch, where we arrived after a brisk canter of half an hour.

The house was of adobe, and consisted of a long range of narrow rooms, one story in height, utterly devoid of either paint or whitewash; slightly Americanized, however, by the addition of a piazza in front, under which we found the proprietor enjoying his pipe, which proved to be his constant companion; for, during the time we remained upon the ranch, it was scarcely out of his mouth.

He was an American about fifty years of age, tall and angular, with a stoop in the shoulders, but with a decidedly pleasant face, that fairly beamed with good-nature, when we addressed him in the Saxon tongue.

"'Light, 'light!" said he as we rode up. "I'm glad ter see somebody that kin talk somethin' besides Greaser and Injun. I hain't heerd a man speak 'Merican for nearly a year, till t'other day, when I was up to 'Frisco, and hired that worthless cuss you've got thar, just ter have a man 'bout that couldn't talk Mexican. Whar'd you pick him up? 'Light, 'light: I'm glad ter see yer."

We briefly informed him of the circumstances under which we had made the acquaintance of Dennis, to which he replied, —

"He's allers gittin' inter some kind of a scrape; there hain't bin a day sence he's ben here, that he hain't done some cussed thing or other: I've had more fun though, than his wages 'll come to;" then, turning towards Dennis, he said, "What yer settin' thar for? Take that hoss down ter the coral, and tell Pedro ter look out fer him; and if I ever ketch yer a-huntin' catermounts again, when I send yer on an arrant, I'll take every inch er hide off that mis'rable back o' yourn. Yer hear me, now."

"Faith, I do that same," said Dennis: "will I take the lether, afut?"

"No, give it ter me, and the pistol too: it's a wonder yer brought that back."

"Sure, it ain't my fault that I did," replied Dennis as with a comical leer he rode away.

Our host insisted upon sending our horses to the

coral, and that we should remain with him over night, offering to send down a message and have the camp moved up near the ranch; adding, "But stay yer must, cause 'twill tickle the old woman and gals to hear somebody that kin talk 'Merican," shouting out,—

"Halloo? ma'am, gals! Here's some chaps that'll talk 'Merican for yer: come out and see 'em."

"That is a needless request," remarked I; "for the pleasure of spending an evening in the society of ladies, will more than compensate for our delay, or the inconvenience of repacking."

Our host offered to send one of his men down with the necessary orders relative to removing the camp; but Sile would not permit it, preferring to attend to the matter himself.

While awaiting Sile's return, Mr. Maverick informed us that he came from Mississippi, through Texas, to California in 1849; but instead of turning his attention to mining, as did most of the emigrants of that date, he located in Southern California with his family, shortly afterwards, purchasing his present ranch from an old Spaniard; and that he now owned two thousand head of horses, three thousand sheep, five thousand head of cattle, and three hundred pigs, employing about fifty Mexicans and Indians to look after his interests.

His family shortly made their appearance: it consisted of his wife, a sour-looking, sallow-complexioned, slatternly dressed woman; two daughters, tall, gaunt, and evidently much given to "dipping;" and a barefooted, bareheaded, hopeful son, about Hal's age, who proclaimed himself a "California buck" who could out-wrestle, out-fight, out-ride, out-shoot, out-smoke and out-swear, any boy of his age in the State.

A couple of hours later, when visiting the coral, I chanced to overhear a conversation between Hal, Ned, and Moses (for that was this young buck's name), that greatly amused me.

"Dad sold five hundred colts last spring," said the boy, "and would 'er sold a thousand more, only they wouldn't pay enuff."

"Why, are all your father's horses, colts?" inquired Hal, evidently disposed to doubt the truthfulness of the statement.

"In course they ain't," was the answer.

"He said he only had two thousand in all," said Hal.

"Dad don't never count ther colts," replied the boy.

"How much did he get apiece for them?"

"Five dollars," was the reply. "Say, don't yer want ter play monte? I'll make a lay-out for yer;" and the boy produced an old pack of greasy, well-worn cards.

"Don't know how," was Hal's reply.

"What! dunno how ter play monte?" repeated the boy. "You uns ain't much count, be yer? What do yer know?"

"We know how to read and write: do you?"

"No, but dad does. I hain't had no schoolin': he says if a boy's got the genii (genius), he don't need no schoolin'; and, if he hain't got none, there ain't no use of it."

"What's the genii?" inquired Ned.

"I dunno: suthin' boys hev. I heerd dad tell ma'am, I'd got it big. Say, I can lick you uns."

"Did you ever kill an Indian?" asked Ned.

"More'n a hundred of 'em, you bet. Dad's killed more'n a thousand."

"I don't believe it," said Hal, rather abruptly.

"Yer mean ter say I lies, does yer?" asked the boy, evidently ready to engage in a set-to.

Thinking it time to put an end to conversation that could result in no good to either party, I stepped forward and said, —

"Here, boys, don't let's have any trouble."

"Wal, yew make him quit callin' my old man a liar, or I'll come from ther shoulder; I will," remarked the young hopeful.

Bidding Hal and Ned pay no attention to the remarks of the boy, but to return immediately to camp, I started toward the house for the purpose of paying my respects to the ladies.

As soon as my back was turned, Mose caught up a lasso that was lying near by, and began making casts for the purpose of "noosing" the boys, who were proceeding to camp in obedience to my commands. So much dexterity did the young rascal evince, that it required considerable effort on the part of Hal and Ned, to avoid being caught.

The "old man," seeing the ineffectual efforts of Mose, hastily caught up a strap that chanced to be near at hand, and, before Mose could dodge it, succeeded in laying it vigorously over the boy's shoulders, two or three times, shouting as he did so, —

" What er ye doin' on thar? Hain't I allers told yer, I'd lick yer if I ketched yer playin' it on strangers? an' hain't yer found out that old Sam Maverick' word's as good as his note, when he passes it? I've a thunderin' good notion ter give yer a tarnal lickin' for not makin' better casts, anyhow. What's the matter with yer? Can't yer ketch nothin' nohow?"

" I'se only foolin'," replied the boy.

" Yes, and you're gittin' fooler an' fooler ev'ry day er yer life. Clar out, now, an' don't let me see yer agin ter-night, or I'll lick yer sartin'. Yer hear *me*, now."

Muttering something that sounded to me very much like, " You'll hev ter ketch me fust," the boy quietly disappeared around the corner of the coral, with a look in his eye that boded mischief towards somebody; and mine host and myself continued our way towards the house.

CHAPTER XX.

THE MAVERICK FAMILY. — DIPPING. — MUSIC. — THE SHOTS. — "IT'S A GRIZZLY." — A RUSH FOR CAMP. — THE CINNAMON BEAR, AND WHO SHOT IT? — "AND YOU AIMIN' AT THE EYE OF THE BASTE." — OLD SAM'S WORD. — WE MAKE A TRADE. — WHO WAS SCARED?

UPON reaching the house, we found "ma'am" seated upon the threshold of the door, puffing away vigorously at a corn-cob pipe filled with the most "flagrant" of "navy plug." Squatting by her side, upon the floor of the piazza, were the two daughters, each with a saucer of snuff and a soft pine stick, engaged in the filthy, but old-time Southern practice, of " dipping."

Seating ourselves, we were saluted with, —

"Me'n the gals reckoned, as how you'n the old man was a-gwine ter leave we uns, ter fight it out erlone ter-night."

I replied that I had no intention of doing any thing of the sort; for, as the society of ladies was the motive that induced us to move our camp, I did not intend to forego the anticipated pleasure.

"Gals, yer hear what ther stranger says, now;

yer want ter take keer and do yer puttiest, 'cause he's a college-larnt chap, and plays ther pianner, I reckon."

"Does yer, stranger?" asked the elder of the two, her mouth full of snuff, and displaying the greater portion of an exceedingly dirty, naked foot, stretched out from beneath the skirt of her well-worn calico dress.

"Do you like piano-music?" asked I, dodging the question.

"You bet we do," cried the younger of the two: "we never heerd one but onct, and that was just scrumptious, you bet. Kin yer play the fiddle? Pedro plays, he does, powerful."

"Can't we have a little music?" asked I: "I'm very fond of the violin."

"Pshaw, now! yer ain't, be yer? wal, I'll fetch him." Placing the saucer upon the piazza, with the stick in her mouth, she ran towards the end of the house, shouting at the top of her voice, —

"You Pedro! you Pedro! fetch that 'ere fiddle o' yourn." Calling several times without receiving any answer, she returned, and, seating herself by her sister's side, said, —

"Dad, that onery cuss has *vamosed;* gone down ter the camp ter swap lies with some of them Greasers thar, I'll bet a hoss. — You Mose," continued she, calling that young hopeful, whom she discovered coming around the corner of the coral, lasso in hand: "come here'n pat ther juba, and whistle fer this' ere stranger."

But Mose only answered by placing his thumb beside his nose, and giving his fingers a twirl, as he vanished into the coral, where, a moment after, we saw him endeavoring to lasso a piebald stallion.

Thus left to our own resources, conversation lagged for a time. Ma'am puffed away at her corncob, the old man pulled at his clay, the girls plied their sticks vigorously, while I industriously labored to consume the smoking contents of my meerschaum, enjoying, meanwhile, the splendors of a California sunset, and speculating upon the feasibility of a contemplated excursion into Mexico after our return to the ranch.

While thus enjoying our *otium cum dig.*, it was rudely and unexpectedly broken by the almost simultaneous discharge of two rifles, followed a moment later by the report of a third, from the direction of our camp.

Springing to my feet I listened attentively; but nothing more disturbed the stillness that reigned about us, save the sharp, shrill neigh of a horse from the neighboring coral.

"I wonder what that meant," said I in a tone of inquiry.

"'Pears like them youngsters o' yourn are out huntin'," was the reply of mine host, without moving.

"Practisin' with them 'volvers o' theirn, more like," replied his wife.

"The reports were those of rifles, I think," said

I; and the next moment I saw Dennis break from the cover of the woods, rush frantically towards us, waving his arms, and shouting, —

"It's a grizzly, it's a grizzly!"

Starting hurriedly in the direction of camp, Dennis turned back, and, as he accompanied us, briefly explained the situation as follows: —

"I wuz sittin' paceably listin' to the ''Pache bye' [Hal] spakin' of the ways of thim divils, whin we heerd the ould man [Sile] and the wee bye [Ned] who'd bin warkin' intil the woods, both firin' aff their goons, and the next minit we seed a big grizzly runnin' forninst us, wid his mouth wide open, and his teeth more'n tin inches long; so ther ''Pache bye' let aff his goon at him, and the bear tumbled over onto his head sure, and I runned aff ter call yez; bedad, but 'twas a foine shot, so it waz. There they be now," continued he, pointing to the group, who as we approached separated, disclosing to our view the carcass of a full-grown cinnamon bear.

"Who shot him?" inquired I.

"This is the lucky feller," replied Sile, pointing to Hal; "me 'n Ned both fired at him, but somehow or ruther onaccountably missed; leastways we don't find no sign er our bullets. I never seed any thing drop so quick though, as he did arter Hal fired; he sent his bullet right threw the critter's eye, clean inter his brain. 'Twas a stavin' good shot. It beats all nater, squire, how that boy does shoot."

"Bedad, didn't I spake till mesilf, whin I saed the

bullet lave the goon, sayin', 'There goes for his lift eye'? and begorra, it's the lift eye, sure enuff," said Dennis, who was standing in front of the carcass.

"But it's the bear's right eye that was hit," said Ned, laughing.

"D'ye think I dunno my right hand from my lift?" queried Dennis. "Ain't this me lift hand, and ain't that lift eye on the same soide?"

"Well, you are facing one way, and the bear's facing the other, ain't he?" queried Ned.

Whereupon we all laughed heartily, in the midst of which Dennis shouted, "So he is, be jabbers;" then seating himself astride the bear, he continued, "Sure, it's the right eye I was spakin' of all the toime."

"Wal, we don't want no more o' your gab; so, if yer can't keep quiet, clar out now," said Mr. Maverick, roughly addressing him.

"An' me not spakin' a word, but as whist as a ded mon all the time," interposed Dennis, with a sly wink at Ned.

"That 'ere was a mighty lucky shot, my boy,— lucky for me ez well ez for you, 'cause I reckon that's the identercle chap as has killed more'n forty sheep for me in the last six months. He's bin seed about, a heap er times; but there ain't nobody wuth shucks ter shoot 'round here. You've made a bully good shot, my boy. I never seed no man as could do better nor that," declared our host.

Hal, who well knew that the shot was a chance

one, after listening to the meed of praise bestowed upon him, became gradually impressed with the idea that, after all, it was owing to his superior skill as a marksman, and not to a fortunate chance, that he had been so successful: this impression shortly grew into a firm belief, which so magnified his idea of his own accuracy, that, when turning towards him I said, —

"You are certainly entitled to congratulation on such a fortunate shot, Hal. It's no small thing to shoot a cinnamon bear dead, at the first fire: they are about as hard to kill as a grizzly," he promptly replied, —

"I knew that when I fired at him: that's the reason I aimed at his eye. I saw," continued he, swelling with importance, as he more fully realized the unusual result of his single shot, "I saw, that every thing depended upon my nerve, after Sile and Ned missed him; and I determined that that, shouldn't fail me."

"But what made you think we had missed?" inquired Ned.

"Think?" queried Hal contemptuously. "I didn't think: I knew. Couldn't any one see, that instead of hitting him, your shots were driving him straight into our camp?"

"Bedad, don't I know that mesilf?" interrupted Dennis; "for whin I saed yer hands a-shakin' so yer could hardly clutch yer goon aff the ground, and yer face a-lookin' so white and scart loike, I sed, spak-

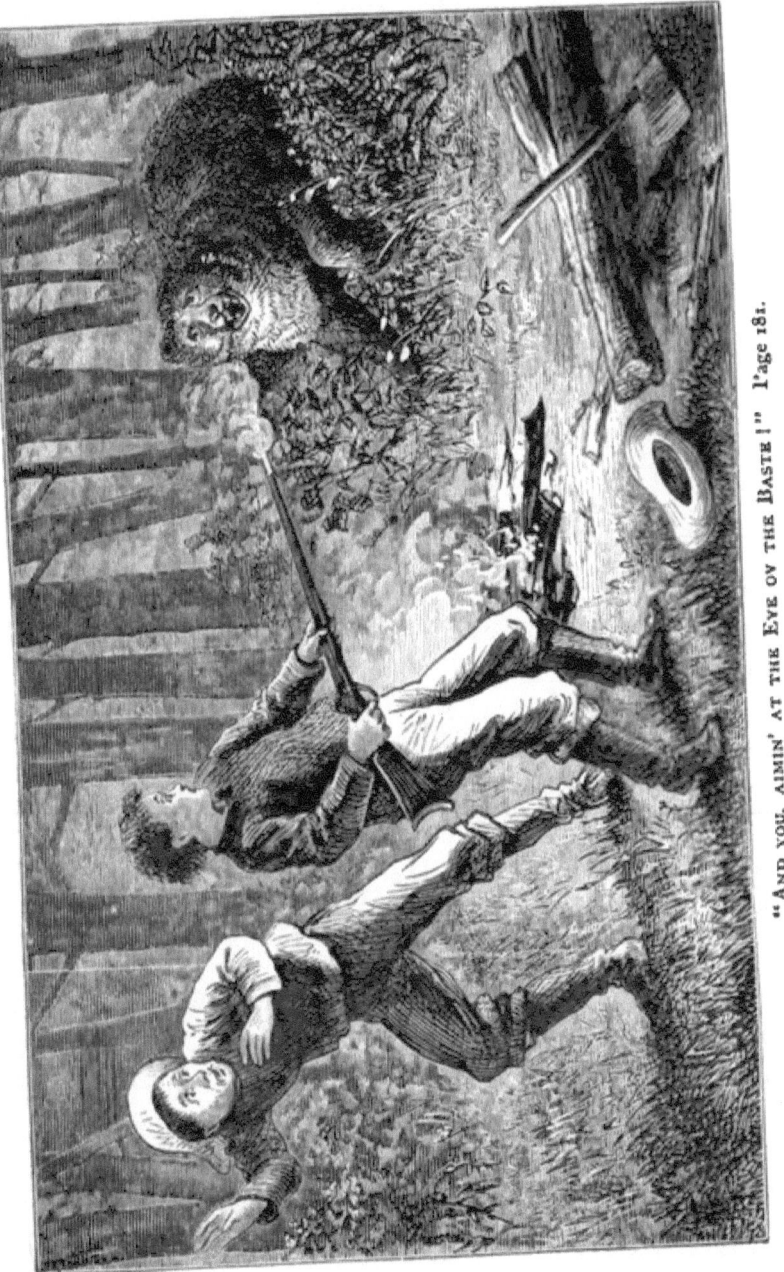

"And you, aimin' at the Eye ov the Baste!" Page 181.

in' aizily to mesilf, 'Dinnis Burke, it's no place for the loikes of yersilf;' and jist as I was lavin' for the ranch ter spake to the masther there, didn't the goon go aff afore yeez got it to yer shouldher, sure, and you all the toime, aimin' at the eye of the baste."

"The gun was up to my face, and I wasn't scared," declared Hal, giving his warm-hearted admirer a look calculated to wither anybody a little less obtuse than Dennis, into silence. "Besides, how could I have hit him in the eye, if I hadn't aimed at it?"

"Ov coorse ye couldn't. Don't I say it mesilf? Didn't I sae ye wid my own eyes, takin' aim at the eye of the baste, and your two hands all the toime so thremblin' wid agerness, ye could bairly clutch the goon aff the ground?"

This explanation of Dennis brought a hearty laugh from us all, in which Hal joined quite as merrily as any one, notwithstanding he evidently regarded the statement as a compliment of a somewhat doubtful character. He was speedily re-assured, however, when Sile, placing his hand upon his shoulder, kindly said, —

"The bar's, nuff for us: we know it's here, and we know you shot it, and there hain't nobody else killed one like it. Cinnamon bars is scace and hard tew kill."

"That ere shot o' yourn's, saved me many a dollar's worth er stock, I reckon; and if yer come hum this way, my boy, you stop at Maverick's ranch, and old Sam'll give you a dozen er his best ewes, ter mak a start er your own."

Hal's eyes sparkled, and his face fairly beamed with happiness, as he said, —

"Truly, will you?"

"Old Sam Maverick's word's as good as his note any time, when he passes it. I tell'd yer you should have 'em, and so yer shell," was the reply.

"But we ain't coming home this way, are we?" said the boy, his face clouding over with disappointment as he remembered the plan of our trip.

"Maybe the squire can buy his cattle here, as well as he can ter go clar on ter San José," suggested Sile.

"But we want to see the quicksilver-mines," said Ned.

"Wal, that needn't interfere, nohow: we kin go on an' see them, and come back this way a'ter the cattle, if the squire kin make a trade that suits him here," replied Sile. "S'pose yer talk with the old man, then, while I git off this bar's jacket. I kinder guess Hal'll want this 'ere skin tew sleep on, some 'er these nights."

"How is it?" said I, turning to Mr. Maverick: "do you want to sell some of your cattle?"

"Cattle, why, er course I do. That's what I've got 'em for."

"Then the only question is the price," said I.

"Wal, squire, that shan't stan' in yer way; for I'll sell 'em a dollar a head cheaper, than yew can buy 'em from any other man in Californy."

"Then there's no need of looking any farther," remarked I, with a smile.

"Yew bet, squire, yew heerd me; an' old Sam Maverick's word's as good as his note any time, when he passes it."

The boys, who, with the balance of the camp, had been watching the process of flaying the bear, now, as the probabilities of a trade became more apparent, began to manifest some interest in the conversation; for, leaving Sile, they joined Mr. Maverick and myself, just in time to hear the former remark.

"I've got as likely a lot of cattle as kin be found in the State; and'll sell yer four hundred head er two or three year olds, as cheap as any other man."

"You said you'd sell 'em a dollar a head cheaper than any other man," interposed Ned rather abruptly.

"So I did, youngster; an' old Sam Maverick's word's as good's his note any time, when he passes it; but I was talkin' with the squire, I beleve."

"You were, indeed, Mr. Maverick," was my reply; "and I'm astonished that Ned should have interrupted you. He must have forgotten the old adage which was taught me, in my younger days, that 'boys should be seen, and not heard.'"

"Wal, boys thinks they know a heap more'n old folks, in these days. Now, there's my Mose; yer can't tell him nothin': he knows it all, or at least he thinks he does, an' that's the next thing ter knowin' it."

"I don't imagine that I do," replied Ned; "and I ask your pardon for interrupting you. I didn't think."

"That's the great trouble with us all, Ned: we don't think, consequently act too hastily. Now, if you and Hal wan't to hear, I've not the slightest objection; but don't interrupt again."

"I never do," declared Hal: "you don't catch me interrupting anybody."

"Wal, squire, I'll tell yew what. I'll go up to the house, an' hev a talk with ma'am, an' give yer the figgers on them cattle in the mornin'. Yer ain't a-goin' ter be in no hurry 'bout startin' nohow."

"Very well; take your own time, Mr. Maverick: only remember that we must buy cheap, if we conclude to purchase here."

"All right, squire. I'll be on hand in ther mornin'. You Mose!" called the old man, looking about him to find his hopeful son; but Mose had mysteriously disappeared in the darkness, and after shouting once or twice more, without eliciting any reply, the old man solaced himself by declaring that, —

"That boy's a heap wus ter find, than a yearlin' colt, an' I s'pose he's gone off up ter the house. Mighty sing'lar, though," continued he in a reflective tone: "I never know'd him ter do sich a thing afore;" and he was forced to take his departure alone.

No sooner was he fairly on the road, than the boy and Dennis both put in an appearance; and when informed that they were wanted, Mose replied, —

"I heerd him holler. He's allers wantin' somethin'. I ain't a-goin' hum till I git a chunk of that bar-meat. I never et no cinnamon bar, and I'm a-goin' ter try it ter-night."

The bear was soon dressed, and in a very few minutes, we all had a piece of the meat nicely roasting upon sticks, set up before the roaring camp-fire; and, although we could not smother it in honey, succeeded in making a hearty supper, which, although not served in the most *recherché* style, was as toothsome as if eaten from the most delicate Sevres china.

"I didn't think cinnamon bear meat was so much better than grizzly," said Hal, after eating heartily, "but it's a great deal nicer."

"Maybe that's 'cause you killed it," said Sile, "and maybe, it's 'cause you're hungry. I don't reckon there's much difference: the grain er both's kinder coarse, and my old pard used ter say, that ther cinnamon warn't nothin' but a cross atween the grizzly and black."

"Did you ever meet many of these fellows in your travels, Sile?" inquired I.

"Never seen but one on 'em, and that was 'bout four year ago, over in Calaveras County, whar ther big trees air," was the reply.

"Those are something that I should like to hear about," said I.

"But tell us about the bear too," exclaimed Hal. "They are mighty scarce in this country, ain't they?"

"Thar's lots on 'em 'bout here," declared Mose, "and 'tain't no ways likely that this 'ere's the one that's bin killin' dad's sheep; but ther old man reckons 'twas, and I hain't nothin' ter say, only he's a durned ole fool ter say he'd give yer ten sheep ter pay for killin' of it, anyhow."

"These fellers air mighty fond er sheep," said Sile. "They make putty quick work when they git amongst a flock, I tell yeou."

"How do you know it ain't the one?" inquired Hal of Mose.

"Dunno nothin' 'bout it," replied Mose, "only 'tain't no ways likely 'tis; an' if 'twas, you hain't arnt no sheep by killin' of it, 'cause 'twarn't nothin' but luck, nohow. I heerd what Dennis said."

"He didn't say so," declared Hal. "Did you, Dennis?" appealing to him.

"Av coorse I didn't. Didn't I sae yez takin' aim straight at the eye av the baste, and didn't I say so, be jabbers?"

"You said he was scart anyhow," stoutly maintained Mose.

"Faith, I didn't spake a word 'bout his bein' schart. He was no more schart than I was, and Dennis Burke never was schart in his life."

"Warn't yer scart when that puma got after yer?" inquired Mose.

"Me schart at the pumel? will, now, ask any one of these gentoilmen here, if I was schart. The pumel don't live that can scare Dennis Burke — or any other wild baste," added he, after a moment's hesitation.

"Come, Sile, it will soon be bedtime, and if we're

to hear that story to-night, it's high time you began," said I, somewhat rudely interrupting the discussion.

"I'm ready any time, squire: I was only waitin' for 'em tew find out which one was scart."

"Well, never mind about that: go ahead with the bear story. We'll hear about the trees another time," said I.

CHAPTER XXI.

A CAMP IN A BIG TREE. — SILE'S CINNAMON BEAR STORY. — HOW JOSH CURTIS FETCHED FRESH MEAT FOR BREAKFAST INTO CAMP. — TREED BY A BEAR. — A STAMPEDE. — "MOIGHTY POOR LUCK." — AMONG THE QUICKSANDS. — A DANGEROUS CROSSING. — BAD LUCK. — A NEW FORD. — HAL IN MORE TROUBLE.

AFTER filling and lighting his pipe afresh, Sile commenced as follows: —

"Four year ago this spring, my old pard Ike McKenzie and a young chap that we picked up down in Tuolumne, was a-comin' up threw Calaveras on our way to Sacramento, and camped in the holler of one er them big trees one night."

"Made your camp in what?" inquired Hal rather incredulously.

"Made it in the holler er one er them big trees," replied Sile.

"I'd like to know how big that tree was," said Hal with a very knowing air.

"Wal, as nigh as we could figure, the one we camped in, was 'bout three hundred feet high, and eighteen or twenty threw; leastways, thar was room enuff for a dozen or fifteen men tew sleep in it, easy enuff."

" Do you mean to tell me that there was a tree big enough for "— Here he was interrupted by Sile, who said with some asperity,—

" Neow look a-here, sonny: if you want this 'ere bar story, you jest keep still, and don't bother me no more."

" Hal's the one who never interrupts," remarked Ned rather maliciously.

" Never mind Hal, sonny: see that you, don't do it," good-humoredly replied Sile.

" Wal, we was a-comin' up from Tuolumne, and camped in ther big grove; and airly in the mornin' I said tew Curtis, that I wished he'd fetch some fresh meat inter camp for breakfast, 'cause, yer see, we hadn't had nothin' but *pinole* [1] for two days, and a feller can't stan' it tew ride many miles with that, for a steady diet.

" Curtis was a young chap thet hadn't bin in Californy long, and hed a big idee that the only thing he wanted, tew make him a 'complished hunter, was tew be able tew say he'd killed a grizzly.

" Arter he'd gone, I started out and took the hosses down tew a swale ter feed a little, and on the way down I seen Curtis, and asked him if he'd seed any game. He said ' Nothin' worth shootin',' and I told

---

[1] *Pinole* is made of parched corn, ground upon a *metate*, or Mexican household mill. It is then mixed with sugar and water, making a very pleasant and palatable article of food.

him I was goin' tew leave the hosses tew feed awhile in the swale, and for him to hurry up, 'cause we was all hungry; but," says I (knowin' his weakness) "yeou hain't lost no grizzly this mornin', so don't yer try tew find one.'

"'Never yeou mind about givin' me advice: I'll bring some fresh meat inter camp, or my name ain't Josh Curtis,' says he. So I went back tew camp, and crawled inter Ike's blankets tew take a little nap; 'cause I've found thar ain't nothin' that'll satisfy yer when ye're hungry, like a nap — 'specially if yer can't get nothin' ter eat.

"I hadn't laid thar long, afore I heerd Ike sing out 'Sile!' I knowed from the way he hollered suthin' was up, so I grabbed my rifle, and broke out, and the fust thing I seed was the hosses a-comin' tearin' along, as though there was forty Injuns arter 'em. Then we seen Curtis with his hat off, followin' along behind them, and yellin', 'Oh, Lord! oh, Lord!' whenever he could ketch breath enuff ter speak. He'd throwed away his rifle and pistils, and was jest stripped for runnin'. Wal, we didn't know what tew make of it at fust; but in a minit more we seed what I thought, was the biggest grizzly I ever see, comin' right straight fur camp, arter him.

"The hosses went plumb threw camp as hard as they could go, and just as though they hadn't no right tew stop thar; and Josh was makin' stavin' good time arter 'em, I tell yer, when Ike sung out, 'Take keer, Sile, it's a cinnamont,' and took towards a little tree, and clim' up. I'd often heerd old trappers tell that when a cinnamont got riled, he was a heap worse'n a grizzly, 'cause he was tougher and uglier like; and I seen that this one was mad clean threw: anybody could 'a' seed that, if they wasn't lookin', 'cause he made sich a infernal kind of a noise a-runnin'.

"Wal, when I heerd Ike sing out, I was kinder scart for a minit, and dropped my rifle, and started to shin up a tree myself; and just as I got out 'er reach, Josh come tearin' along, and grabbed a limb that hung low, er the same tree, and swung hisself off er the ground quicker'n I could say 'scat.'

"The critter stopped right under the tree, tew kinder take breath, I s'pose; and I yelled ter Ike, tew give him a shot, for I didn't hev nothin' tew shoot with, 'cause I'd throwed my rifle down, and left my pistil under my blankets, when Ike woke me up hollerin'.

"As soon as Josh could git breath enuff tew speak, he sung out, 'I've fetched yer fresh meat inter camp, Sile; and if yer don't take it 'tain't my fault.'

"'Yes,' said I; 'and a nice mess you've made of it, too.'

"'I'm goin' tew wait whar I am, till it's better cooked, afore I take any more of it,' said he, laffin'-like.

"Wal, Ike had fired all the shots he had; and thar we was, all er us, roostin' in trees; our hosses had stampeded, nobody knowed whar; and a yaller bar as big as a cow, a-settin' lickin' his chops, and waitin' for us tew come down.

"We knowed ther critter hed seven er Ike's bullets in him; but he didn't seem ter mind 'em any more'n he would so many paper-wads. He sot thar jest as though he meant tew stay; and if one on us moved the least bit, he'd look up and growl, as much as ter say, 'Come down and try it, if yer think yer want to.'

"What on airth ter do I didn't know; and I see Ike was as much puzzled as I was; and, as for Josh, all he did was to set'n laff, an say, 'I've done's I agreed; I've fetched yer fresh meat inter camp: why don't yer cook it?'

"We was gittin' mighty hungry, as well as cur'rus 'bout our hosses; and we all knowed suthin' hed got ter be done, though none on us seemed ter care 'bout doin' of it.

"Putty soon the bar diskivered my rifle layin' on the ground; and arter pokin' it over and over, two or three times, he grabbed it in his mouth, and took his paws and bent the bar'l almost double, in less'n a minit.

"That made me mad, for I knowed I shouldn't get another rifle like it in Californy; and I said tew Ike, 'I ain't goin' ter stay up here no longer: we'll shin down at ther same time, and if he starts to chase either on us, the one he takes arter must keep runnin' 'round a tree, while the other one tackles him with his knife.' Wal, boys, as sartin as you're livin', we didn't neither of us 'member that we hadn't got but one knife atween us, till we was all ready ter drop. Yer see, I'd left my knife with my pistil-belt; Josh he'd throwed his away when the bar started for him; and Ike was the only one that hed a knife: and thar we was, and thar we sot all day, waitin' fer that critter ter leave. We was enamost starved tew death, too; for the critter never left till night, and then we darsn't move for fear he hadn't gone.

"I never seed a feller so mad as Ike was at the idee of bein' treed by thet bar. He cussed and swore more'n I ever heerd him afore; for he was mad clean threw 'bout the hosses stampedin', as well as t'other thing.

"Ther more he swore, the more Josh laughed; and that didn't please him none too much, I kin tell yer. Wal, we sot ther night out, and as soon as 'twas light, and we could see that ther old feller'd really gone, we come down; and as quick as we could git the kinks outer our legs, we started for camp, glad enuff tew git some *pinole*, you kin bet.

"As soon as we got a good share er that, we started off arter the hosses, and found 'em 'bout ten mile away, feedin' as quiet as though they'd never heerd of a cinnamont bar.

"That's the only scrimmage I ever had with one o' these critters; and seein's I missed this one, 'pears like I don't hev any sort o' luck with 'em."

"Faith, I think ye hez, moighty poor luck, I does," said Dennis.

"So I do," replied Sile; "but my old mother used ter say, 'Try ag'in; better luck next time;' and I ain't noways discouraged, 'cause I mean tew git one on 'em, one er these days."

"Did you ever see any thing more of the bear?" inquired Ned.

"No, nor never wanted to," said Sile. "I never told ther story afore, and shouldn't now if it hadn't bin fer missin' this critter ter-night."

"I'll bet a hoss, yer never sent that other feller out ter fetch fresh meat into camp agin, did yer now?" inquired Mose.

"Halloo, youngster, you here? well, you'n the Irishman hed better be makin' tracks for the ranch, or you'll hev the old man down arter yer," was Sile's answer.

"He's as mad as he kin be now, so we may as well stay it out," responded Mose.

"It's high time tew go ter bed anyhow," said Sile. "So yer may as well start along towards home. Come, boys, you and me'll turn in," addressing Hal and Ned, "so's tew be on hand ter hear that bargain in the mornin'."

"But we want to know about those big trees to-night," persisted Ned.

"I sha'n't say another word to-night. You'll hev tew wait till 'nother time," and Sile went out to pay his usual visit to our animals before retiring; ignoring the thanks offered for the evening's entertainment, in a very unusual and uncourteous manner.

Early upon the following morning, our camp was visited by Mr. Maverick, whom we had invited to breakfast with us; and after partaking of a remarkably fine juicy bear-steak, and drinking a cup of excellent coffee, a bargain was concluded for the sale of four hundred two and three year old heifers, at a very moderate price per head, to be delivered at the coral upon the ranch, any time after one, and within three weeks, from that day.

This business being satisfactorily arranged, we once more set out upon our journey to the famous New Almaden quicksilver-mines, from thence intending to return directly to Maverick's ranch.

For the first few miles our trail led through a magnificent country, beautifully diversified with forest and plain and hill and valley.

Sile and myself had fallen behind, leaving Hal and Ned in charge of the train, which about noon arrived at the bank of a broad but apparently shallow stream.

With his accustomed impetuosity, Hal rushed in to pilot the way across, calling upon the muleteers with the train, to follow him.

This they did; and when Sile and myself arrived upon the bank, a few moments later, it was to find the heavily laden animals floundering about in a dangerous quicksand.

Hal's pony was already up to his back, and the boy himself, wading towards the shore. Two of the lightest loaded mules, and one of the muleteers' animals, were just emerging from the stream, while the balance of the train with the exception of Ned's pony, were in such peril, that it was evident, unless help shortly reached them, they would be unable to extricate themselves from the loose shifting sand.

Sile comprehended the situation at a glance, and hastened to the rescue, giving his orders with so much coolness and deliberation, that the men at once recovered their presence of mind, and labored so faithfully, that we succeeded in saving all but Hal's pony and the mule that bore our tent.

We made every effort to rescue the pony, whose frantic exertions to liberate himself were pitiful to behold; and when at last, he could no longer move, and it became evident that he must certainly perish, Sile put his pistol to the poor creature's head, and discharging it instantly ended what must otherwise have proved, a slow and painful death.

We all felt sad at the fate of the poor fellow, for he was a great favorite with every one, being unusually intelligent and very fleet.

"What made you forsake him, Hal?" inquired I, after we had reached the bank.

"I felt him sinking, and trembling under me at the same time, and thought that if I left him, he would be able to get through easier, than with me on his back," was the reply.

"You've already had one experience in crossing the quicksands: why didn't you profit by that?" said I.

"A fellow can't always remember every thing, when he gets into a scrape," said the boy.

"True; but you should have remembered that when in a similar trouble a few days since, Sile told you, that if you ever again found yourself obliged to cross a bed of quicksand, you should sit lightly upon your horse, with feet well out of your stirrups, keep a firm, steady hand upon the rein, and, if you felt the animal sinking, apply the spur sharply. Did you think of those directions to-day, Hal?" inquired I.

"You see, it was so unexpected, that I hadn't time to think of any thing: the ford looked so easy that I never dreamed of its being dangerous."

"That's no excuse, Hal: in the first place, you are not competent to select a fording-place, or to pilot any one across a stream. You should have waited for Sile to come up. You see the consequences of acting without proper consideration. You have lost your pony, and our *cargas* have got so thoroughly wet, that we shall be obliged to remain here all day I expect, to dry the loads, saying nothing of the damage they have sustained by the wetting."

"There couldn't any one have known there was quicksand there, and I don't believe Sile would have brought 'em over any better than I did."

"I'll venture to say that Sile would not have lost an animal; at least he would have acted with more caution. His experience has taught him to do that, if nothing else."

"When you come to talk of experience, I've had

as much of that, as any one; while I was with the Apaches I learned the art of woodcraft, and I hain't forgotten what I learned either."

"You don't pretend to know as much about fording streams, as Sile does, Hal?"

"But I've killed a cinnamon bear," retorted the boy, "and that's more than Sile ever did."

Just at this moment Sile, who had been superintending the unpacking of the *cargas*, came up, and, overhearing the latter portion of Hal's remark, good-humoredly replied, —

"That's so, sonny; you've got me on that; I own up beat. But how come yer tew miss the ford?"

"I didn't miss the ford," replied Hal.

"Wal, somebody did, sonny; leastways I've just been across and back on foot, with a good hard bottom, and the water not up tew my knees."

For once, Hal was evidently nonplussed, and found no excuse to offer; but even went so far as to acknowledge that every person was liable to make a mistake, declaring, that he never would attempt to pilot another party across a stream as long as his name was Hal Hyde.

CHAPTER XXII.

WE BUY A NEW HORSE. — MR. HITCHCOCK. — THE BIG TREES. — WHAT THE BOYS THOUGHT. — A NEW-ENGLAND HOME. — HAL'S CHOICE. — HOW HE BROKE HIS HORSE. — PLUCK AND GRIT. — HAL VICTORIOUS. — CONGRATULATIONS. — ON THE ROAD ONCE MORE.

"WELL, Hal, what are you going to do for a horse to ride?" said I a few hours after the conversation narrated in the previous chapter.

"I suppose I shall have to ride one of the muleteers' until we can buy one," coolly replied the boy.

"That won't do," was my reply: "neither of them can be deprived of their animals; they need them constantly."

"I can walk, can't I?" he asked.

"I suppose so; or perhaps Ned will ride 'tie and tie.' — What do you say to that suggestion?" said I, turning towards Ned: "will you permit Hal to ride your pony part of the time?"

"Why, of course I will," responded he: "I intended to ask Hal to ride him."

"There, Hal, I don't see but you are provided for," said I.

"Do you suppose I'm going to share a horse with anybody?" angrily inquired Hal. "No, sir: if I can't have a horse to myself, I'll either walk, or go back to old Maverick's ranch and stay, until you return there."

"There ain't much danger of your going to the ranch, I guess," said Ned; "for I heard Mose tell you, he'd lick you the first time he caught you alone."

"I'm not afraid of Mose, or you either, Ned Brown," said Hal belligerently: "I want you to understand that. I'm able to take care of myself, without any of your help."

"I presume you are; but if you'd taken my advice, and waited a few minutes this morning, for Sile to come up, instead of rushing into the water to pilot the train over, you'd have had your horse now," replied Ned, who was rather fond of saying things that he knew would provoke Hal.

"What do you know about it, any way? I guess I've had experience enough to find my way across a stream like that, without waiting for Sile or anybody else," retorted Hal in an angry manner.

Just at this moment Sile came up, accompanied by a stranger on horseback, whom he introduced as a Mr. Hitchcock, informing us that he was the owner of a ranch lying a couple of miles to the east of us, from whom we could purchase a good saddle-horse, as well as a mule to take the place of the animals we had lost.

Mr. Hitchcock proved to be a very pleasant, intelligent gentleman, originally from New England, who had been a resident of California about four years, and was the owner of the nearest ranch; and after some further conversation Sile, the boys, and myself decided to go over and see if we could suit ourselves from his herd. While riding along, I chanced to refer to the size of the pines and redwoods that grew so abundantly about us, when Mr. Hitchcock remarked, that he had just returned from a visit to the grove of big trees, situated about thirty miles north of Sonora, in Calaveras County.

As at this time but comparatively few persons had visited these wonders of the forest, it was with no small degree of satisfaction that I embraced the opportunity to converse with one, who was enabled to describe them from personal observation.

As soon as the boys discovered that Mr. Hitchcock had himself seen the grove, they rode up beside us, manifesting the most lively interest in all that was said concerning it.

"There," said Mr. Hitchcock, pointing to an enormous redwood at some little distance, "that is the largest tree I have seen in this section."

"How tall is that?" inquired Ned.

"A hundred and fifty feet," was the answer.

"Are the trees there, much larger than that?" asked Hal in a quizzical way.

"Yes; many of them are quite three times as tall," replied Mr. Hitchcock.

"Why, that would be four hundred and fifty feet," said Hal.

"Did you ever see Bunker Hill Monument, boys?" inquired Mr. Hitchcock.

"Why, of course we've seen it: we're from Massachusetts," said Ned with some pride.

"So am I," replied Mr. Hitchcock; "and, being from Massachusetts, we Yankees will look at the trees with Massachusetts eyes. Bunker Hill Monument is two hundred and thirty feet high, and thirty feet square at its base, if I remember right. Now, if we could bring that monument here, we could easily conceal it in the hollow of one of the trees that I saw, and its top would not reach as high as the lowermost branches."

Upon hearing this statement, the boys looked at one another in evident surprise; but, seeing that neither Sile nor myself betrayed any signs of incredulity, wisely kept silence.

"How old do you suppose the trees are?" inquired Ned.

"One that has recently been felled, had just been examined by a scientific gentleman, whom I met at the grove, who estimated the age of the fallen monarch to be three thousand two hundred years, at least."

"I'd like to know how they cut it down," said Hal.

"They bored it down with long augers; and it took four men twenty-five days to fell it, and they worked hard at that, cutting it six feet above the level of the ground."

"What was its diameter at that point?" inquired I.

"Twenty-five feet from inside of the bark to inside. I measured it myself," was the reply; "and it took sixteen good days' work, to smooth off the top of the stump."

"Was that the largest one in the grove?" asked Hal.

"No. I saw several that were over four hundred feet high; and there was one that lay on the ground and was hollow, that I rode this very horse through, for more than sixty feet, without being able to touch the top with my hand."

"How big around, I mean, what was the circumference of the largest you saw?" inquired Ned.

"I measured several that were over a hundred and ten feet," was the reply.

"Well, those are the biggest trees I ever heard of," remarked Hal. "I thought Sile must be 'yarning' when he told me about three of 'em camping in the hollow of a tree; but I reckon he wasn't, after all."

"I saw several trees in the grove, that could boast of a more commodious room than can be found in nine out of ten miners' cabins in California," said Mr. Hitchcock. "But here we are at the Pino Alto[1] ranch," continued he, pointing to a very pretty story-and-a-half cottage, painted white, with green blinds, and a broad, comfortable piazza stretching around it. "There is the only genuine New England home

[1] Tall Pine.

in this section. Let me bid you welcome to it. Come up to the house."

I looked at Sile, who shook his head saying, —

"I'm obleeged tew you, sir, but it's bin so long sence I've seed a New England hum, it would only make me sick; besides, it's gettin' nigh night, and you must 'cuse me, for I want ter go and look at the stock. My old mother used tew say, 'Business fust, and pleasure afterwards:' so I'll see the critters, and git back ter camp."

I therefore declined Mr. Hitchcock's kind invitation; and we rode down to the coral, where Sile soon made a selection of a couple of animals. Hal, however, protested so earnestly against Sile's choice of a horse for him, that I finally told him to select for himself. This he did, choosing a clean-limbed, dark bay stallion, which Mr. Hitchcock told me was of fine blood, but not thoroughly broken.

Sile and myself both endeavored to convince Hal that the horse was unsuitable for his use; but he insisted that he could break him as easily as any person living, declaring his willingness "to risk it, in any event," seeming so anxious and determined to have it, that I finally yielded, and purchased the animal, against Sile's judgment; he assuring us "that the boy would hev a heap er trouble with the critter, afore he got threw with it."

Having completed our purchase, Sile rode back to camp with the animals, leaving myself and the boys to a pay a visit to the family of Mr. Hitchcock, which consisted of his wife and two very intelligent and agreeable young ladies, his daughters.

We found it indeed a New England home, in every sense of the word, and a most charming one at that. After partaking of a bountiful supper, and spending a couple of hours in pleasant conversation, we reluctantly took our departure for camp, declining their pressing invitation to spend the night with them.

As we rode back, I could not avoid calling the attention of the boys to the contrast between the two families we had so recently visited, as showing the results of early training and education; proving plainly, that a residence upon the frontier need not of necessity be devoid of refinement, or culture.

Early the next morning we made ready for the day's journey. Both Sile and myself felt no little curiosity to witness Hal's first attempt to ride his new purchase. We had expected trouble, nor were we disappointed.

The animal quietly submitted to being saddled and bridled; but when Hal placed his foot in the stirrup, preparatory to mounting, it became exceedingly restive and uneasy, manifesting its impatience in so positive a manner that it was with difficulty the two Mexicans, who were holding him for Hal to mount, could retain their hold of the bit.

The instant the horse felt Hal's weight upon his back, and the Mexicans had quit their hold of the bridle, the spirited creature gave one bound into the air, and then firmly planting his fore feet upon the ground, and elevating his hind, sent Hal in an attempt to describe the parabola of a circle, causing him to alight upon his back on the earth, at least ten feet in advance of his horse; which did not offer to move, but stood contemplating its would-be rider, with a look that seemed to say, "I thought you were on my back a second since: I wonder how you got so far ahead of me, so suddenly."

Hal picked himself up with a somewhat surprised expression upon his face, remarking, —

"I wasn't quite seated: he can't do it again," proceeding straight to the animal's side, which he once more prepared to mount.

"Hadn't you better let one of the Mexicans git on and ride him a while, afore you try him again?" inquired Sile.

"Do you suppose a Mexican can do what I can't with a horse?" exclaimed Hal. "No, sir; I'm going to ride this horse, and nobody else shall ever back him but me. I wasn't fairly seated before."

"Listen to reason: let some one who's more used to breaking horses try him before you do. It will be poor satisfaction if he breaks your neck," said I.

"I mean to try him again anyhow: I'll risk my neck," replied the boy.

The Mexicans once more seized the bit, while Hal again vaulted into the saddle. Evidently convinced that he was master of the situation, the animal stood perfectly quiet, as though for the purpose of giving Hal ample time to seat himself after the most approved style; and then, without moving from his track, he again sent the boy flying through the air.

Hal picked himself up, cast a hurried glance about him to ascertain if his mishaps had excited our risibility, and, seeing that we regarded the scene with sober faces, nothing daunted he again approached the horse, who stood as quietly as a thoroughbred, waiting for his master to mount.

Gathering the reins firmly in his left hand, Hal with a bound once more sprang upon the animal's back. For an instant the creature stood as still as though carved out of stone; then with distended nostrils, flashing eyes, and quivering flanks, he uttered a snort of rage, and with a tremendous leap alighted upon the earth with his four legs stiffened, at the same moment, lowering his head in such a manner that Hal, in spite of himself, slid gently over the creature's neck to the earth, where he lay for a moment, horse and rider staring each other in the face, and presenting such a comical picture that we all burst into a hearty laugh.

This seemed to arouse all the lion in Hal's nature. Springing to his feet, he declared that he would ride the beast, anyhow. Borrowing a huge pair of Spanish spurs from one of the Mexicans, he firmly adjusted them upon his feet, and, stripping off the saddle, vaulted upon the animal's bare back, with such a look of determination upon his face, that I could not avoid saying to Sile, —

"Hal will certainly break that fellow before he leaves him."

"Somethin'll break, I guess, though it's as likely to be the boy's neck as any thing," said Sile in reply.

Again the creature, snorting with rage, gave a fearful bound; but not before Hal succeeded in clasping his arms tightly about the animal's neck, and at the same instant thrusting his spurs deep into the creature's quivering flanks with such force that he started violently forward as though for the purpose of escaping the unexpected and hitherto unknown instrument of torture that had so violently assailed him.

Recognizing this partial triumph, Hal again applied his spurs so vigorously, that in sheer desperation the maddened creature shot forward, and the next instant was coursing over the plain at a rate of speed that astonished us all.

As long as they remained in sight, we could see that Hal kept plying his spurs vigorously; and when at last they disappeared, Sile turned towards me with the pithy remark, —

"He's got him, sartin."

Anxiously we waited the boy's return; and when, a couple of hours later, Hal quietly rode the panting animal into camp, his foam-flecked sides, quivering nostrils, and bloody flanks, told us that he had at last found his master; while there was that in Hal's face, which plainly said that the boast, uttered in a moment of anger, had proved no idle one.

As the boy dismounted, Sile, Ned, and myself hurried toward him, and warmly congratulated him upon the determination, pluck, and skill he had shown in so quickly and thoroughly conquering the noble animal which now so loyally acknowledged him its master; and a splendid creature he proved to be, bearing his owner in after-years safely through many scenes of hardship and danger, and proving one of the most trusty, sagacious, and valuable animals I have ever seen upon the frontier.

Although we had been ready to move for some time, we delayed our departure a little, that the horse might have a rest after his severe exercise, watching with no little curiosity the experiment of placing the saddle upon his back; but the animal's will had been thoroughly broken, and he permitted Hal to mount, and then ambled along beside us, as quietly as though he had been in our ranks from the first.

"That ere critter's goin' tew be wuth his weight in gold, some of these days," said Sile, addressing Hal.

"You didn't think so last night, and wanted me to take that old plug of a thing that you picked out. Why, I'd just as soon have had a cow," replied the boy.

"Wal, yer see, you've bragged so much and done so little, ever sence you started, that I had no idee you'd try ter break the critter in yerself, and I kind'er thought some one else'd hev tew do the ridin' for yer," responded Sile with great deliberation.

"Bragged so much!" repeated Hal. "I haven't bragged at all: you're the one that's done the bragging, and I've done the work. Who killed that cinnamon bear, I should like to know, if I didn't, after you and Ned had both fired at and missed it?"

"All right, sonny," said Sile, with a quiet laugh. "You've done a good thing in breakin' in that hoss, and yew desarve credit for it, for he was a tough one."

CHAPTER XXIII.

HAL'S HORSE. — A BEAUTIFUL VALLEY. — NED AND I TAKE A TRAMP. — THE LION AND THE GRIZZLY. — A TERRIFIC FIGHT. — IT CONTINUES ALL THE AFTERNOON. — WE TAKE NO NOTE OF TIME. — DARKNESS. — WHAT SHALL WE DO? — A SLEEP AND A TERRIBLE AWAKING.

NO one of the party exhibited more pleasure at Hal's triumph than did Ned, who we thought would never tire of calling attention to " the points " of Hal's newly acquired prize.

All day he travelled beside us, the only manifestation of dislike at the imposed restraint, showing itself in an uneasy champing of the bit, and a disposition to resent the too close approach or familiarity of the other animals; in all other respects evincing, as Sile remarked, " an idee of tendin' strickly to bizness," that promised well for the future.

Our trail, which for some time past, had been growing more rocky and uneven, now entered the heart of the Coast Range, through the foot-hills of which, we had been journeying for several days.

The deeper we penetrated, the more completely were we surrounded with dense forests and towering rocks that hemmed us in on all sides, shutting out the bright sunlight, and casting a gloom over the whole party, that was in marked contrast to its cheerfulness in the early part of the day.

About three o'clock in the afternoon, we entered a beautiful little valley, containing some twenty acres of luxuriant grass, through which flowed a stream of excellent, clear, cold water. It was so lovely a spot, that I at once proposed making our camp here for the night; a suggestion that Sile received with no great favor, declaring that "we spent two-thirds er the time packin' an' onpackin'," to which remark no reply was made; but in a very short time the animals were unsaddled, and cropping the sweet grass about us with an avidity that plainly showed they, at least, appreciated the fancy that induced our early halt.

While stretched upon my blankets, lazily admiring the symmetry of the magnificent oaks that here and there dotted the beautiful verdant lawn about us, I heard Ned say, —

"I'd like to take a stroll along the side of that hill there," pointing to an eminence that loftily towered above us, covered with the most luxuriant verdure.

Springing to my feet, I shouted, "A good idea, Ned: we have plenty of time to do it before night. I'll go with you as soon as I ascertain if our fire-arms are in good condition." These were soon freshly loaded; and, with our rifles on our shoulders, we set out on our tramp.

"Don't git lost," shouted Sile.

"See if you can kill a cinnamon bear before you come back," cried Hal.

"Or drown a horse," retorted Ned, laughing.

For nearly an hour we travelled through the dense forest, without seeing any game save a few grouse or tufted quail, although we frequently came upon the huge tracks of a grizzly or brown bear, and occasionally saw those of the elk, indicating an abundance of game in the country.

"It would be sport if we should happen to come across a cinnamon bear, wouldn't it?" said Ned, as we stood for a moment looking at the succession of lofty and rugged mountains that lay before us.

"There might not be much sport in it, and I, for one, had rather not meet any; but it's well enough to keep eyes and ears open, lest we should stumble upon something of the kind," was my reply.

We pursued our way through deep ravines and dense thickets, now winding along the side of a steep hill, here picking our steps carefully upon the verge of some frightful abyss, to again emerge into a vast grove of lofty pines, whose tall trunks, entirely destitute of branches, stretched for a hundred feet above our heads, when suddenly Ned said, —

"Hark! what's that noise?"

We both listened attentively; for a moment the silence of the vast solitude was broken by the sweet notes of some deep wood-songster, and then we distinctly heard the low, deep, angry growl of some creature, accompanied by a sharp, quick cry, as of a person in mortal anguish.

"It's over this way," said Ned. "Come on till we see what it is."

Carefully we made our way in the direction of the sound, every faculty on the alert, every sense quickened. Shortly we came to a huge, sloping rock, that barred our path: from behind this, the noise seemed to come.

Slowly and with difficulty we climbed to the top, and peered over into the ravine below, when to our amazement we saw a large lion[1] and a medium-sized grizzly bear engaged in deadly combat over the carcass of a deer. It was a terrible sight, — those two huge, powerful creatures, biting, scratching, tearing, and gouging each other in the most horrible manner.

When we first saw them, the bear held his enemy with his paws tightly clasped about the fore-shoulders, while the lion's teeth were firmly fixed in the side of the grizzly's throat, who appeared to be endeavoring to crush his opponent with his enormous fore-arms.

While it was evident at a glance that the bear, which was undermost, was the stronger of the two, it was equally plain that the lion was the more agile and wary. The bear occasionally uttered a low, wheezy growl, but whether from pain or rage we

[1] Properly the puma, but more commonly known in the country as the California lion.

could not tell; while the lion, its teeth firmly set, hung to the bear's throat, with a tenacity that was wonderful to behold.

After many desperate but fruitless efforts, the bear succeeded in turning its adversary, and for the instant taking the uppermost position, which, however, it held but a moment, when the lion again recovered it, and the two began rolling over and over upon the ground, snarling, writhing, kicking, and raising such clouds of dust, that for a moment they were completely hidden from our view.

After this struggle was ended, each, as if by mutual consent, separated, for the double purpose of taking breath, and gaining fresh strength for another encounter.

They withdrew a few paces, laid themselves down upon the ground, and began to lick their wounds. This continued for several minutes. The lion lay stretched at full length, evidently resting, its tawny fur streaked with blood, and showing many evidences of the desperate encounter in which it had taken part.

Suddenly its large eyes began to restlessly move in its small head; its ears assumed an erect position; its long red tongue, from which the saliva had been falling in drops, was drawn into the mouth; its supple body gracefully undulated with a movement not unlike that of a cat when about to spring upon its prey; while its tail angrily lashed the ground, from side to side.

In the mean time, the bear, the better to enable itself to reach its wounds, had slowly risen upon its haunches, the blood from the wound in its neck trickling in a little stream down its gray flecked sides, when, with a quick, sharp cry, the lion sprang towards it.

Uttering a deep, angry growl, the bear raised itself erect upon its hind-legs, and, as the lion reached it, quicker than a flash, dealt it a tremendous blow with one of its enormous paws, that sent it rolling over and over, a dozen feet away.

It was a critical moment for the bear; the blow had been bravely dealt; and, from that instant, our sympathies were on the side of the grizzly monster.

Forgetting himself, Ned, on the impulse of the moment, shouted out, —

"Bully for you, old fellow!"

In an instant, both animals came to their feet, and looked sharply about them, as if actuated by a common desire to detect and punish the intruders. We quickly withdrew from sight, and, after the lapse of a few moments, again cautiously returned to our post of observation.

The animals had resumed the relative positions occupied by them, previous to the blow dealt by the bear. Each appeared to be closely watching the other, although ostensibly engaged in licking their wounds; nor did either appear anxious to renew the fray.

Soon it became evident from the movements of the

lion, that it was preparing for another spring. The bear saw it, and uttered a low, hoarse growl of warning, which had the effect of causing the lion to crouch closer to the earth, and gather itself for another spring, — this time over the bear's head; then, wheeling like a flash, it fastened itself upon the animal's back, before that unwieldy creature could turn and properly receive it.

And now ensued another desperate struggle, so fierce and terrible, that Ned and myself fairly held our breath, so intense was the interest with which we watched the deadly combat.

Over and over they rolled, growling, snarling, and biting, now enveloped in a cloud of dust, now showing the bear uppermost, and the next moment revealing the tawny fur of the lion in that position.

How long they maintained the struggle, I have no idea: it must have been nearly an hour, although in our excitement it seemed scarcely a minute.

Suddenly it became evident that the bear had somehow gained a decided advantage: for the lion, slowly but sullenly withdrew from the contest, leaving the bear, who manifested not the slightest disposition to renew the fight, master of the field; and, while we were wondering what its next move would be, it suddenly disappeared in a neighboring thicket.

Then, and not till then, did Ned or myself draw a long breath; and it was with a feeling of very great relief, that we were finally able to withdraw our gaze from the sylvan arena, and look at one another.

So intense had been our interest in watching the combat, that we had entirely forgotten two very important things to us, — first, that we had our rifles with us; and, second, the lapse of time.

Now that the struggle had ceased, and the contestants vanished, we suddenly remembered both; for the shades of evening were falling, and the forest was shrouded in a deep gloom that would effectually prevent our returning to camp that night.

"What shall we do?" asked Ned, looking sharply at me.

"There's but one thing to do, and that is to remain just where we are until daylight; then we can easily find our way back to camp. We had better gather a lot of dry wood and brush, before it gets any darker, so that we can keep up a fire to-night."

"But the woods are full of wild beasts," suggested Ned.

"They are always afraid of fire: it's the best protection we could possibly have against these fellows. Besides, we have our rifles and pistols, a fact that I had entirely forgotten up to this minute."

"So had I," returned Ned. "I'm glad we didn't think of 'em before; for we should have been tempted to have shot those fellows, and I wouldn't have done it for any thing."

"Why not?" inquired I, picking up a stick of wood.

"You wouldn't have done it, I know," said Ned. "It would have been a shame to have shot either of 'em. I wouldn't have missed that sight for a good deal. Which did you want to have whip?"

"Well, I am some like the boy who wanted to know 'who beginned the fight' before he expressed his sympathies."

"Which do you suppose began it?" persisted Ned.

"I suppose the bear must have been the aggressor," said I.

"Then I'm sorry I shouted for him. I'd a great deal rather have the lion whip. Ain't this wood enough? It's getting so dark we can't see any more."

"No: there isn't half enough. We must gather a big pile to keep a fire going all through the night."

"Give me a match, and let me light it: we can see better then."

I handed the boy a match, and the next moment a little puff of bluish-white smoke curled up from the pile of brush collected, which soon increased in volume; and then, little tongues of flame began to make their appearance, which in a few moments shot far up into the air, crackling and sparkling, and burning with a brightness that not only drove away the deep gloom of the forest, but the depressing effect which the murmuring of the pines always has upon the sensitive mind of a boy. It lighted up our surroundings, and imparted a rosy tint to the cold gray surface of the rocks about us, that Ned pronounced "just lovely."

"Well, here we must stay until morning, Ned. I

wish you had your blankets. You lie down close beside the fire, and take your nap while I watch; then I'll wake you, and you shall keep 'watch and ward' for awhile. 'Turn about is fair play,' you know.

"But you won't wake me if I fall asleep, I'm afraid. You must promise me that you will, or I won't do it."

"Won't I wake you?" was my answer. "You wait and see. Do you think I'm anxious to sit alone all night? Don't fear on that score."

Thus assured, Ned laid himself down upon a bed prepared of pine-boughs, and in a very few minutes was fast asleep.

I piled a quantity of wood upon the fire, seated myself in a comfortable position with my rifle on my lap, and my back to the rock, and began thinking over the events of the day,—Hal's persistent determination to ride his horse; our camp in the beautiful little valley; the tramp upon the hillside; the savage encounter between the wild beasts, and the forgetfulness it engendered in both Ned's mind and my own; and then, my thoughts wandered to a trip I once made through Sonora and Durango in Mexico; and, while thus musing, I fell asleep.

How long I slept, I do not to this day know; but I awoke with a sudden start and a presentiment of danger near.

The fire had died down, and the few smouldering embers that remained, showed just enough light to enable me to distinguish Ned sleeping quietly upon his piny couch. All around me was darkness: the thick dense tops of the pines above me, prevented my seeing a single star; and, for the moment, I was at a loss to remember my exact situation.

I soon recovered myself sufficiently, to be aware that I ought to rise and replenish the fire, and was about to do so, when a quick sharp sound like the snapping of a dry twig arrested my attention.

Holding my breath, I cast my eyes in the direction from whence the sound came, and saw what I supposed for the moment to be two coals of fire, lying upon the hillside beyond me.

I gazed at them for an instant, in a dreamy, half-conscious way, wondering how coals from our fire could have got so far above it, and suddenly became aware of the fact, that there were not two coals only, but the ground about me seemed fairly alive with them.

I opened my eyes in astonishment, looked again and again, and at each look, saw that their number increased until there seemed to be millions of them. Was I dreaming? What could it mean? I asked myself the question a dozen times, seemingly unable to answer it satisfactorily.

I listened for some sound; but nothing save the night-wind sighing through the tree-tops disturbed the silence that oppressed me like a horrid nightmare, paralyzing my senses, and rendering me alike incapable of thought and action.

While thus looking, I fancied that these coals of

fire were approaching nearer to me; then came the thought of fire-balls, and then, that they were the eyes of animals glowering at me — hungry, roving, restless, glaring eyes, that fascinated me to that extent, that I cared not to end the spell they had wrought. I thought not of the rifle that lay in my lap, thought not of the sleeping boy near me, thought not even of saving our lives; but contented myself with wondering if they were the eyes of lions, panthers, bears, ocelots, or fiends; wondering if it would be an easy death to be torn limb from limb, and devoured by wild beasts; and then, wondering how long it would be before they would spring upon me.

Suddenly Ned called out in his sleep, "Sile!" the spell was broken in an instant. Like a flash I recognized all the horror of my situation, saw our danger, knew that we were surrounded by wild beasts, and that nothing but instant action would save us.

Quickly drawing my revolver, I placed it in my lap: then raising and cocking my rifle, I spoke in an ordinary tone to Ned, who instantly awoke and sat upright.

"Throw some of that wood by your side upon the fire," said I.

The boy did so: the next moment a dry twig caught, and a bright flame shot up, lighting with a lurid light our surroundings for an instant; then, dying down, left it darker than before.

Speaking in as unconcerned a tone as possible, I said, "We are surrounded by wild animals, Ned: take your rifle, and come close beside me."

The boy instantly obeyed; when, as if to give particular unction to my words, the terrible silence that had so long oppressed me was broken by the quick, snarling howl of a wolf, seemingly at my very elbow.

It came, not unexpectedly, but so suddenly that for an instant I was startled; my heart almost ceased to beat, and I felt my hair fairly rise on end, as the terrible sound fell upon my ear: the next moment it was answered by a hundred snarling, blood-curdling barks, apparently from all portions of the forest about us.

CHAPTER XXIV.

WOLVES. — WHAT WE DID. — OUR FIRE GONE. — OUR LAST RESOURCE. — NED DOES HIS SHARE. — A VERY UNPLEASANT SITUATION. — A CONCERT. — DAYLIGHT. — I RISK A SHOT. — ITS EFFECT. — WE START FOR CAMP. — A RIFLE-SHOT. — WHAT IT SAID. — SILE. — CAMP AT LAST.

"SET your cocked rifle carefully against the rock," said I, giving Ned's hand a warm pressure for the purpose of re-assuring him. "Keep your revolver also cocked in your left hand, and when you see me grasp one of those blazing brands, and advance suddenly towards the hillside, follow my example. Handle your revolver carefully. Don't fire unless you are obliged to, and, whatever you do, don't shoot me. Remember that our whole salvation depends upon keeping that rock at our backs and that fire burning until daylight, — two things that must be done at all hazards."

"I understand it, and will do my share, you bet," exclaimed Ned. "There's some excitement about this: it's jolly. Don't those fellows howl though! They keep up a regular concert."

"When we start, Ned," said I, "seize a brand,

wave it above your head for the purpose of keeping it in a flame, and rush to the right. I'll go to the left; but in no case go so far as to enable one of those fellows to slip in between you and the rock. When I count three, we'll make the sally."

During the whole of this time, the wolves were keeping up the most infernal din; chattering, barking, snarling, and yelping, until it was with the greatest difficulty only, that I could hear myself speak; being obliged to fairly shout my instructions into Ned's ear.

Of one thing, however, I was certain: if he understood them, I could depend upon his obeying them to the letter, and, in that case, felt perfect confidence in being able to maintain our position until morning, which I supposed, must be near at hand. Had I known then, the long, weary, anxious hours that must intervene ere daylight should come, I could hardly have regarded the situation as cheerfully as I did at the time.

As soon as the brands were well on fire, Ned and myself each seized one, and started with a rush towards the foe. As I had expected, they retreated before us; but upon our return followed, until it seemed to me, they approached nearer to our position than before. I did not mention my fears to Ned, but proceeded to pile more fuel upon the fire; and in doing so, discovered, to my horror, that our supply was nearly exhausted, and this fact filled me with an indescribable dread. I knew that when that was gone, if some other plan of safety were not devised, all was lost; for it was impossible to gather a fresh quantity of fuel, with a pack of gaunt, hungry wolves surrounding us.

I did not dare speak of this new trouble to Ned, lest the boy, who was doing bravely, should become disheartened and discouraged; and I knew that as long as we could keep the fire burning in front of us, and the rock at our backs, we were safe. For some time we occupied this position, without experiencing any particular fear of molestation; using the fuel meanwhile as sparingly as possible.

Occasionally we would sally out with a blazing brand; the wolves would again retreat before us, and upon our return, again advance; all the while uttering their sharp, shrill cries in concert, until our ears fairly ached with the horrible din.

Our pile of fuel was fast dwindling down: but a few sticks remained. Something must be done ere long, some means devised, to avert the terrible fate that stared us so inevitably in the face.

How long before morning? I asked myself the question many times over. The deep gloom that shrouded the dense forest about us could vouchsafe me no reply. What should we do? Again and again I turned my eyes towards the tall stems of the stately pines around us, but they offered no solution; for to climb one, was impossible.

"Well, Ned, we'll give 'em another charge; what say you?" shouted I, in as cheerful a tone as I could command.

"I'm ready," screamed the boy in return.

"You take the left this time, and I'll go to the right; it'll be a little change for us," shouted I, forcing a laugh.

"It would be more of one if they'd stop their howling, and clear out and leave us alone," answered the boy, with a smile; "but here goes, come on."

Whereupon we each seized one of the brands, and again made a sortie; as usual, the wolves retreated as we advanced, but upon our return followed even nearer to the dying embers of our fire than they had ever done before.

I felt that the crisis was fast approaching; but, with as brave a heart as possible, piled the last of the wood upon the bed of coals; this consumed, what then?

The dry sticks quickly caught, and blazed up with an unusually bright glare, illuminating the huge trunks of the tall pines about us, bringing into bold relief the cold gray surface of the rocks, and revealing, at the distance of twenty or thirty feet in front of the fire, the broad spreading branches of an ironwood tree, apparently not more than eight or ten feet from the ground.

To see was to instantly act. Turning towards Ned, I shouted as unconcernedly as possible, "You see that ironwood in front of us, don't you? Well, take your rifle, and come with me."

Taking one of the blazing sticks from the fire in my hand, and swinging it before me, I walked towards the tree; and found, with no little satisfaction, that the trunk was smooth, and the lower branches at least eight feet from the ground.

"Get up into this tree, and climb as high as you can, Ned," said I.

Without a question the boy obeyed.

"Now take my rifle, carefully," said I, handing it to him with one hand, while with the other I kept the brand in motion.

Then I turned; the wolves, as though enraged at our temerity in venturing so far beyond the dying embers of our fire, now approached within a very few feet of the tree. I could even distinguish their long, gaunt, gray forms, revealed, it seemed to me, by the fire from their hungry eyes, that glared so terribly at me through the almost Stygian darkness; and I even fancied that I could see their open mouths, lolling tongues, and gleaming white teeth, as they angrily snapped their jaws together, in anticipation of the feast they soon expected to enjoy.

They were getting too bold for comfort; but I knew, if I killed one, the smell of the fresh blood would so madden the rest, that the terrors of the fire-brand would no longer restrain their impatience.

Once more I vigorously swung the brand, while I seized a limb of the tree with my left hand, and, gathering all my strength for the effort, hurled the blazing stick into the midst of the howling pack, and drew myself up among the branches of the tree as quickly as possible.

The next instant they were upon us. I drew my feet up beneath me, and closely watched the fiery eyes that swarmed below; for it was now too dark to distinguish any thing else.

After a few moments of terrible suspense, I became satisfied that they could not reach our position; and then, for the first time, I completely gave way.

I soon rallied, however; for the savage creatures appeared to realize that we had escaped their fury, and gathered in countless numbers beneath the little tree (whose trunk was scarce five inches in diameter), hurling themselves against it with such force that it fairly shook from their terrible onslaught; during which, they continued snarling, barking, howling, and yelping, until it seemed to me that Bedlam had fairly broken loose.

Occasionally one or two of this number, larger or more vigorous than the rest, would leap almost up to our resting-place; and we could distinctly hear their jaws snap together, as, foiled in their purpose, they fell back among the howling pack, realizing the inability of their efforts to reach us.

So terrific was the horrible noise they made, we found it impossible to hear ourselves speak even, much less converse together; consequently were forced to pass the long time until day, without communicating in any manner with one another.

Thus passed the weary hours of that terrible night, which seemed to me like an eternity spent in the society of the damned; nor can I, even at this late day, recall it without shuddering: it was too frightful for description.

Daybreak came at last, however; and as the light gradually penetrated the gloom, and found its way into the depths of the vast forest, our assailants one after another stole away; their gaunt, gray forms disappearing from our view, until finally, when the last one seated himself upon his haunches, at what he thought was a safe distance, and elevated his sharp nose into the air to give us a parting howl, I could not resist the inclination to bring my rifle to my face, and give him the contents, even though it should bring the hungry pack back upon us.

He fell over upon his side, and after a few convulsive struggles was still in death.

"Thank God it's over! it's been a tough night for us, Ned," said I, for the first time addressing the boy since daylight.

"The toughest one I ever saw; it was just terrible, and I'm fairly deaf from the horrible noise they made: my legs are all knotted up, and I'm almost starved, to say nothing of being completely chilled with the cold," was the reply.

"Never mind it now, it's all over, and I reckon we may as well make a run for the camp: we'll be there in time for breakfast." said I, dropping to the ground.

Ned followed suit; and, as soon as we could stand, we took up our line of march for camp.

"Well, Ned, we've had such an experience during the last twenty-four hours, as we little anticipated when we left camp," remarked I, as we walked along.

"Yes, and it came near being a dreadful one too," replied the boy.

"I must say that I feel more comfortable than I did last night at this time, and am glad we are safe and sound and but a short distance from camp," said I.

"That may be true; but we don't know exactly where to find it, do we?" asked the boy in a tone of inquiry, watching my face very narrowly in the mean time.

"Why, what do you mean? I shall take you to camp as straight as the face of the country will admit," said I, with a tone and manner calculated to inspire the boy with confidence in my ability to do as I said; adding, "You can't lose me if you try."

"I wonder what Sile and Hal think of our absence," queried Ned, after a short silence.

"Sile thinks that I'm able to take care of you as well as myself; and Hal thinks, that if we had a little of his experience, we should be a great deal better off," said I, laughing. "I shouldn't wonder if they were out hunting us though, this morning."

"Nor I," said Ned. "I think you, ought now, to be able to appreciate Hal's and my situation when we were treed by the wild hogs on our trip through Texas. I believe, after all, though, I was more scared then, than I was last night."

"I fancy I can imagine your feelings rather better this morning, than I could yesterday," remarked I.

At this moment the crack of a rifle came faintly up from the valley below us. Never was sound more welcome. Waiting a few moments, I answered it by discharging my own, and then listened for the reply.

It came presently, bounding up the mountain-side, echoing and reverberating among the crags and peaks, until it was lost in the vast forest above us.

"Answer again, Ned," said I, my heart so full of thankfulness I could scarcely speak; and answer he did; and, as the last reverberation died away in the distance, I turned towards the boy, and said, —

"There, Ned, that spoke louder than words, saying, 'Camp and friends, and a good breakfast, and sleep.'"

In less than half an hour we heard Sile's voice below us, saying, —

"Give 'em one with that old *escopeta*[1] of yourn, Juan: that'll wake the echoes."

I instantly replied, —

"Don't trouble yourself, Sile: I'd much rather Juan would give us some breakfast."

"Hurrah!" shouted Sile, "there they be, hungry 's ever. Hurry down and get breakfast ready for 'em, Juan."

The next moment we stood face to face.

"Wal, squire," said Sile, grasping my hand with a

[1] An old-fashioned bell-mouthed Spanish musket.

warmth that plainly betokened his joy at seeing us, "I come nigher bein' scart about you when it got dark last night, and you didn't come in, than I ever will be again, you bet. I might 'a' knowed yer was all right.— And the youngster," addressing Ned, "How are you? lookin' a leetle holler, hey? Wal, you'll be all right arter yer get five or six pounds er venison-steak tucked under yer jacket."

"Where's Hal, Sile?" inquired I.

"Out huntin' yew. He's bin awfully worried ever sence yer didn't come in tew supper last night, ter think he didn't go with yer, so's yer could 'a' had the benefit of his 'sperience 'mongst the 'Paches," answered Sile with a laugh.

"We've had something of an experience of our own since we left you last evening, which you may be able to induce Ned to relate, after he has had his breakfast; but here we are in camp once more," said I, as we emerged from the dark forest into the beautiful little valley which had so pleased my fancy the day previous.

"*Poko tiempo, señor*,"[1] said Juan, as we passed by the spot where he was busily engaged in cooking our breakfast.

"All right, Juan: first a bath and then breakfast, you know."

"*Esta bueno, señor*,"[2] was the reply.

[1] In a little while, sir.   [2] Very good, sir.

CHAPTER XXV.

CONGRATULATIONS. — A VISIT TO THE SCENE OF OUR ADVENTURE. — WHAT WE FOUND. — MORE GAME. — WE RETURN TO CAMP. — ON THE ROAD. — ARRIVAL AT NEW ALMADEN. — WHAT WE SAW. — VISIT TO THE FURNACES. — HOW THE ORE IS TREATED. — SOMETHING ABOUT QUICKSILVER.

WHILE we were eating breakfast, Hal returned. His face became wonderfully bright as he caught sight of us; and, on coming up, he exclaimed, —

"I declare, I'm glad to see you, for I was terribly afraid you were lost. I went up the hill a little way myself, and it was as much as I could do to find my way back to camp. I was afraid you'd get lost when you started out yesterday."

"Hold on a minute, Hal," said I, with my mouth full of venison-steak, and with difficulty making myself understood. "You're entirely wrong in your premises. Neither Ned nor myself has been lost for a single minute, since we left you here yesterday afternoon."

"Not lost!" repeated the boy in tones of astonishment. "Why, what on earth made you stop out all night, if you were not lost?"

"That's just the question, Hal. Why did we stop out all night?"

"I'm sure I don't know," replied the boy. "I thought you must be lost."

"Well, Hal, Ned will explain the reason, after he has finished his breakfast," said I.

This, as I expected, aroused the boy's curiosity to that extent, that it was really amusing to witness the many attempts made to draw us out, before finishing our meal.

Nothing was gained, however; and after Sile came up, we threw ourselves down beneath the shade of a splendid oak, while Ned narrated the substance of the story given above; ending with, —

"Now, Sile, which do you suppose began that fight, the lion or the bear?"

"The bar, of course," was the reply. "I guess the lion ketched the deer, 'cause grizzlies ain't spry enuff tew do it, as a gen'ral thing; but he diskivered the lion eatin' of it, and tried tew drive it off: the lion wouldn't be druv, and that's what started 'em at it. I'd 'a' give a good deal tew 'a' seen that scrimmage, squire."

"It certainly was a sight well worth seeing, Sile: I really had no idea what ferocity meant until I saw those beasts engaged in combat."

"Didn't that grizzly make you think of the cinnamon bear I killed the other day?" queried Hal. "He was a pretty ferocious sort of a fellow."

"Well, I don't know but he did, Hal, now you remind me of it. I declare, I had forgotten all about the cinnamon. I'm going to spread my blankets, and nap it a couple of hours; and, Ned, you had better do the same. Don't let any one disturb us, Sile; and after I wake, I'd like to take a tramp up and visit the scene of our last night's adventure. I have a fancy that we shall find the remains of one of those animals near by; and I predict it will be the bear. What say you?"

"Like as not; but bein' as I didn't see the scrimmage, I can't judge. I s'pose you ain't thinkin' of leavin' here ter-day, be yer?"

"We've only one more day's ride before reaching the mines, have we, Sile?"

"Thet's all, and a short one at that; we ought tew git in by three o'clock ter-morrow arternoon."

"Then we won't leave here until morning: so govern yourselves accordingly. And now for a snooze. Where's Ned?"

"Ned was asleep some time ago," answered Hal. "Can I go with you and Sile when you go up the mountain?"

"Certainly, if you wish to, and Sile has no objection."

With this promise Hal took his departure, and I my nap. When I awoke, three hours later, the sun was in the zenith: Ned was lying near me, sound asleep; Hal and Sile were lolling beneath the shade of a neighboring oak, waiting for me to awake; the

Mexicans were cooking their dinner, and the animals peacefully feeding in the meadow about us, the emerald green of which, furnished a strong contrast to the darker verdure of the dense forest that surrounded us upon all sides.

I lay for a few minutes gazing at the quiet beauty of the scene spread out before me, and then, rousing myself, called, "Sile!" He instantly came towards me, followed by Hal.

"Are you ready for a start?" asked I.

"All ready, squire. We'll hev a little grub fust, and then travel; it's bad bizness trampin' on a empty stomick on the frontier, for ye're likely tew git ketched out over night ena'most any time — 'specially if yer ain't 'spectin' tew."

Half an hour later, I was again toiling up the steep hillside, and picking my way through deep ravines, or along the edge of some steep precipice, or pushing through a dense thicket, over the path I travelled the day previous, until at last we stood in the same grove of lofty pines that silently witnessed our adventures of the night.

"Here we are, Sile; here's the little ironwood, and that's the rock from which we witnessed the battle."

"Yes; and here's the wolf that you shot: nothing's touched him," interrupted Hal.

"It's a putty place; but let's get down inter that ravine," said Sile. "I guess I've got about as much currosity as any Yankee you ever seed, if I have bin away from Maine risin' of fifteen year."

We were soon at the bottom of the gorge; and in a very few minutes Sile discovered bloody tracks, which we followed for some distance towards a dense thicket of juniper. As we rather carelessly approached the spot, there suddenly issued from out the cluster, a low, deep, menacing growl.

"Thunder! the critter's in thar, and 'live tew, as sartin' as you're born. We must be mighty keerful; 'cause if he's wounded, he'll be as ugly as Satan."

"If it's the same old fellow I saw yesterday, Sile, I believe I'd rather go back to that rock, and shoot from there," said I, by way of a joke. "But who's going to poke him out? we ought to have a dog."

"P'r'aps Hal'll play dog, and drive him out for us," suggested Sile, with a roguish look about the eye; adding, "He's the smallest of the three."

"I didn't come here to be insulted, Sile Carter; if you want the bear got out, get him out yourself. After your remark, I shall render you no assistance, but go immediately back to camp;" and Hal turned from us with all the dignity imaginable.

"Come, Hal, this won't do," said I; "if you're afraid of the bear, say so, and clear out; but don't pretend it's because you've been insulted."

"I'm afraid of no bear," said Hal. "My courage has been tested. I shot that cinnamon bear the other "—

"Git out er the way; here he comes!" shouted Sile.

And sure enough, he was coming. The junipers

were as violently agitated as though a gale of wind was sweeping through them; and the next moment there rushed out, not a dying grizzly or a wounded lion, as we expected, but a large, active, ugly black bear, apparently about as mad as he could be at being disturbed from his lair.

He came boldly out with a rush, paused for a moment as if to estimate the strength of the foe; and, as he did so, we all fired. He took a step forward, uttered a low growl, partly raised himself upon his haunches, and then fell over upon his side, dead.

As we approached the spot where he lay, Sile said, —

"It's well enuff tew be kinder keerful: thar might be 'nother of 'em in thar; but them black bars ain't much 'count, nohow. This 'ere skin's good; fur's fust rate: s'posin' I jerk it off? it'll be a good thing to have about the ranch;" and without more ado, Sile went to work.

While he was engaged in flaying the bear, Hal and myself began a cautious exploration of the underbrush in the immediate vicinity, and, after a short search, were rewarded by finding a portion of the carcass of what Sile immediately pronounced to be a large grizzly. Every particle of flesh was gone, only a few of the larger bones and bits of the hide remaining, which Sile unhesitatingly said had lain there but a few hours; expressing the decided opinion that it was that of the hero of the previous day's fight.

"What makes you think so?" asked Hal.

"'Cause the critter hain't bin ded but a little while, in the fust place; then ther wouldn't be likely tew be a second grizzly killed so near ther place of ther fight as this; then agin, we know sartin thar was a pack of wolves about here last night, and this 'ere wounded grizzly was what bringed 'em tergether. Yer kin see yerself how they've polished ther bones off. Wal, if we was tew come back here in ther mornin,' there wouldn't be as much er that 'ere carcass left, as ther is er this; 'cause ther bones ain't so heavy, yer see. I 'spect it's 'bout time we was startin' for camp. I kin pack this skin on my back, and we'll start along down."

"This has been about the stupidest trip I ever made, any way," said Hal, as we slowly descended the hillside.

"I'm sure we've found all we came to find, and more too: and, if in every expedition through life we are so fortunate, we sha'n't have much to regret at the end, shall we?" replied I.

"Of course I don't mean that," explained Hal; "but shooting a black bear seems so tame and commonplace, after killing a cinnamon, that there's no excitement or fun about it."

"If we hadn't happened to have struck that feller in the right place, we'd 'a' seed fun: you kin be sartin er that," remarked Sile.

"I always aim at the right place myself," said Hal.

"I declar, I forgot ter see which of ther bullets

hit this feller in the eye; I 'spose though 'twas yourn if you aimed at it," suggested Sile.

"Of course it was," declared Hal, falling completely into the trap Sile had so cleverly laid for him.

"Well, I've got the critter's skin here on my back, and, when we git down ter camp, we'll sarch for ther holes: them'll tell," replied Sile.

This was rather more than Hal had bargained for when he asserted the fact so positively: at first he appeared somewhat disconcerted, but finally said, —

"There's a chance of my missing it, of course: no person always hits the mark, does he?"

"No, sir," declared Sile very emphatically: "ther best shot'll miss sometimes; but there's a chance for yew now," said Sile, pointing to a fine large red buck, browsing a little distance ahead of us.

Before Sile could unsling his pack, and bring his rifle to his face, Hal fired; but the buck bounded away, apparently unharmed.

"There's the proof of what I was sayin'," remarked Sile dryly.

Nothing more was said; and in a few moments we arrived in camp, Hal evidently feeling very much crestfallen, and disposed to remain unusually silent.

At my suggestion, nothing was said concerning the shot at the black bear; and, as we were all somewhat fatigued, we retired at an early hour.

The next afternoon about two o'clock we came in sight of the little village of New Almada, situated at the foot of the Coast Range, about thirteen miles east of San José, at the head of the beautiful valley of the same name.

We camped just outside the town, in a grove of magnificent oaks and sycamores, interspersed occasionally with clumps of firs and redwoods; the latter towering high above all the others.

As soon as we were fairly settled in camp, I rode into the town, which consisted almost entirely of buildings belonging to the company, and paid my respects to Mr. Young, the superintendent of the mines. This gentleman received me very kindly, and after informing him who I was, and our object in visiting the mines, expressed much pleasure at seeing me, offering his services in showing us all the points of interest about the premises, as well as those of his engineer in conducting us through the mines, the entrance to which is about a mile from the furnaces, at an elevation of nearly a thousand feet above them.

Thanking him for his politeness, and promising to be on hand at an early hour the following morning, to avail ourselves of his kind offer, I took my departure for camp, well pleased at my reception, and anticipating much pleasure in the proposed visit.

During the evening, while seated about our pleasant camp-fire, Hal suddenly asked, —

"What is there so funny about these mines?"

"Nothing funny," was my reply. "There are but very few quicksilver-mines in the known world; probably not more than half a dozen, and but three or four of those, of sufficient value to pay for working: besides which, this is the only quicksilver-mine that has yet been discovered in the United States."[1]

"I wish you'd tell us all about quicksilver," exclaimed Ned: "I'd like to be posted before I go up there to-morrow."

"So would I," was my reply, "for the fact is, I know so little about it myself, I hoped to have learned something on the subject this afternoon; but Mr. Young was so busy I didn't like to ask too many questions, so concluded to wait until to-morrow."

"What do they do with quicksilver, anyway?" demanded Hal.

"It is largely employed in collecting gold-dust, in extracting gold and silver from their ores, in the manufacture of looking-glasses, in gilding, and in plating. In its native state, it is the pigment known as vermilion, used in coloring sealing-wax, and by the Indians in painting their faces, besides a hundred other purposes that I can't now think of."

"Of course the Indians didn't know any thing about this mine," remarked Ned.

"On the contrary, they first discovered it, and had dug some thirty or forty feet into the mountain to obtain the cinnabar, before its commercial value was discovered."

"What is cinnabar?" inquired Hal.

---

[1] At the time of our visit, no other mine of this kind was known to exist in the United States. Since then, it is claimed that one or two others have been found, but no paying ones.

"The ore from which the quicksilver of commerce is obtained; technically it is the sulphide or sulphuret of mercury, which, when pure, is a natural vermilion, from which fact the attention of the Indians was drawn towards it, I suppose."

"Haven't they always had quicksilver?" inquired Ned.

"You're getting me into pretty deep water with your questions, Ned; but I'll try and answer this one. If I remember right, Pliny gives the first account of cinnabar. He states that the Greeks imported red cinnabar from Almaden in Spain, seven hundred years before the birth of Christ, and that in his own time seven hundred thousand pounds were received annually in Rome from the same mines; it was used as a pigment by the painters of that day, as well as by the Roman matrons for the purpose of beautifying their faces."

"How pure is this ore, and what does it look like?" inquired Hal.

"You'll have to wait until to-morrow for that information, when I doubt not Mr. Young will be able to answer all your questions much more intelligibly than I can."

"All right; let's turn in now, and be up in good season in the morning," remarked Ned.

"I never saw such a sleepy-head as you are, Ned Brown. I believe you'd go to bed at sundown and get up at sunrise the year round, if you had the choice," said Hal.

"He's right about it tew," remarked Sile. "My old mother used tew say, bed was ther best place in ther world tew keep a boy from gittin' inter mischief; and I've found she was right's, a general thing."

"She might have been right for those days, but there's a different state of things now. Boys ain't kept under as they used to be," declared Hal.

"The more's ther pity for ther boys. They'll never make half the men that ther boys er them days did. A boy was a boy then till he got his time, a freedom coat, and a hundred dollars, all in the same day; then he knowed he was of age. But now, why, there's many a boy of sixteen that thinks he knows more'n all the men livin';" and Sile turned, and went out to pay his nightly visit to the stock.

CHAPTER XXVI.

WHAT WE SAW.—DESCRIPTION OF THE MANNER OF REDUCING THE ORE.—ITS SPECIFIC GRAVITY.—INTERESTING EXPERIMENTS.—HAL AND NED DELIGHTED.—A FINE ENTERTAINMENT.—VISIT TO THE MINES.—HOW THEY ARE WORKED.—WHAT WE SAW UNDERGROUND.—RETURN TO CAMP.—WHAT SILE SAID.

THE boys were up betimes the following morning; and about nine o'clock Hal, Ned, and myself started for the village, leaving Sile in charge of camp.

We found Mr. Young at the company's office, waiting for us. He greeted us kindly, introducing Mr. Bester the engineer, and a Mr. Walkinshaw, one of the proprietors, who resides near the mines; and after a short conversation, accompanied by Mr. Young and Mr. Walkinshaw, we set out upon our visit to the furnaces, &c., reserving the mines until the following day, when Mr. Bester was to take us in charge.

The village itself is pleasantly located, and contains the company's furnaces, storehouses, machine-shops, offices, and dwelling-houses for both officers and men; these buildings are generally constructed of brick in a substantial and durable manner.

Our steps were first directed towards the furnaces; and, while on our way there, Mr. Young informed us that when the company first commenced their experiments, having in view extracting quicksilver from cinnabar, they labored under many disadvantages; for they were entirely ignorant of every thing connected with the operation, there being but one other mine in the world (that of Almaden in Spain), where it was carried on successfully; and, although every effort was made to ascertain their manner of treating the ore, the attempts were all unsuccessful; the proprietors of a mine holding such a monopoly of course refused to impart any information that would benefit what might prove to be a dangerous rival to their interests. "Consequently," added he, "we were all in the dark, but we are gradually getting light upon the subject: it's rather expensive light though, for the cost of starting has been enormous; but we are learning every day.

"We have six of these furnaces now in operation; and, as you can see, they are simple, and the cost of running them is comparatively light.

"The ore is brought down from the mine, sorted, and piled up close by the furnace-doors; we throw the ore on, keep up a steady fire night and day, until it is thoroughly heated, and the quicksilver sublimed."

"Will you tell us what that is?" inquired Ned.

"Certainly, my boy; and if at any time you want to ask a question, don't hesitate to do it. I'll be very glad to answer it.

"By sublimed I mean, converted into vapor by heat, and then recondensed into a solid form, when it of course falls by its own weight, and is conducted by these pipes, which lead along the bottom of the furnaces, to reservoirs which I am going to show you, buried in the earth; these hold between one and two gallons each."

"What are they buried in the earth for?" asked Hal.

"To assist it in cooling. From these reservoirs the quicksilver is carried into this storehouse, where it is deposited, as you see, in these cast-iron tanks, or vats, which are set in solid masonry."

"How much is there in this one?" said Ned, standing beside one of the tanks about five feet square. "Over twenty tons," was the answer. "Pull off your coat, my boy, roll up your sleeve, and plunge your arm down into this vat."

Ned did so, quickly withdrawing it, and exclaiming, —

"Ough! how funny it feels!"

Hal and myself followed suit. The sensation experienced was, as Ned declared, a "very funny one," or perhaps I can better describe it by saying that it was something between a funny and a chilling one; so peculiar, in any event, that neither of us cared to repeat the operation.

"There," said Mr. Young, handing Hal a small piece of very light porous wood, "hold that in the tank a minute."

Hal did as requested, and, upon withdrawing it, found that the metal had penetrated, even in that short time, through every fibre of the wood, making the weight of the stick almost as much as that of a like quantity of pure quicksilver.

"Now," said Mr. Young pleasantly, "one more illustration, and you young gentlemen will have a pretty good idea of the specific gravity of this metal."

Taking a piece of oak plank about three feet long and twelve or fourteen inches wide, he laid it upon the surface of the quicksilver in the vat, then said, —

"Now you boys both stand upon that piece of plank."

"Why, we shall sink it," exclaimed Hal.

"It'll let us in, sure," said Ned.

"It will do neither one nor the other," replied Mr. Young: then turning to me he said, —

"Come, judge, you try it with me."

I stepped upon the plank with him (not without some misgivings, I confess), and the next moment was floating upon a mass of pure quicksilver, and to my surprise found that its specific gravity was so great, our united weight made scarcely a perceptible difference in the buoyancy of the plank.

"There," said Mr. Young as we stepped upon *terra firma* once more, "that's better explained than words would have done it."

"Yes, and a good deal more satisfactorily," replied I.

"From the storehouse to the warehouse is but a step, you see," continued Mr. Young; "and here we prepare the metal for market, by putting it into these wrought-iron flasks, each one of which holds seventy-five pounds: these are imported by us from England, because they are just as good as, and cost much less, than those manufactured in the United States."

"How do you fill them?" asked Ned.

"With these ladles, from which it is poured into the flask, through an ordinary tin tunnel; one of these screws is then fitted into the mouth of the flask so as to render it absolutely tight, and the quicksilver is ready for market. It is carried from here to the ocean in ox-carts, from thence shipped to San Francisco, and from there to China, Japan, and elsewhere."

"What is the average product per month of your mines?" inquired I.

"Last month we shipped nearly two thousand flasks or about one hundred and fifty thousand pounds, and we hope to double the amount during the coming year."

"Don't the laborers who are constantly inhaling the vapors arising from these furnaces suffer from salivation?" inquired I.

"Oh, yes! they have to take a rest every three or four weeks, and we are obliged to set a fresh gang at work; then we lose some twenty or thirty horses and mules every year from the effects of the mercury; but the miners, and those who merely handle the ore are not affected in the least."

"How long do you run your furnaces without drawing their fires?" inquired I.

"It generally takes seven or eight days to fill the furnaces, extract the quicksilver, and remove the residuum, which is the worst part of the entire business," said Mr. Young.

"Why the worst part?" asked Hal.

"It's the most dangerous, because the men employed at it appear to suffer more from the effects of the mercury; that is, they are salivated the worst."

"What is salivation?" asked Ned in an aside.

"I suppose it would be termed an excessive or unusually large flow of saliva," said I.

"Is that injurious?" continued the boy.

"It is considered very much so, I believe," replied I; and just here Mr. Young turned and said, "Now, gentlemen, I was requested by Mr. Walkinshaw to bring you up to his house to lunch; the ambulance is harnessed, and I shall be most happy to drive you up if you will allow me."

I was at first inclined to refuse the invitation so cordially extended; but Mr. Young was very decided in urging our acceptance, and I finally yielded a reluctant assent, and accompanied him to Mr. Walkinshaw's beautiful residence about a mile distant from New Almaden.

This gentleman, an Englishman by birth, had for many years been a resident of Mexico and California, where his long and fortunate experience with mines and mining, had rendered him a most desirable and valuable resident owner and counsellor.

After partaking of a substantial lunch, we spent several hours in viewing and admiring our host's extensive and elegant grounds, the natural beauties of which had been greatly augmented by the addition of many rare and valuable plants and flowering shrubs; we then returned to our camp, well pleased that the day had brought us not only pleasure, but much valuable information.

The boys entertained Sile until a late hour, relating the incidents of the day with so much spirit that they succeeded in awakening sufficient curiosity in Sile's mind, to induce him to accompany us in our visit to the mine the following morning.

We set out about nine o'clock, and found Mr. Bester waiting for us with mules, just back of the storehouses, at the point where the ascent to the mine commences.

The road, which is about a mile in length, winds up the side of the mountain for that distance, rising about twenty-five feet in every hundred, until the opening is reached.

On our way up we stopped a few minutes at the *adit* or tunnel, which the company was constructing for the purpose of intersecting the main shaft. This had already been dug through the solid rock for nearly a thousand feet; and Mr. Bester informed us that he expected to reach their objective point after penetrating fifty feet farther.

The expense of constructing this adit, which was nearly ten feet in width by eight in height, must have been very great; but the company believed it would more than compensate for the cost, in the great saving of labor that would accrue from its use.

The apex or top of the mountain, which is conical in shape, rises for two hundred feet above the entrance to, or main shaft of the mine, which is on a level with and but a short distance, from the village where the laborers and their families reside.

As we approached the opening, and saw the nearly naked miners swarming in and out, with their huge leather sacks swung upon their backs, the busy scene reminded me more of the entrance to a beehive than any thing else.

"What are those men doing?" inquired Hal.

"Bringing up the ore from the mine," was the answer.

"They don't bring it up on their backs, do they?" continued the boy.

"Yes; we have no other means of hoisting it, save in these sacks, upon the backs of the men," was the response.

"It must be a very expensive process," remarked I, in a tone of inquiry.

"Yes; for not only the best ore, but the refuse, must be brought up as well, before it can be separated: it is done by contractors, however, who, as you see, employ none but Mexicans."

"Wouldn't Americans do as well?" asked Ned.

"Undoubtedly; but Americans could hardly be employed as cheaply as these men, and I doubt if they would answer the same purpose," replied Mr. Bester.

"They look more like Apaches than Mexicans. Don't they ever wear any more clothing than they have on now?" inquired Hal.

"Not when at work; the handkerchief and breech-cloth constitute their sole dress," was the reply.

"I don't see as these *arrieros* are much better off," remarked Sile. "It's a mighty comfer'ble way er dressin', anyhow."

"Yes," remarked Mr. Bester, "that extra calico shirt can't well be called superfluous clothing."

"How many trips to the surface per day do these miners average?" inquired I.

"Generally from fifty to sixty," was the answer.

"And the *arrieros?*" continued I.

"Two trips each day; that is, from the mine to the furnaces twice, and return. They are about loading the train; if you would like to remain and witness the operation, before descending into the mine, we will do so."

The mules to the number of seventy-five, sleek looking, splendid animals, were brought up, each with a pair of panniers, made of rawhide, slung across their backs. Into these, three hundred pounds of the ore was piled : this constituted a *carga ;* each one of which was weighed, the company paying so much for bringing it to the surface, and so much for carrying it to the furnaces.

After witnessing the operation of loading and starting the train, we prepared for our descent into the mine.

We were first each provided with tallow candles tied to the end of a pine stick, which Mr. Bester rather facetiously denominated torches, and with these in our hands entered the mine.

About ten feet from the entrance we came to a little niche cut into the solid rock, in which the workmen had set up an image of their patron saint, gaudily attired in silk and velvet; and Mr. Bester informed us that "every man, before entering the mine in the morning, falls upon his knees before the image, and invokes its protection for the day. "Indeed," said he, "the mine was opened in the winter of '46 and '7 ; and, although we employ about two hundred workmen, we have been so singularly fortunate as never to have had an accident thus far, — a fact that the men all attribute to the protecting influence of this saint."

After advancing horizontally about sixty feet, the shaft took a turn downwards ; and in a short time we came to a notched log, down which we climbed with difficulty, steadying ourselves with one hand, and holding the torch with the other.

"Why don't you have regular ladders instead of

these notched logs?" inquired Hal, after reaching the platform upon which the log rested.

"This is a ladder, the same now in use in nearly all the mines throughout Mexico. Workmen prefer them to any other; and I believe that I like them quite as well myself, since I have become accustomed to them."

"It seems to me a mighty awkward way of getting up and down in the world, anyhow," laughingly remarked Hal.

"Yes, to you; but see with what facility the miners climb them, with those heavy leathern sacks upon their backs," replied Mr. Bester.

"I suppose it's every thing in getting used to it," said Ned.

"Now if you are ready we will go on down; here we have ten stone steps to descend;" and so we went on, here following an inclined plane for a short distance, then climbing down another notched log, and then more stone steps, until at last we stood at the bottom of the mine, two hundred and forty feet beneath the surface.

From different points numerous passages extended in all directions, following the lead of the different veins of ore, there being over nine thousand lineal feet of these excavations; some of the passages were four or five feet in diameter, others barely large enough to admit the working of a single miner with his pick and drill.

With boyish curiosity, Hal and Ned of course

insisted upon exploring each of the different passages, so that several hours elapsed before we found ourselves slowly climbing the notched logs or ascending the rudely cut stone steps, in our journey towards the light of day.

We reached it finally; and after emerging into the bright sunshine, and once more inhaling the sweet, fresh air, Sile expressed the feelings of our entire party, when after drawing a long breath he exclaimed, —

" I've tramped these 'ere mountings and valleys for nigh about ten year; but I'll be blessed if I ever know'd the vally o' fresh air and blue sky afore;" adding as he looked about him, " Ef yer ever ketch Sile Carter so far under ground ag'in, yer may set him down for a dead man."

Not many months after this, upon emerging from the exploration of a silver-mine of vast depth in Old Mexico, I ventured to remind Sile of the above declaration, to which he replied, —

" I ain't a-goin' tew deny it; but, if any man thinks I'm dead, he'll fin' me the livest corps he ever tried ter bury. I ain't the fust Carter either thet's hed ter foller his team inter mighty onpleasant sitooations."

It was four o'clock in the afternoon, before we reached the furnaces once more, on our return to camp. Here bidding adieu to our new-found friends, and thanking them for the many courtesies extended to us, we set out for camp, well satisfied with the result of our visit to the New Almaden quicksilver-mines, but very tired from the unusual fatigue of the day.

I went to bed early; and the last thing I remember was listening to a discussion between Hal and Ned, regarding the probabilities of finding a quicksilver-mine in the mountain range near our ranch, and the possibility of successfully working it.

CHAPTER XXVII.

HAL AND NED DISCUSS A POINT. — THE TWO INDIAN CHIEFS. — A QUESTION. — SHALL WE GO, OR STAY ? — THE DECISION. — HAL OBJECTS. — THE STRAY HORSE. — A LONG TRAMP. — A PROPOSITION. — HAL APOLOGIZES.

"I WISH old Jerry was here this morning," said Ned, seating himself before a plate piled high with juicy venison-steak.

"I don't, because he'd be sure to snub me if I spoke about the Apaches, or ventured to give an opinion upon any subject. I wonder though, what he'd say about that cinnamon bear I killed," replied Hal, helping himself to a flap-jack.

"He'd probably say what everybody else says, that 'twas a mighty lucky shot," answered Ned.

"A mighty lucky shot," responded Hal, mimicking Ned. "That's all the credit I ever get when I do a good thing. If anybody else had killed him, it would have been a splendid shot; but, because it was me, it's a 'mighty lucky' one. I don't care, Ned Brown: I didn't go out and get lost, and have to stay up a tree all night because I was afraid to come down in the dark."

"No, but you and I both got scared at a drove of hogs when we were coming through Texas, and were glad enough to climb a tree in daylight, to get rid of 'em," replied Ned.

"Don't say I was scared: I wasn't frightened a particle," said Hal.

"Then what did you cry for?" asked Ned.

"Cry! I didn't cry: you was the only one that shed a tear about the matter," asserted Hal.

"Didn't Hal cry when he was up that post-oak in Texas?" asked Ned, appealing to me.

"If I remember right, he did," was my reply; "but you boys must settle your own differences without reference to me."

"Well, I meant that I didn't cry because I was scared," said Hal, a little disconcerted by my answer.

"What did you cry for, then?" inquired Ned.

"I shouldn't think you'd ask such a question, Ned Brown, when you knew that I only cried out of sympathy with you," said Hal.

"That reminds me of the story of two Indian chiefs who were once invited to dine at a white man's table," said I. "One of them seized the mustard-pot, and conveyed to his mouth, a spoonful of the contents, which were so strong that it brought the tears to his eyes.

"The other observing this said,—

"'What'ee cry for, eh?'

"'Umph! me tinkee my fader; die tudder day,' was the answer.

"In a short time the other Indian seized the pot, and conveyed the spoon to his mouth, which immediately brought the tears to his eyes.

"Observing this, the chief who had first tried it asked in a triumphant manner,—

"'What make'ee cry for, eh?'

"'Umph,' responded his companion, 'me cry 'cause you no die when oo fader did.'"

"I don't see how that story applies to me," remarked Hal to Ned, who was laughing.

"Yours was the same kind of sympathy that made the Indian cry; wasn't it?" asked I.

"Of course it was," said Ned: "Hal cried because he couldn't help it, and so did the Indian."

"Well, I don't see any point to the story," remarked Hal; "but I'd like to know if we are going to stay here all day, or not."

"Suppose when Sile comes, we take a vote, whether we spend the day here, or go back to the little valley near where we had the bear-hunt," said I.

"Well, for my part, I'm tired of hunting, and had rather stay where we are," remarked Hal.

"All right; here comes Sile: we'll take a vote, and the majority shall decide. What say you, Sile? shall we spend the day here, or return to our old camp in the valley for a day or two?"

"I'm for goin' back, squire: we kin hev a day's huntin' there, for I hain't seen no place sence we started, where thar's so many signs er game, as thar is 'bout that place."

"And you, Hal, what say you?"

"I just told you. I'm for staying where we are."

"And Ned?" inquired I.

"I'm for going back. It's a great deal pleasanter there," was the reply.

"Well, I'm very certainly in favor of returning," remarked I. "Three to one, Hal. — Catch up, and we'll start, Sile."

"You needn't catch my horse, Sile. I want to stay here awhile, and will come on and overtake you before you get into camp," said Hal.

"I guess I'd better hev him ketched up, 'cause maybe he'll bother you if you try to ketch him when he's alone. Yer see, he's used tew runnin' with a herd, and " —

"Well, don't you trouble yourself about my not being able to catch him. I don't want him caught now, anyway," said Hal decidedly, angry at the idea of being advised by any one.

"Let the horse alone, Sile," said I. "Hal thinks he's able to take care of himself. Let him catch his own animal."

"All right, squire, just as you say; but he'll hev a job a-ketchin ther critter, or I'll lose my guess."

"Well, it's one of his own seeking: so let the horse be."

In about half an hour the animals were packed, our horses saddled, and we on the road, leaving Hal behind, lazily reposing beneath the shade of one of the oaks.

"You look rather lonesome, Hal: hadn't you better conclude, after all, to come with us?" said I as we passed him.

"I'm going to take a nap before I start," replied the boy.

"That hoss'll foller us, as sartin as you're a livin' man," remarked Sile in a low tone, as we wheeled into line.

"Then Hal will have to shoulder his saddle, and travel after him. It won't hurt him to walk a few miles, and may learn him a lesson," replied I.

We rode on, and in a few minutes a turn in the trail hid our camp from sight. We looked back as we turned: Hal was lying in the same position as when we left him, and his horse was quietly feeding near.

"I don't believe the horse'll offer to follow us," remarked Ned: "he's quiet enough now."

"All right, sonny. Hosses is hosses, the world over; and I never seen one yit, that didn't like company: much more them as is used tew it," replied Sile.

"How far is it from the furnaces to that valley, Sile?" asked Ned, after we had been on the road an hour or more.

"I guess 'tain't over ten mile," replied Sile.

"There's no chance of Hal's getting lost, is there?" inquired the boy.

"Not a bit; he couldn't do it onless he tried: but there's a right smart chance of his hevin' tew walk in, or my guess ain't wuth a cent."

"Do you really think his horse will follow us?" asked Ned.

"'Tain't wuth while talkin'; wait a while and see," responded Sile confidently.

We rode on for perhaps half an hour longer, when we suddenly heard the sound of horse's feet behind us, and the next moment a loud neigh, which was immediately answered by Ned's pony; and then Hal's horse, without saddle or bridle, but with his long lariat trailing behind him in the dust, galloped past us, and fell into line with as much precision as an old cavalry-horse.

"What'd I tell yer?" asked Sile. "Somebody'll hev tew take that hoss back now."

"Not a bit of it," said I, speaking very decidedly. "Hal may overtake us the best he can: if he don't come in before we get ready to leave the valley, we'll send back after him; but we'll give him plenty of time to walk, and perhaps it may teach him to take the advice of those who are older, and know more than he does. Have some one catch the horse, and coil that lasso, so that it won't be dragging in the dust behind him."

This was soon done, and we rode along without further delay, until we reached our camping-place about three o'clock in the afternoon.

Dinner was soon prepared, and after a little time, Sile and Ned began to make preparations for our hunt the following day. I took this occasion to write up my journal, and the Mexicans amused themselves by catching one another with lassos.

About six o'clock Sile announced that Hal was just coming through the woods, with his saddle upon his shoulder; and in a few minutes he appeared, considerably blown, and looking exceedingly cross and uncomfortable.

Throwing his saddle and bridle down upon the ground, he turned towards Sile, and said, —

"You served me a pretty trick, didn't you? — coaxing my horse to follow you off."

Sile only laughed.

"What's the matter, Hal?" inquired I.

"Why, when I went to catch my horse, he started off into the woods; but I knew I could get him well enough, because his lariat was dragging behind. I followed him for a mile or two, but he kept just far enough ahead of me to prevent my catching hold of the rope; after chasing him awhile I saw that he was going to keep the trail, so I went back after my saddle and rifle, and when I came up to the place where I left the trail it very suddenly disappeared; and I'll bet I walked a dozen miles, hunting for him in the woods."

"Well, what had Sile to do with that? If you had followed his advice you wouldn't have lost your horse."

"I should have been all right if he hadn't taken off the lariat."

"All right!" repeated I. "How so?"

"Why, I was trailing him by the lariat; and when I lost the mark in the dust, I supposed of course that he had gone into the woods."

"That's the strangest thing I ever heard — a boy with the experience upon the frontier that you claim to have had! Hal, I'm astonished. You should have been able to have tracked your horse by the prints of his hoofs, not by the rope he dragged behind him. You ought to have seen, not only the mark of the man's feet who alighted to coil the lasso, but you should have known where his horse stood when he dismounted. Ned and myself also stopped there for some time, while Sile was catching the horse. Besides this, you should have known that the animal would have followed the herd, any way. Sile and myself both urged you to allow him to be caught; but you persisted in having your way, and now you have got your punishment for it. Instead of coaxing your horse away when he overtook us, Sile wanted to send him back; but I refused to permit it. If you are tired I'm not sorry, for I hope you have learned a lesson from your experience to-day, that will be of service to you in future. You've done Sile great injustice, and I believe you'll show yourself manly enough to apologize to him for it; remember, it's only a coward who is ashamed to acknowledge himself wrong, when convinced of his error."

This was the longest lecture I had ever given Hal; but he received it without attempting any justification of himself or making any reply, and, when I had finished, marched up to Sile, and handsomely apologized for his indiscreet statements.

It was readily overlooked, for Sile knew and understood Hal's impulsiveness far too well to take any offence at his ill-advised and foolish speeches.

"Well, Hal," said I, as he joined us after eating his dinner, "are you going to accompany us up the mountain on our hunt to-morrow?"

"Of course I am. I wouldn't miss it for a great deal," was his reply.

"Is your rifle cleaned, and every thing ready?"

"No, sir; but I'll have it ready before I sleep;" and the boy started with alacrity to make the necessary arrangements.

In about an hour Hal returned, and announced himself ready for the morrow's hunt; seeing how fatigued and weary he looked, I said "Now, boys, it's high time to retire: and I know that Hal won't object to 'turning in' early, after his walk to-day, especially as we must be off in the morning in right good season: so let's to bed for once, before the fire burns down;" and in ten minutes the camp was quiet.

CHAPTER XXVIII.

EARLY RISING. — MORNING THE BEST TIME FOR GAME. — THE ANTELOPE. — THE BOYS' SURPRISE. — SILE TRIES HIS LUCK. — SPECKLED BEAUTIES AND RED FLANNEL. — HAL THE DOUBTER. — A CHALLENGE. — THE FIRST SHOT.

AS the first faint streak of dawn flashed athwart the eastern sky, the following morning, the boys were astir.

"Ain't you up rather early?" inquired I, as I heard them discussing the chances of the coming day's sport.

"No, sir: I don't mean to be behind in any thing to-day," responded Hal.

"We're going for game, we are," put in Ned; "and Sile says morning's the best time for it."

"That's no reason why you boys should disturb every one in camp by getting up in the middle of the night; so I advise you either to go back to bed again, or make less noise," said I, sleepily turning in my blankets.

"Halloo! what's the matter?" asked Sile. "What's the use of routin' a feller out at this time er night?"

"Why, we are going out on a hunt to-day, and want to be in season: that's all," responded Ned.

"Wal, I advise yer tew go back ter bed agin, and stay there, for you're *out* er season now, anyhow," said Sile.

"But we don't want to go back to bed: we are going to start up the fire, and have an early breakfast," replied Hal.

"Then, don't make any more noise than you can help, and stop your talking," remarked I, by way of a squelcher.

The boys withdrew, and both Sile and myself turned over for another nap. We had not been sleeping long, ere I was aroused by the discharge of two rifles, — not a very startling sound, it is true, in a camp like ours: still it awoke me; and being awake I sat up to ascertain the cause, fully determined to give the boys a lecture that they would not soon forget, for disturbing us.

While waiting to catch sight of them, I heard Hal's voice with wonderful distinctness, saying, —

"I've found it, Ned."

And a few minutes later I heard Ned respond in unmistakable tones of triumph, —

"I've found mine too, Hal. Won't they stare when they see what we've made by getting up in the morning? Sile said, morning was the best time for game, and I believe him."

Supposing that they might have shot a couple of wild geese, immense flocks of which were constantly flying over, I laid myself down once more, and was soon fast asleep.

When I again awoke, the sun was just peeping above the horizon, gilding the summit of the mountains about us with a halo of crimson glory, which penetrated the depths of the vast forest extending far up their rocky sides, and awakening to life and song the innumerable dwellers therein.

Springing to my feet, I was for the instant surprised and bewildered by the sight of the carcasses of two antelope, ready dressed, suspended from one of the limbs of the tree under which I was lying.

For an instant I stood trying to remember how they came there, when I was startled by the shouts of the boys, who sprang out from behind the trunk laughing in great glee.

"Who says we aren't hunters?" demanded Ned.

"What have I always said about my shooting?" queried Hal.

"Please tell me what this all means," suggested I.

"It means that Hal and myself have begun our day's sport," replied Ned.

"It means that we ain't afraid to shoot with the best of you," responded Hal, evidently very much elated.

"Who shot those antelope?" inquired I, a little disposed to doubt the evidence of my own senses.

"We did,— Hal and I," responded Ned.

"Who dressed them?" asked I.

"Ned and I," answered Hal.

"What! Did you do it alone?"

"No, sir. Sile stood by, and showed us how. We did all the work though," replied Hal.

"You've made a good start, boys. Where did you find them?"

"We saw a herd feeding down yonder, just after we got up; but we didn't know what they were at first: and, when we discovered, we crept down through the tall grass, until we got within range, and brought those two fellows. Ain't they fat and nice, though?" explained Ned, proudly caressing one of the carcasses with his hand.

"They are indeed. If you boys keep on as you've begun, you'll beat Sile and myself all hollow before night," was my reply.

"That's just what I told Ned," remarked Hal; "but he only laughed at me."

"Hain't them boys done fust rate fur a beginnin'?" inquired Sile, at this moment approaching us.

"Splendidly," was my reply. "They'll beat us, if we don't look out, Sile."

"They will, sartin, if we don't git to work afore a great while. How's this fur a start?" continued he, holding up a fine string of speckled trout, which he had been carrying behind him.

"Where did you get those?" inquired I.

"Oh! what are they? Where did you catch 'em?" shouted the boys, in the same breath.

"They're speckled trout; and I ketched 'em out er the brook thar," was the answer.

"Out of this brook, right here?"

"Sartin sure. I was down there, and seed 'em dartin' back and forth in the water; and, thinkin' a few fish might be good for a sort of change for breakfast, I stopped and ketched 'em."

"What did you catch 'em with?" inquired Hal.

"A hook and line, of course," responded Sile.

"I didn't know there was one in the party," remarked Hal.

"Ever sence I larnt tew trap, I hain't never bin without a line and hooks," said Sile, producing a small silk line and half a dozen hooks from the pocket of his hunting-shirt.

"If I'd known there were trout in that brook, I'd had a mess long before this," declared Hal. "What did you use for bait? worms?"

"Worms?" repeated Sile, in an inquiring tone. "Where would I git worms, I'd like to know?"

"Out of the ground, of course," responded Hal indignantly: "you don't think I supposed they grew on trees, do you?"

"I'll give yer a ninepence apiece for all the angle-worms you'll find atween now and night," remarked Sile.

"You will, and won't back down, Sile Carter?" anxiously queried the boy.

"Sartin, sure; I don't never back down on my word," responded Sile.

"I'll find you worms enough to take what money you've got with you," declared Hal, starting up.

"Hold on a minute, Hal," interrupted I. "I'm ashamed of you. Don't you know that you can't find angle-worms in the wilderness,—that they always follow, never precede, civilization?"

"Why, when I was with the Apaches in Texas, I used to see plenty of 'em," declared Hal.

"Think again; are you sure? for I have never known them to be found in a wilderness or unsettled country, in my life. However, you can try for them while Sile has the fish cooked for breakfast: that's by far the most important consideration at present."

"I can prove your theory wrong in five minutes," remarked Hal, going in search of the spade.

"I should be very glad to be set right," said I.

"While Hal is a-findin' them angle-worms, I'll go and cook these trout myself, 'cause I never knowed a Mexican, cook fish decent; leastways, nothing but catfish," remarked Sile, starting towards the camp-fire.

"I thought we were going to get such an early start, this morning," said Ned; "but here it is after sunrise, and we haven't even had breakfast yet."

"I'm afraid the delay has been caused by my laziness, Ned. I slept later than usual. I reckon we shall find the day long enough before we return, however," said I.

"I believe I should given the same answer that Hal did, if any one had asked me about angle-worms," said Ned.

"I've never found them in a new country; and settlers and trappers have always told me that they have never seen them there. You'd better think again, and see if you can remember having found them."

"Well, what kind of bait did he use?"

"He probably cut a bit of red flannel from his shirt. Trout are not nearly so fastidious in the wilderness as in the thicker-settled portions of the country."

"I mean to go and ask him," said Ned, starting in the direction of the camp-fire, where Sile was busily at work cooking his fish.

In a few minutes, Ned shouted, "Breakfast!"

We had hardly seated ourselves to partake of it, ere Hal made his appearance with his spade upon his shoulder, saying, —

"I don't give it up yet; but I ain't going to be cheated out of my breakfast for all the angle-worms in California."

"Satisfy yourself, Hal: that's always the better way," remarked I.

"Sile did bait his hook with red flannel," said Ned, addressing me.

Hal was holding a trout by the tail, but stopped in the act of conveying it to his mouth, and with a look of astonishment said, —

"Baited his hook with what?"

"Red flannel," replied Ned.

"You ain't such a goose as to believe that yarn, are you, Ned Brown?" queried Hal.

"I believe what Sile says, of course," answered Ned.

"Well, I don't," retorted Hal. "I've caught too many of 'em myself, to swallow that nonsense. I never heard of such a thing before."

"Likely's not," replied Sile. "I guess thar's a good many things you never heerd on, 'bout roughin' it or ketchin' fish, either, for that matter."

"You can't teach me any thing about fishing for trout, Sile Carter. There was a trout-stream within a mile of my father's house in Berkshire County, that I've fished in many a time," replied Hal.

"Maybe," said Sile; "but, you see, trout out in this country ain't much like them in Massachusetts: they ain't so used ter dodgin'. I dunno how 'tis in Berkshire County, but down in Maine there used tew be two fishermen to every trout."

"I'm ready for a start after that shot," cried Ned, jumping up.

"And so am I," was my response.

Ned and myself left Sile explaining to Hal the philosophy of fishing on the frontier, while we went after our rifles and equipment, and on our return found Hal, expressing a desire to try fishing for trout with "Sile's new-fashioned bait."

"It seems to me, Hal, that you have laid out a pretty good day's work," said I: "between digging for angle-worms, fishing for trout, and hunting in the mountains, you'll have your hands full, won't you?"

"Oh! I don't expect to do every thing to-day," replied he. "I shall have plenty of time after I get back from the hunt."

When at last we were ready for a start, I found that the boys, who were greatly elated at their success of the morning, had been arranging a plan of operations which was soon formally announced by Hal,— himself and Ned, proposing to shoot against Sile and myself.

At first I was inclined to humor the proposition as quite a joke, but soon became convinced that they were in downright earnest about it.

I endeavored to show them what I regarded as the absurdity of the plan, telling them that the forest was a vast one, in which they were likely to get lost, or meet with wild animals with which they would be unable to successfully cope.

They asserted that there was not the slightest danger of their getting lost, as they should never be out of hearing of the sound of our rifles, and could easily call us in case they should meet with any thing in the shape of wild animals that they could not overcome.

"Let 'em try it, squire," whispered Sile. "They'll get sick of it afore they've bin out two hours; and you might talk from now till night, yer couldn't convince 'em er nothin'. As my old mother used ter say, 'the least said, the soonest mended.'"

"But suppose they get lost, Sile?"

"I don't b'lieve there's any danger, but if they do we kin find 'em."

"If they should happen to meet a grizzly?"

"They'll let it alone, you bet," confidingly asserted Sile; "and, if they do, 'twon't bother 'em."

"It would be just like Hal to attempt to capture it alive," said I, laughing.

"Talkin' 'bout capturin' a grizzly and doin' it's, two things. Hal's fust-rate at talkin' 'bout what he will do; so I say, give the boys a chance."

"Well, if they go, Sile, you must take the responsibility, for I don't care to assume it."

"All right, boys," said Sile, turning towards them. "The squire says yer may go. Here's my pocket-compass; get the bearin's er camp, and be sure and meet us here at four o'clock, and don't git out 'er the sound of our rifles."

Away started the boys in high glee, declaring that they would show us what hunting meant, before night.

As Sile and myself slowly made our way up the mountain's side, he remarked, —

"I declare, if 'tain't 'sprisin'; now, who'd thought that boy Ned could ever hev bin got to start on sich a lark as he's gone on ter-day? I wouldn't hev b'lieved it. I s'pose though, Hal's kinder made him think he kin do most any thing sence they shot their antelope this mornin'."

"They did well, Sile. I had no idea of it until I saw them hanging, all dressed."

"Yes, they was a-laffin' tew think how s'prised you'd be when you waked up. Halloo! look at that now," said Sile, bringing his rifle to his shoulder; the next instant a fine grouse came tumbling down from the top of a small pine.

"I didn't know as we were to count grouse," said I, laughing.

"Every thing with legs, is the rule in this country," replied Sile, reloading his rifle.

A moment later we heard a loud "Halloo!" Sile answered, asking, "What do you want?"

And in a few minutes both boys came rushing breathlessly through the bushes, shouting at the top of their voice, —

"What'd you shoot? what'd you shoot?"

Waiting until they had nearly reached us, Sile held up the grouse, saying, "This ere's the critter."

"Pshaw! is that all?" inquired Ned.

"I could have killed half a dozen of those fellows if I'd been a mind to," remarked Hal.

"Every thing that wears legs, is the rule in this country," responded Sile.

"All right; now that we know it, we'll give you enough of it before night," said Hal. "Come on, Ned!"

"I believe I'd rather stay, and we'll hunt all together," remarked Ned, in reply to Hal's solicitation.

"That's just like you, Ned Brown: we've got a chance to show that we're as good hunters as any one, and you are afraid to try it," urged Hal.

"I ain't afraid; but I believe we should have a

good deal more fun if we all stuck together," replied Ned.

"Oh, nonsense! come on," cried Hal rather impatiently. "We'll beat 'em: I feel it in my bones."

Thus urged, Ned reluctantly threw his rifle over his shoulder, and the two disappeared in the forest.

CHAPTER XXIX.

OUR GAME. — WE CALL THE BOYS. — IN CAMP. — LOST. — THE EFFECT OF A BLUNDERBUSS. — A SLEEPLESS NIGHT. — ON THE TRAIL. — THE LITTLE LAKE. — THE CAMP-FIRE. — THE GENTLEMAN FROM PIKE. — HAL DISCOURSES. — FOUND. — " TOOK SICK." — WHY HAL REFUSED TO GUIDE US IN.

TWO b'ars, a fox, two deers, four wolves, and a even eight pair er grouse," said Sile, counting over our game while we were making ready for our return to camp, late that afternoon. "Not so bad a show, arter all: we'd do better ter-morrow. We've got the ears er them bars and wolves, the tail er the fox [sticking it in the band of his hat], two saddles er venison, and the grouse; and I guess they'll make 'bout as big a load as me'n you'll want tew pack inter camp ter-night, ef 'tis all the way down hill. I guess afore we start, we'd better gin them boys a call; and maybe, I shouldn't be much s'prised if they was so light loaded theirselves, they could help us pack some er our grub in."

Whereupon we discharged our rifles three times in rapid succession, and waited for a response.

None came.

We repeated the call, and again listened for the reply; but the echo of our own shots, reverberating among the crags upon the mountain-side, and finally dying away in the distance, was our only answer.

I looked towards Sile, who was busily engaged in tying one of the saddles of venison over his shoulder, and said, —

"Funny they don't answer; ain't it?"

"I guess they got kinder tired er shootin' by theirselves, and hev gone down tew camp: we hain't heerd 'em shoot once ter day, hev we?" asked he as we slowly started along.

"I haven't," said I "and that seems to me rather strange."

"That's why I kinder think they've gone inter camp; 'cause Hal would hev shot at somethin', if it hed bin his shadder."

"I reckon we shall find them there, for I fear they haven't had very good luck," remarked I.

"Considerin' thar's so many signs er game 'bout, we, hain't hed no sort er luck ter day," replied Sile: "still it's better'n nothin'. Thar's some days when ther best on 'em don't see nothin' bigger'n a chipper. It's all a streak, anyhow."

"What shall we do, Sile, if we don't find 'em in camp? I'm half afraid they've met with some mishap," remarked I.

"I guess they're thar, sure enuff," was the reply. "'Tain't best tew borrow trouble, nohow: it allers comes fast enuff. If they ain't thar, we'll hev to find 'em, that's all."

"It was a foolish idea, their starting out alone: I ought never to have permitted it," said I.

"What's done can't be helped; 'tain't no use tew cry for spilt milk: if they've got lost, we must find 'em;" and Sile strode on at a pace that required no small exertion on my part to keep up with him.

"They took that pocket-compass, and you showed them how to take their bearings, didn't you?" inquired I.

"Sartin I did. We shall know in a few minutes now; thar's the smoke from our camp-fire," said Sile, pointing to a thin column of light smoke curling up from a point far below us. "They hain't had nothin' tew do with that fire though, I know."

"How do you know that?" said I.

"'Cause it's a Mexican smoke," was the reply.

"Well, Mexican smoke or not, I'll have to put this saddle of venison down, and rest a few minutes: you're walking awfully fast," remarked I.

Sile unslung the venison from his shoulder, and, laying the grouse beside it, threw himself down upon the hillside, and, after a few moments' silence, turned towards me, and said, "Yer see, a Injun allers builds his fire er dry twigs, and sich stuff as don't make much smoke; leastways he does onless he's telegraphin', and smoke's what he's arter. Wal, a Mexican won't use nothin' but dry wood neither, but he burns branches and bigger sticks than a Injun, 'cause he won't take the trouble tew pick up so much small stuff; but a 'Merican'll pile on any thing that'll burn, green or dry, and ther nat'ral consequence is, he makes a big smoke that allers shows whar his camp is. Injuns allers laugh at us Yankees, 'cause they say we build sich big fires, ther can't nobody sit near enuff tew 'em ter git warm. S'posin' we go along down: be yer rested yet?"

I replied, that I was, and we once more started. In half an hour we reached camp. My first question was, —

"Where are the boys, Juan?"

"*Quien sabe, señor?*"[1] was the answer.

Throwing our burdens upon the ground, we looked one another in the face. Neither of us spoke for at least a minute; then I said, —

"They're lost, Sile: what shall we do?"

"Find 'em," was the laconic answer.

"What's the first thing to do?" inquired I.

"Wal, the fust thing is tew git our supper. While we're eatin' it, I'll send Juan up ter that big rock yonder with his old *escopeta*, and they can't help hearin' it, if they're on this side er the mountain."

"And alive," added I.

"Nonsense, squire! of course they're alive. Why shouldn't they be?"

"I certainly can't answer that; but I have a sort of feeling that they've met with some accident, and we ought to start out in search of them at once."

[1] Who knows, sir?

"We shouldn't do nothin' if we did, 'cause it's nigh 'bout dark now. We'll hev tew wait till mornin', anyway, and we may as well make the best on't."

A moment's reflection convinced me that Sile was right, and we must wait till daylight if we hoped to accomplish any thing.

In the mean time, Juan mounted the rock with his *escopeta*, and, turning its huge muzzle towards the head of the ravine, discharged it.

The report sounded like that of a small cannon. The silence of the grave followed it for a single instant; and then we heard it echoing and reverberating among the far-away cliffs and crags, now loud and clear, again faint and indistinct, dying away in the distance into a feeble and confused murmur, to be suddenly caught and for a moment retained by some overhanging precipice, then hurled back by an invisible power, to once more echo and re-echo louder and louder, sharper and sharper, clearer and clearer, until finally it ceased, and profound silence once more environed us.

Breathlessly we listened for a response. The echo was gone, and the stillness of death had settled over and about us.

Again and again did Juan discharge his musket.

Again and again did we anxiously listen for an answer, to be as frequently disappointed.

At last I said, —

"It's no use, Sile. They would certainly have heard those reports if they are alive."

"Or hadn't got 'round on t'other side ther mountain," interrupted Sile. "That Hal's a master hand tew 'speriment. We'll take their trail in ther mornin' from that place whar I shot that fust grouse, and 'twon't be many hours afore we'll overhaul 'em, you bet. Leastways we can't do nothin' ter-night, can we? So we may as well make the best on't, and rest easy."

Sile's advice was good. I knew it, but found it impossible to act upon it; for, do what I would, my thoughts dwelt constantly upon the boys.

I knew something of the perils to which they would be exposed, passing the night alone in this vast forest; and I feared for their safety.

"I ain't half so anxious 'bout 'em as I should be if Ned wa'n't along: he's a kind er balance-wheel tew t'other one; and with sich a night as this, why, it couldn't hurt a baby to sleep out," remarked Sile.

"I'm not afraid of any thing but their meeting wild beasts," said I.

"Thar ain't one chance in a dozen of thar meetin' any thing that'll hurt 'em. 'Cause yew happened tew git 'mongst a pack of wolves t'other night, you needn't 'spect they're allus hangin' round. I'll risk 'em. I ain't no ways 'larmed 'bout that."

In conversation like this, passed the long hours until bedtime; it was evident that, notwithstanding his assumed indifference, Sile was very uneasy. A dozen times had he started up and abruptly gone out to consult with Juan or one of the *arrieros*, and a dozen times had he returned without deriving any satisfaction from his conference with them.

At last we went to bed, but not to sleep. That "sweet restorer" visited not our eyes during the long and weary watches of the night. With the first signs of dawn, one of the *arrieros* was sent to the top of the highest eminence, in the hope that his keen eyes might detect some traces of their whereabouts, through the smoke from their camp-fire. He returned in a couple of hours, saying that there was "a white man's smoke" far to the south of us, in an entirely different direction from that taken by the boys when they left.

As soon as we could fairly see to distinguish any tracks in the forest, four of us set out in the hope of discovering their trail; agreeing that the signal of the first sign should be the discharge of three chambers of a revolver, in rapid succession.

We had gone barely half a mile from camp, when we were suddenly brought to a halt by hearing the hoped-for signal. We all started in the direction from whence the sound came; and in a few moments reached a spot where Juan had discovered the trail of two persons, which crossed a small piece of moist land.

Sile immediately pronounced the tracks to be those of the boys, made recently, but leading towards the south, instead of the north-east, the supposed course taken by them.

After a consultation with the Mexican, Sile decided to take the trail from that point, and on it we started. Occasionally Juan would discharge his *escopeta;* but it brought no answer save its own echo, or the cry of some bird, frightened from its resting-place by the terrible and unusual sound which penetrated every portion of the vast solitude about us.

After proceeding in this way for more than an hour, Sile, who was in the advance, paused, and, pointing to a spot beneath a tall pine, carefully examined the ground about it, all the while talking with Juan. After a little, he turned to me, and said, —

"They stopped a while to rest here, squire: thar ain't no doubt about that. Here's whar they sot, and thar's ther mark whar they sot their rifles, with the muzzles leanin' agin the tree: it's all fresh too, like as though 'twas made yesterday afternoon. But I can't see what they're doin' down here. Juan thinks they started for camp, and went by, within half a mile of it: it does look so, that's a fact; but I can't hardly b'lieve it. However, we're on the right trail, thar ain't no two ways 'bout that: so we'd better git on as fast as we kin."

Again we started, following the tracks through the underbrush which each moment grew thicker and more dense, obliging us to proceed slowly, although the footprints were more clearly defined, owing to the dampness of the ground in which they were embedded.

Following them for some time, we suddenly came

to the shores of a small lake of beautifully clear water, on the pebbly beach of which, at a distance of about a quarter of a mile from the spot where we stood, were to be seen the still smoking embers of a camp-fire.

Hurrying towards it we found every proof that the boys had passed the night there; among them, the feathers that had been plucked from a grouse, also the sticks upon which portions had been broiled over the fire.

"They're all right, squire," said Sile, with gladness in his tones: "with plenty of grouse tew eat, and water tew drink, thar ain't no sort er danger of thar dyin', you bet."

"My mind is certainly very much relieved," said I; "but the question still is, where are they now?"

"We'll have Juan give 'em a shot with that 'er blunderbuss er his'n once more: that'll fetch 'em," replied Sile.

At this moment the Mexican came up with the information that his *campañiero*[1] had discovered a cattle-trail leading from the shore into the woods, and that he had discovered the boys' tracks upon the dust of this trail.

We immediately sought the trail, and on following it for about half a mile, suddenly came upon a small open place, in the midst of which we saw four or five *bronco* horses, quietly feeding with a couple of cows, an old steer, and half a dozen yearling calves.

[1] Companion.

Between two old and well-worn wagons was burning a small fire, beside which were a few old cooking-utensils, and over them was squatting a very seedy-looking old man, "bent, slim, and hollow." At a little distance, there stood a tall, angular, gaunt-looking female, arrayed in a faded, limp calico gown, with an antiquated pasteboard sun-bonnet upon her head, puffing away at an old clay pipe, well blackened with age, while, like the old man, she was attentively listening to the two boys; who, seated in low, straight-backed, splint-bottomed chairs, were evidently explaining the circumstance of their appearance in the camp.

I was so overjoyed at the sight of them, that I was about to rush forward, but was detained by a motion from Sile, who whispered in my ear, "Pikes, for sartin."

For an instant I was at a loss to comprehend his meaning; then it flashed through my mind that by the term "Pike,"[1] in California, was meant that class of poor whites who had emigrated to the country from many of the Southern States, and were shiftless, uneasy creatures, travelling about and living in their wagons, rarely ever known to do an hour's work; stopping here to-day, moving on to-morrow, but always bearing off the palm for owning the most prolific cattle in the world; every cow or steer producing from four to five calves a year, which a

---

[1] The name given to many of the first emigrants to the State, who found their way there from Pike County, Missouri.

"Pike" never found any trouble in converting into bacon, coffee, or sugar, as the needs of his family required.

"So the boys have found their friends from Pike, have they?" said I, laughing outright from joy at the sight of them.

"See them young ones," remarked Sile, pointing to seven or eight half-naked, dirty little brats, who were peering out at the strangers from behind the wagons, evidently scared nearly out of their wits at the sight of them.

"Come on; let's go forward," said I, impatiently addressing Sile.

As we emerged from the woods, the children were the first to discern our approach; but, like young partridges, fled to cover without uttering a warning note.

Next the old man saw us. Straightening his tall, bent form, and shading his eyes from the glaring sunlight with his hand, he looked steadily for a moment, and then, grasping the barrel of his long Kentucky rifle, he shouted in a hoarse voice,—

"Stan' off yar, strangers!"

This at once attracted Hal and Ned's attention; who, upon looking around, sprang to their feet, and rushed towards us, laughing, shouting, and crying, at the same moment.

"Whar's yer game?" asked Sile as unconcernedly as possible, and speaking as though we had but just returned from the hunt. "We've come tew count up with yer;" then, without waiting for their answer, he walked towards the old man, who still stood as though half expecting an attack, and held out his hand, exclaiming, —

"How d'y, old pard? Pre-emptin', hey?"

"What are you doing so far from camp, boys?" said I, speaking in as natural a tone as I could command.

"Why, we got lost, and couldn't find the camp last night," said Ned. "How'd you find us so quick? We haven't been here more than half an hour."

"That's just like you, Ned Brown, to say we were lost. We weren't lost any more than we are now," said Hal.

"Well, where are we now, Hal? I'm sure I don't know," said I, appealing to him. "What sent you here instead of into camp? I'd like to know that."

"Why, you see we made a big tramp yesterday, and camped last night on the shores of a real pretty little lake, and this morning made up our minds to stop and talk with the old man here, and get something to eat, before we started for camp."

"I think you were very wise, Hal," said, I laughing. "We'll hear your story by and by. I must go and speak to the old man now, for I see Sile is beckoning to me."

I at once asked the wife, who still stood watching us intently, and puffing away at her pipe, if she could not provide something for the boys to eat, promising to pay her liberally therefor. In a reasonably short time, some bacon and corn-pone and a cup of tea were served on a board which answered for a table, supported upon one of the wagon-tongues; and, from the way the boys devoured the provisions, the most casual observer would have become convinced that substance, not style, was their greatest need.

Meanwhile I had been conversing with the ancient "Pike," who informed me that he had "bin a-livin' in them yar wagons er his'en for eight year: he'd kinder got sot ter stay a heap er times; but somehow either ther old woman took sick, or neighbors begun ter come in, or suthin' or other turned up ter start him on. He'd just found this yar place, but reckoned may be 'twan't healthy; 'peared like thar might be shakes round, so he 'lowed he'd hev ter move on afore long."

The boys having finished their meal, I cheerfully paid the old woman the half-dollar demanded, and was extremely sorry to be unable to comply with her request for "'bacca;" but unfortunately not one in the party had a supply with them.

Bidding the "Pikes" a hearty good-by, we left them to move on in search of a locality where the "old woman wouldn't take sick, and thar was no danger of ther shakes," while we took up our line of march for camp.

Upon reaching the shores of the lake, I said,—

WHY HAL REFUSED TO GUIDE US IN.

"Come, Hal, you must show us the way to camp now."

"Me!" exclaimed the boy, "me, show you the way? Why don't Sile do it?"

"Perhaps, like myself, he don't know where we are," replied I.

"It ain't my business to guide the party to camp; but if Sile says he can't do it, I'll try," said Hal.

At this moment, we saw Sile, who had tarried behind to converse with the old woman, coming up; but, before I had an opportunity to explain, Hal said, —

"Sile, do you know the way back to camp from this place?"

"Why, in course I do," was the reply.

Whereupon without further remark, we started, "homeward bound."

CHAPTER XXX.

THE PROOFS. — HAL'S EXPLANATION. — HOW TO COOK GROUSE. — ON THE ROAD. — CAMP. — DENNIS BURKE AGAIN. — "THE OULD MAN'S IN THE HURRY." — OLD MAVERICK'S RANCH. — THE CATTLE. — SEÑOR ESCARRITO. — CALIFORNIA AS IT WAS. — THE CONTRAST UNDER AMERICAN RULE. — READY FOR A START AT LAST.

"YER see," said Sile, poking the fire with a long stick, and sending up shower after shower of sparks, supplemented by a bright blaze that made our camp as light as day, "yer see, we've got tew settle yet. I'm bound tew know what yer did with yer game. Yer was tew beat the squire and me, 'all holler.' Now here's our proofs," producing six pair of ears, and a fox's tail; "thar's the two saddles of venison and the grouse hangin' under that tree. Now we want you, tew show with us."

"We haven't got any thing to show," replied Ned. 'We only killed one grouse, and eat that up before night; so you'll have to take our word for it."

"Sartin', I'm willin' tew do that. But what was yer doin' all day? that's what I want ter know."

"Why, hunting for game, of course," replied Ned.

"Wall, the woods was full er it: why didn't you shoot somethin'?"

"We should have shot it if we had seen it, of course," replied Hal.

"You see, we hadn't been out more than a couple of hours, before Hal looked at his compass, and the needle wouldn't move at all; he shook it, and did every thing to make it work, but something was the matter with it," explained Ned.

"I s'pose you didn't slip the ketch, did yer?" inquired Sile.

"What catch?" asked Hal.

"Why, the ketch that holds the needle up agin the glass, tew keep it from wabblin'," responded Sile.

"I didn't see any catch," said Hal, producing the compass from his pocket: "the old thing ain't worth a cent, any way."

"It'll take more cents than you've got tew buy it, sonny, or use it either, I guess by the looks," remarked Sile, springing the catch, and letting the needle loose, which instantly flew around to the north. "What d'ye want tew pint straighter'n that?"

"It wouldn't work for me that way, anyhow," retorted Hal.

"It would if yer'd knowed any thing 'bout it. — But go on with yer story, Ned: I want ter hear what yer did all day."

"Well, after we found the compass wouldn't work, Hal said there was no use going any farther from camp, and we'd go back. We weren't a great way from you any time, because we could hear your shots every once in a while. We wanted to get back to camp alone, or we should have answered 'em; and that was why we got lost."

"*I* didn't get lost, Ned Brown," interrupted Hal.

"Then why didn't yer come inter camp, when you was so near it?" asked Sile.

"Near it! why, what do you mean?" queried the boy.

"Why, when we found yer trail, it was less 'n half a mile from this ere camp."

"Less than half a mile!" repeated Hal, looking very much confused.

"Yes, less'n er half a mile. Now, if yer wasn't lost, why didn't yer come inter camp? Sartin' there warn't no use tew go clear down tew 'old Pike's' camp, just tew ask him the way back, was thar?" inquired Sile.

"Come, Hal, acknowledge the corn: you were lost, and you know it, as well as Ned and the rest of us. It's no use trying to dodge the issue. Be frank and own up: every one will think the better of you for it. This making excuses, and evading a direct answer, is one of your greatest faults; try and overcome it," said I.

"I didn't know I was so near the camp; that's a fact," replied Hal; "but, if I'd stopped to think, I might have known it. I don't want to deceive any one, I'm sure. Now, when I shot that cinnamon bear, Dennis tried to make out that I didn't take aim, but I know "—

"Never mind that, Hal. Were you lost or not, last night? Answer the question honestly, yes or no."

"I suppose "— began the boy.

"No, no, that won't do: let your answer be squarely, yes or no," interrupted I.

"Well, yes, I was."

"Now, Hal, why wasn't it better to admit it at once, instead of contradicting Ned when he made the statement?" asked I.

"Because I was afraid that you and Sile would laugh at me," was the reply.

"That's a coward's reason, Hal. One ought never to be ashamed to own the truth under any circumstances. We didn't laugh at Ned, and we should have been no more likely to do so at you. Think this over, Hal, and try and correct it, and we'll say no more about it to-night. To-morrow we must start for Maverick's, and I hope you'll be on hand in good season in the morning."

"I guess we're all tired enuff tew go tew bed. Ned's bin layin' asleep thar for the last half-hour," remarked Sile.

"I must say I didn't sleep very well myself last night," said I.

"Nor I neither, squire: too much on the old man's mind, kep' him putty wide awake; so I'll turn in myself, as soon as I see to the critters," and Sile walked out to take his nightly survey of camp.

The next morning we were up bright and early, making ready for the road.

"It'll be a putty long stretch tew old Maverick's," remarked Sile. "We can't git in till late, any way, and sha'n't stop fer no dinner: so yer may as well eat a hearty breakfast, boys."

"How long before we shall be ready to start, Sile?" inquired I.

"In a couple of hours, I guess," was the reply.

"Why can't I roast some of these grouse so that we may take them along cold, for a lunch?" asked I.

"That'll be a fust-rate idee, squire. Ther boys can pick 'em for yer, while we're gettin' packed," said Sile.

"Oh! but I propose to roast 'em feathers and all," remarked I.

"Who ever heard of such an idea?" said Hal, who had just come up to where we were standing.

"I have, Hal, and eaten many a bird roasted in that manner."

"I don't want any of 'em," replied the boy; "besides, I don't believe it can be done."

"Very well: remember, please, that you are to have none.—Now, Ned, we'll go to work."

Ordering one of the Mexicans to replenish the fire with plenty of short dry sticks, so as to make a large bed of coals, I selected a couple of the plumpest birds, and carried them to the brook, where, after properly removing the entrails, I made a thick paste of clay, with which I plastered the birds completely over, leaving this covering to dry a little by exposure to the air.

I then carried them to the fire, and, making two hollows in the warm ashes, completely buried them beneath the hot coals.

In about an hour, we uncovered and removed them from the fire, when, a gentle tap with a stick upon the breast, caused the clay covering, as well as the feathers and skin of the birds, to peel nicely off, leaving the flesh as plump and white and juicy as the most fastidious gourmand could have desired.

"There, Ned," said I, disposing them neatly upon a plate, "there is a roast fit for a king; and when you eat a portion of one cold, to-day, if you don't acknowledge it, why, you must do your own cooking in future."

"I didn't believe it could be done," remarked Hal, who had been regarding the birds with a watery mouth ever since the clay covering had been removed. "If they only taste as nice as they look, they'll be pretty good."

"Who's to solve the question for you, Hal? You know you declared, before they were cooked, that you didn't want any of 'em," said I.

"Well, since they are cooked, I'll change my mind and try them; for, with all my experience upon the frontier, I never heard of roasting fowls in that manner, before."

"That statement only shows how limited your

knowledge of frontier life really is, Hal. This method of cooking has been practised for hundreds of years by the Indians and Mexicans. I saw a wild turkey roasted in this way upon the lower Rio Grande, more than ten years ago, and never ate a more deliciously cooked bird than that.

"The Indians frequently prepare fish in this style, which are said by travellers to be very nice.

"So you see, Hal, that by disputing statements you may hear made upon any subject with which you are not familiar, you only make a lamentable display of your own ignorance. No one person is expected to know every thing; and any such pretension must of necessity subject the person making it to frequent mortification and chagrin."

"I didn't say that it couldn't be done," remarked the boy.

"No; but you implied that it couldn't, which was quite as bad."

"Ned didn't know any more about it than I did."

"Very true; but he said nothing, being content to wait and see, before he pronounced an opinion upon it."

Our conversation was interrupted at this point by hearing Sile shout, —

"All ready; saddle up!" and in a very few minutes we were once more on the road.

We met with no adventure worthy of record during the day; for, under Sile's guidance, we forded without the least inconvenience the stream which had proved so disastrous on our previous crossing, and about dark reached our old camping-place near Maverick's ranch.

It was so late, and we were all so weary, that we did not notify Mr. Maverick of our arrival that night, but retired early that we might get thoroughly rested in readiness for the labors of the coming day.

I was awakened shortly after sunrise the following morning, by hearing Hal shout, —

"Halloo, Dennis! where did you come from? Have you seen any 'pumels' lately?"

A minute afterwards I heard Dennis respond, —

"Well, begorra, if that ain't the 'Pache bye agin! Ould Maverick's bin a-lookin' fer yez, this two days gone bye."

"Here we are, Dennis," said I, sitting up in my blankets. "Has Mr. Maverick got the cattle up?"

"Sure he has, sir; a hape on 'em too," was the reply.

"How is Mr. Maverick and his family?" asked I.

"The ould woman's ailin' a little, but the gal's all right," replied the man, winking at Hal.

"Will you tell Mr. Maverick that we have returned?" said I.

"Sure, then, masther sint me over to ould Escarrito's to have him come over and sae if he could find any of his cattle amongst our'n; and he's in a hurry too," said Dennis, remaining quietly seated upon his horse.

"Then why don't you go along?" inquired Hal.

"Faix, it's the ould man that's in the hurry, not me," replied Dennis, with a comical leer.

"Have you lost any more sheep since I killed the cinnamon bear?" asked Hal.

"How the divil would I know? It's in the pig business I am, wid nothin' to do wid shape," was the reply.

"I didn't know but you might have heard some one say something about it," suggested Hal, in rather a disappointed tone.

"Ould Maverick's spachless wid me about his mathers entirely, so he is; and it's spachless I'll be mesilf if I don't go afther ould Escarrito, sure," said Dennis, putting spurs to his horse, and galloping rapidly away.

He was scarcely out of sight, ere Sile and Ned rode up, having been to the coral to inspect the cattle, which they reported were a superior lot and in very fine condition.

Breakfast over, we all set out for the ranch, where we found about two thousand head confined in the corals, from which, we were to select the number required.

Mr. Maverick and his *vaqueros* were on hand, and in about an hour after our arrival, we were fairly at work. And now began a similar scene to that described in a previous chapter, for each animal purchased must be "cross-branded," i.e., the seller re-brands upon the shoulder, as a sign that his title to the animal has passed; otherwise he can claim it wherever found, it being felony for any person but the owner, to destroy or obliterate a brand.

During the course of the day *El Señor* Escarrito (Mr. Maverick's nearest neighbor), attended by his body-servant, rode up mounted on a splended jet-black stallion, whose flashing eyes, distended nostrils, arched neck, clean limbs, and ambling pace, at once proclaimed a favorite saddle-animal; for these old Spaniards are noted, the world over, for possessing the finest saddle-horses known.

I was not only surprised but delighted to find, upon being introduced to the gentleman, that he spoke English fluently; and in conversation with him I learned much that interested me concerning the early life of the old Californians, which I have since found to have been almost identical with that of the Spanish hidalgos living at the present time in Mexico.

Indeed, when travelling through that country a few months later, scarcely a day passed that I was not reminded of incidents related by Señor Escarrito in my conversation with him at Maverick's ranch.

"Ah, yes! you Americans have destroyed the charm of our Californian homes," said the señor. "Ours was a simple, quiet, and very peaceful life; we had our own amusements, our own habits and customs, and were undisturbed by the commotions of the outside world. We had no crime in the province until you came, nor was there a single prison upon the coast. A traveller might ride the entire distance from Monterey to San Diego, without spending a cent of money, and yet have a fresh horse to mount each morning. Ah! those were the days when a man could enjoy life! Such magnificent riding, such wonderful feats of horsemanship, as we used to witness at our *rodeos* and our *festas!*

"But those times have passed now. No *vaquero* then presumed to address the *padrone*,[1] or any member of his family, without first removing his hat: now he never thinks of it. Then, a traveller could call at any ranch, and, if he was in need, borrow one, two, or three hundred dollars upon his simple word: now, the only thought is, how best to rob the unfortunate *cavallero* of what little he may possess. Then every ranch made its own bread, butter, and cheese, wove its own blankets, made its own wine, dressed and tanned its own skins, and, in truth, provided every thing necessary for the comfort and happiness of its people: now our people are no longer industrious, simple, and happy, but have become lazy, shiftless, and miserable; and we purchase our necessaries, from your American stores.

"Ah me! but since you Americans have taken possession of our country, *Valgame Dios*, how every thing has changed! You have stolen our cattle, killed our *vaqueros*, robbed us of our lands, and broken up our families; you have introduced new customs, destroyed our simple amusements, and

---

[1] The master's title.

made our lives a scene of perpetual warfare, a constant fight to retain what is honestly our own.

"Our churches and missions have been turned into jails and prisons. Instead of the thousands of sober and industrious, well-fed, well-clad, and happy Indians, who were glad to labor upon our ranches and in our houses, you find a set of drunken, starving, naked beggars, who are a curse to themselves and to every one else.

"It is you Americans who have done this, who have ruined our country by forcing upon us what you are pleased to term 'your civilization.'"

In this manner the señor discoursed of the past and present of California for nearly an hour, contrasting the country as it was previous to the discovery of gold in 1849, with its status at the present time, in a manner that reflected but little credit upon the American *régime*.

So interested had I become in listening to this native's simple, honest complaints, that I was quite unprepared for Sile's announcement that the work was completed, and it only remained to settle with Mr. Maverick when we should be ready to once more take the road.

It was not without many regrets that I bade the señor farewell, expressing to him the hope that I might frequently meet as simple, honest, and true gentlemen among the *rancheros* of California, as the Señor Escarrito.

CHAPTER XXXI.

THE MORNING AFTER. — ON THE ROAD. — NED'S REQUEST. — WHAT CAME OF A RED BLANKET. — AN EXCITING CHASE. — A WONDERFUL FEAT. — HOME AGAIN. — OLD JERRY'S WELCOME. — A NEW PROJECT. — WHAT JERRY THINKS. — TRUTH STRANGER THAN FICTION. — ADIEU.

"WAL, squire, we've got as fine a lot 'er young cattle as kin be found in the State," said Sile, seating himself to eat his breakfast the following morning. "Old Maverick's goin' tew send five *vaqueros* along to drive an' herd, so that you and the boys can run the train."

"Why, I've got to go along with the cattle," remarked Hal. "I've got my sheep to look out for; besides, I know I can do as much as any two Mexicans on the road."

"Like as not," replied Sile, helping himself to a cup of coffee; "but, if it's all the same tew you, I'll do the drivin' myself."

"But it isn't all the same," declared Hal. "I want to drive my own sheep, and I mean to do it, too."

"Wal, now, see here, sonny, I'll look out for them

sheep myself. I'd rather you'd ride 'long ther squire, than tew be botherin' round ther cattle: that's all," replied Sile.

"That settles it, Hal. You must ride with Ned and myself," remarked I.

"I don't see what the reason is that I can't"—

"The question is already answered, Hal. Sile prefers to attend to the herd himself, and that's enough," said I, speaking authoritatively.

"I think I ought to be allowed to drive my own sheep, anyhow," persisted Hal.

"You know well enough, Hal, that every time that you have insisted upon having your own way, contrary to the advice of Sile and myself, you have made trouble for yourself: this time I propose to have my way."

"I didn't make any trouble by insisting upon selecting my own horse at Mr. Hitchcock's, did I?" inquired the boy.

Just at this moment the *vaqueros* who were to accompany us rode up and dismounted, their huge Spanish spurs clattering like cavalry-men's sabres; and in a short time our animals were packed, our horses saddled, and we on the road, leaving Sile to follow on behind with the cattle.

Suddenly Ned said, "I want to ride back, and see how they get on driving."

"It seems to me, Ned, you had better keep along with us. The cattle are wild, and it may be you'll get into trouble. A very slight thing will sometimes stampede them," said I.

"Oh! I only want to see how they drive. I won't frighten 'em, and I sha'n't be long away either," remarked he, wheeling his horse, and galloping back towards the herd.

The boy was right; for in a very few minutes, happening to turn my head, I saw him coming towards us as fast as his horse could come, followed by a couple of young bulls, whose clean limbs, sleek coats, and long horns seemed each moment to be drawing nearer and nearer the object of their pursuit.

I could hardly imagine what it meant at first; and then I saw, that one end of the scarlet blanket which the boy carried tied to his saddle behind him, had in some manner become unfastened, and was flying loosely in the wind, then I understood the situation at once.

On came the pursued and his pursuers, each doing his best, but the bulls, little by little gaining the advantage, although still too far away for our voices to reach them. There was therefore nothing for us to do but watch the race, which each moment became more exciting.

The pony, as though aware of the situation, was using his legs to the best possible advantage, for it seemed to me that his nose almost touched the ground in his efforts to escape, while Ned was bending in his saddle until his face was nearly on a level with the animal's neck; and, as he came nearer, we could see his feet working as regularly and decidedly as the walking-beam of a steamboat, as he thrust his spurs into his pony's sides.

Behind him the bulls were running like deer, each moment becoming madder and madder at the sight of the red pennon which Ned unconsciously was flaunting so valiantly in their faces.

At first I had felt some alarm for the safety of the boy, but a suggestion of Juan's immediately relieved my mind, and now I was rather enjoying the sight; while Hal, who evidently anticipated no danger to Ned, was fairly yelling with delight at the spirited race.

As soon as Ned came within hearing, I shouted,—

"Drop your blanket, Ned! drop your blanket!"

The boy heard me, and, turning his head, discovered the fluttering scarlet, and at once comprehended my meaning; tearing it loose, and letting it fall to the ground.

The next instant the bulls were upon it, trampling it beneath their hoofs with loud bellows, and expending all their pent-up fury upon the innocent object of their rage.

Occasionally one of them would succeed in raising it upon his horns for an instant: then there would be a terrible contest between the two infuriated creatures, which ended as soon as the blanket dropped to the earth, when they again brought their united efforts to bear to destroy it.

In the mean while Ned, almost breathless from excitement and pale from fear, had ridden his panting pony, whose reeking sides were fairly dripping with blood, into our midst, where he sat gazing, without speaking a word, at the furious efforts of the frantic creatures, whose hoarse bellows of rage we could distinctly hear.

The boy was safe; but what was to be done about the blanket? We knew that if it should be left until the herd came up, it would madden them to that extent that it might delay us for hours, perhaps stampede the entire herd. It must be removed; but how, was the question.

In this dilemma, I turned to Juan. He appeared to understand my wishes instantly, and, turning to his companions, spoke a few words in Spanish; then, accompanied by one of them, he rapidly rode towards the infuriated creatures, who were so intent upon destroying the innocent cause of their anger, that they paid not the slightest attention to the approach of the horsemen, who rode so near that they succeeded in grasping the maddened bulls, each by his tail.

Surprised and bewildered by this sudden and unexpected attack from the rear, the creatures appeared for the moment to forget their anger at the blanket that lay trampled in the dust beneath them, and started upon the keen run in opposite directions over the plain; while the third Mexican spurred forward, and hastily removed the remains of the offending blanket.

And now my whole attention was riveted upon

Juan, who, as soon as the bull started, rapidly wound the end of his tail about his hand, tucking it under his leg, between it and the saddle.

The instant his well-trained horse felt the bull's tail upon his flank, he increased his speed, running in a line parallel to the bull, until, by an apparently slight effort, Juan was enabled with a sudden twist to fling the bellowing and now thoroughly frightened creature heels over head, upon the ground.

It was as fine an exhibition of the *vaquero's* skill as I had at that time ever witnessed, one that caused our warmest expressions of pleasure.

When the surprised and bewildered creature so far recovered from the effects of his sudden somersault as to once again get upon his legs, he seemed to have forgotten the blanket, his rage, every thing, in fact, save a strong desire to join the herd, which could now be seen approaching in the distance.

Juan's companion appeared to have been equally fortunate in his capture; for both the animals were fast travelling towards the herd, without once attempting to look about them, or manifesting the slightest desire to ascertain the fate of the blanket that had so excited their ire.

As soon as the Mexicans had returned to the train, and we had expressed our admiration at the wonderful exhibition of skill we had witnessed, I turned towards Ned, and said, "Well, my boy, how long since you determined to become a *matadōre?*"[1]

---

[1] A bull-fighter.

"Why, do you know, I couldn't imagine what made them chase me? I was riding along quietly when I saw these two, who were a little to one side of the herd, start for me; they looked so mad, and came so fast, that I just turned my pony and cut back as hard as I could come. I tell you, I was scared; and all the time that old blanket was making them madder and madder. It's lucky I didn't know it; if you hadn't called as you did I shouldn't have known what the trouble was, or thought of stopping them in that way. How came you to think of it?"

"It was Juan's suggestion," said I. "You can see, from the skill he has just displayed in tipping that old fellow heels over head, that he has had some experience with the creatures."

"I saw how he did it," remarked Hal, who had been listening to our conversation, "and I don't believe but what I could do it myself; I know I could with a little practice."

"If you're going to practise, I'd advise you to commence with one of your sheep," remarked Ned in a jocose manner.

"If I do, I'll know enough to keep my red blanket out of sight," retorted Hal.

"Come, come, boys: this kind of talk don't pay," remarked I, interrupting the conversation; "besides, I don't want these Mexicans to get the idea that you are constantly disputing about trifles."

"I hadn't any idea of disputing," said Hal, "until

Ned began upon me; and then of course I had to say something, or he'd have talked till this time."

The boys were soon good-natured again, and rode along beside Juan for the purpose of learning the definition and pronunciation of certain Spanish words concerning which there had been some question; leaving me behind, when I fell back to ascertain how Sile was getting on with the herd.

Finding that every thing was progressing nicely, I returned to the train, quietly falling in behind the boys, who were earnestly conversing together.

I overheard Hal saying, in a loud voice, —

"I don't care: I promised her I would come, and I mean to go; and, if he won't give his consent, I'll write home, and get father's, and then he can't stop me."

"I don't believe that he'll want to stop you, Hal," replied Ned.

"Yes, he will; he'll think it's a foolish trip," answered the boy.

"Well, I can't see what's the good of your going, Hal. I must say I think it's a little foolish, myself," responded Ned.

"Of course you can't see, but I mean to see Juanita. She's the sweetest little girl I ever met; and I made up my mind when we were prisoners together with the Apaches, that if we ever got away, I'd go to Chihuahua to see her; and I'm going, Ned Brown, if it takes a leg."

I had long known that Hal had promised to visit Chihuahua, and had more than half made up my mind to make a trip through Mexico myself. I knew that the journey must be made over vast plains that fairly bristled with Apache spears, through mountain fastnesses that swarmed with wild beasts. Yet there had always been a fascination for me, in reading of the land of the Montezumas, for the possession of which, the Spaniards had risked the loss of an empire, and in which, so many brave cavaliers had yielded up their lives while searching for its hidden treasures.

It was a country that I had long wanted to visit; and, as I listened to the boys' conversation, I suddenly asked myself the question, "What is to prevent my going this year? Why not take advantage of Hal's desire, and accompany him?"

I thought the matter over during the afternoon; and in the evening, after we were gathered about our camp-fire, unfolded a plan to make a trip through the Mexican states of Sonora, Sinoloa, Durango, and Zacetecas, to the city of Mexico; thence returning, visiting Chihuahua and the more eastern portions of the Republic.

All appeared to be delighted with the idea, except Sile, who thought that old Jerry would be a better person to accompany us than himself.

We spent the evening until bedtime, discussing the subject; and, although the trip was fully determined upon, the arrangement of the details, time of starting, &c., was left until our arrival at the ranch.

But I do not propose to ask you to follow us step by step, through the remaining days of our journey home.

Suffice it to say, that on the afternoon of the fourth day we came in sight of the live-oaks growing upon our own ranch, and in a very short time thereafter, were shaking hands with old Jerry, who received us and bid us "welcome home," with a warmth and cordiality that left no reason for doubting his pleasure at our return.

Hal and Ned were as happy as two boys could be; and after visiting the corals, and shaking hands with every *vaquero* upon the place, insisted upon extending the same friendly salutation to Jim and Carlo, my two shepherd dogs, who were nearly frantic with joy at again beholding us.

Sile and the cattle arrived a few hours later. Our purchase was critically examined by old Jerry, who took occasion to do a little grumbling, but expressed himself as being —

"On the hull, putty well satisfied, though they was a leetle small, and some on 'em hed amazin' long horns; but then, you couldn't 'spect nothin' better ov Texas cattle, nohow."

When evening came, and the old man's camp-fire was lighted, he brought out his "painter's skin," and, stretching himself himself out upon it, prepared to listen to an account of our recent trip; but the boys were too full of the future to care to recall the incidents of the past, and forthwith began a recital of the plan of our contemplated journey, ending with, —

"Now, what do you say to it, Jerry?"

Rising upon one elbow, the old man looked about him for a moment, and then said with a twinkle in his eye, "Say to it? why, I say that I should think the hull on yer, reckonin' Sile Carter in, hed gone clean crazy, ter want ter go trav'lin' off inter that country that don't grow nothin' 'ceptin' mules and greasers and silver, and is as full er Injuns, as thet 'ere dog Carlo is er fleas.

"I s'pose you'll do's yer mind ter though, but I should think Sile Carter'd know better than to want ter go;" but the old man's eyes flashed with a fire, and his face bore an expression, that strongly contradicted his words.

Having delivered this opinion, he lit his pipe, and remained silently listening to our conversation for nearly an hour; then turning suddenly to me he said, —

"Be yer in airnest 'bout goin', jedge?"

"Certainly I am," was the reply.

"Then I shell go with yer," said the old man.

And thus the trip became a settled thing; and thus it comes, that in a future volume of "The Trail-Hunters'" series, I shall tell you some of the many startling adventures that we encountered in travelling through this wonderful country, that for many years has furnished the most perilous yet fascinating field for adventure to be found upon this continent. In the third volume of the present series, soon to be issued, entitled "THE YOUNG SILVER SEEKERS," will be recounted such actual experiences as will cause all who read them to acknowledge that "truth is stranger than fiction."

NEW AND POPULAR JUVENILES.

By the author of "DOTTY DIMPLE."

FLAXIE FRIZZLE.

24mo. Illustrated. 75 cents. Uniform with "Little Prudy Stories," "Dotty Dimple Stories," and "Little Flyaway Series." This is the first volume of a uniform series, to be known as FLAXIE FRIZZLE STORIES. Of this book, a well-known literary lady, who has read the proof-sheets says, —

"The critic who wrote years ago, 'Genius comes in with "Little Prudy,"' will have to own that it remains with 'Flaxie Frizzle.'"

New editions of other books by same author.

OLIVER OPTIC'S NEW BOOK.

VINE AND OLIVE;
   OR, YOUNG AMERICA IN SPAIN AND PORTUGAL.

16mo. Cloth. Ill. Price, $1.50. This is the fifth volume of YOUNG AMERICA ABROAD (Second Series), which is now published, 5 volumes in neat box, per vol. $1.50, viz.:

UP THE BALTIC, NORTHERN LANDS,
     CROSS AND CRESCENT,
          SUNNY SHORES, VINE AND OLIVE.

New Editions of Old Favorites.

ELIJAH KELLOGG'S NEW BOOKS.

BLACK RIFLE'S MISSION;
   OR, ON THE TRAIL.

16mo. Cloth. Illustrated. Price, $1.25. The fourth volume of THE FOREST GLEN SERIES. Now ready. 4 volumes in box.

THE WINGED LION;
   OR, STORIES OF VENICE.

By Prof. James De Mille, author of the "B. O. W. C." Stories. 16mo. Cloth. Illustrated. Price, $1.50.

SNIP AND WHIP, AND SOME OTHER BOYS.

By Miss Elizabeth A. Davis. 16mo. Cloth. Ill. Price, $1.25.

REV. DR. WISE'S NEW BOOK.

WINWOOD CLIFF;
   OR, OSCAR, THE SAILOR'S SON.

By Rev. Daniel Wise, D.D., author of "Glen Morris Stories." This will be the first volume of a series to be known as the "Winwood Cliff Series." 16mo. Illustrated. Price, $1.25.

A ROUSING BOOK OF ADVENTURE.

THE YOUNG TRAIL HUNTERS;
   OR, THE WILD RIDERS OF THE PLAINS.

By Samuel Woodworth Cozzens. With 25 illustrations. Price, $1.50.

*** For sale by all Booksellers and News Dealers, and sent post-paid on receipt of price by the publishers.

LEE & SHEPARD, Publishers, 41-45 Franklin St., Boston.
678 Broadway, New York.

LEE & SHEPARD'S ELOCUTIONARY SERIES.

CHARLES DICKENS' DRAMATIC READINGS. Selected by himself from his own works. 16mo. Cloth. Illustrated. Price, $1.50.

By PROF. L. B. MONROE.

HUMOROUS READINGS in Prose and Verse. 318 pages. 12mo. Cloth. Price, $1.50.

MISCELLANEOUS READINGS in Prose and Verse. 352 pages. 12mo. Cloth. Price, $1.50.

DIALOGUES AND DRAMAS, for Public, School, and Home Entertainments. 342 pages. 12mo. Cloth. Price, $1.50.

"YOUNG FOLKS" READINGS, in Prose and Verse, for Home, School, and Public Reading. 12mo. Cloth. Price, $1.50.

By GEO. M. BAKER.

THE READING CLUB AND HANDY SPEAKER.

Being Selections in Prose and Poetry, Serious, Humorous, Pathetic, Patriotic, and Dramatic. For Readings and Recitations. Edited by Geo. M. Baker.
No. 1. 16mo. Cloth, 50c. Paper, 15c. | No. 3. 16mo. Cloth, 50c. Paper, 15c.
No. 2. 16mo. " 50c. " 15c. | No. 4. 16mo. " 50c. " 15c.

THE HANDY SPEAKER.

A new collection of choice extracts for School and Home Speaking and Reading. 16mo. Cloth. Price, $1.00.

HANDY DRAMAS.

For Amateur Actors. 12mo. Cloth. Price, $1.50. A new collection of plays, uniform with Amateur Dramas, being the sixth volume of

THE AMATEUR DRAMA SERIES.

6 vols. Illustrated. In neat box. Price, $1.50.

1. AMATEUR DRAMAS.
2. THE MIMIC STAGE.
3. THE SOCIAL STAGE.
4. THE EXHIBITION DRAMA.
5. DRAWING-ROOM STAGE.
6. HANDY DRAMAS.

By LOOMIS J. CAMPBELL.

THE COLUMBIAN SPEAKER.

Consisting of choice and animated Prose, for Declamation and Reading. Selected and adapted by Loomis J. Campbell and Oren Root, Jr. 16mo. Cloth. Price, 75 cents.

PRONOUNCING HAND-BOOK.

Of three thousand words, often mispronounced. By Loomis J. Campbell and Richard Soule. Small 4to. Price, 60 cents. School edition, price, 35 cents.

HANDY BOOKS.

LITTLE PIECES FOR LITTLE SPEAKERS.

The Primary School Teachers' Assistant. 16mo. Illustrated. Cloth. Price, 75 cents. Fancy binding, price, 60 cents.

THE MODEL SUNDAY SCHOOL SPEAKER.

Selections in Prose and Verse. Dialogues for Sunday School Exhibitions. 16mo. Cloth. Price, 75 cents. Half bound, price, 60 cents.

POETICAL DRAMAS.

For Home and Public Exhibitions. Particularly arranged for young ladies' schools. By Mary L. Cobb. 16mo. Cloth. Price, 75 cents. Half bound, price, 60 cents.

⁎⁎* For sale by all Booksellers and News Dealers, and sent post-paid on receipt of price by the publishers,

LEE & SHEPARD, 41-45 Franklin Street, Boston.
678 Broadway, New York.

www.ingramcontent.com/pod-product-compliance
Lightning Source LLC
Chambersburg PA
CBHW021155230426
43667CB00006B/401